2021 - 2022

Elementary School
Contest Materials

ISBN-978-1-387-90778-6

2020-2021 Elementary School Contest Materials
Table of Contents

Thank you for purchasing the 2021-2022 mathleague.org Contest Problem Set series. Good luck to you and your students as you prepare for this year's math contests! Upcoming tournament information and the latest mathleague.org policies and information can be found at our website, http://mathleague.org, and you can reach us at mathleague@mathleague.org.

mathleague.org is eager to help bring local math contests and championship meets to areas where such opportunities do not currently exist. Feel free to contact us if you would like more information on hosting a local contest or setting up a mathleague.org championship in your state or province.

This page intentionally left blank.
[sic]

Place ID Sticker
Inside This Box

Name _____

Grade _____

School _____

1. $12 + 12 =$ _____.

2. The tens digit of 70476 is _____.

3. $293 + 128 =$ _____.

4. $4 + 7 \times 4 =$ _____.

5. $514 - 318 =$ _____.

6. $13 \times 20 =$ _____.

7. The remainder of $63 \div 5$ is _____.

8. $17 + 43 + 43 + 17 =$ _____.

9. $65 \div 13 =$ _____.

10. (estimate) $126 + 231 + 273 =$ _____.

11. $314 - 109 - 106 =$ _____.

12. $12^2 =$ _____.

13. The remainder of $134 \div 9$ is _____.

14. $11 \times 34 =$ _____.

15. $8 \times 5 \times 7 =$ _____.

16. *CCLVI* in Arabic numerals is _____.

17. $22 \times 18 =$ _____.

18. $26 + 39 + 65 =$ _____.

19. $18 \times 35 =$ _____.

20. (estimate) $102 \times 299 =$ _____.

21. $25 \times 28 =$ _____.

22. The GCD of 8 and 18 is _____.

23. If 1 gallon is equal to 4 quarts, then 12 quarts is equal to _____ gallons.

24. $12 \times 15 \div 20 =$ _____.

25. $22^2 =$ _____.

26. $527 \div 17 =$ _____.

27. The greater of $\frac{3}{5}$ and $\frac{5}{8}$ is _____ (fraction).

28. $18 + 24 + 30 + 36 + 42 =$ _____.

29. $\frac{1}{3} + \frac{2}{21} =$ _____ (fraction).

30. (estimate) $29 \times 30 \times 31 =$ _____.

31. $\frac{1}{2} =$ _____ %.

32. $16 \times 99 =$ _____.

33. The perimeter of a rectangle with length 8 and width 6 is _____.

34. 10% of 120 is _____.

35. $45^2 =$ _____.

36. The number of odd whole numbers between 8 and 28 is _____.

37. $34 \times 36 =$ _____.

38. The LCM of 8 and 18 is _____.

39. 180 minutes is _____ hours.

40. (estimate) $23456 \div 112 =$ _____.

41. The remainder of $221 \div 11$ is _____.

42. $8 \times 12 + 4 \times 16 =$ _____.

43. The perimeter of a regular octagon with a side length of 14 is _____.

44. $96 \times 16 =$ _____.

45. The eighth term in the arithmetic sequence $5, 10, 15, \ldots$ is _____.

46. $41^2 - 31^2 =$ _____.

47. $101 \times 21 =$ _____.

48. $3^5 =$ _____.

49. 63_9 in base 10 is _____.

50. (estimate) $539 \times 333 =$ _____.

51. $8\frac{1}{3}\% =$ _____ (fraction).

52. $103 \times 105 =$ _____.

53. The sum of the terms of the arithmetic sequence $4, 8, 12, \ldots, 40$ is _____.

54. 110001_2 in base 8 is _____ ${}_8$.

55. $9^3 =$ _____.

56. The measure of an interior angle in an equilateral triangle is _____ $^\circ$.

57. $\sqrt{2116} =$ _____.

58. The mode of the list $1, 2, 2, 3, 3, 3, 4$ is _____.

59. $125 \times 17 =$ _____.

60. (estimate) $142857 \times 14 =$ _____.

61. Two fair dice are rolled. The probability the sum of the numbers shown is 3 is _____ (fraction).

62. $5\frac{1}{2} \times 5\frac{1}{2} =$ _____ (mixed number).

63. $111 \times 207 =$ _____.

64. $0.\overline{6} =$ _____ (fraction).

65. If $v = 8$, then $v^2 + 8v + 16 =$ _____.

66. The area of a right triangle with a leg of length 6 and a hypotenuse of length 10 is _____.

67. $9 \times 99 \times 11 =$ _____.

68. $79^2 =$ _____.

69. The number 66 written in base 4 is _____ ${}_4$.

70. (estimate) $17^4 =$ _____.

71. The sum of the prime divisors of 1001 is _____.

72. $1002 \times 1003 =$ _____.

73. The number of positive whole number divisors of 30 is _____.

74. If $2^x = \frac{1}{2}$, then $2^{3-x} =$ _____.

75. $\sqrt{18} \times \sqrt{8} =$ _____.

76. The sum of the lengths of the edges of a $4 \times 8 \times 11$ right rectangular prism is _____.

77. $48 \times 25 \times 18 =$ _____.

78. $\frac{1}{3}$ of 25 is $\frac{5}{6}$ of _____.

79. The sum of the terms of the infinite geometric sequence $\frac{2}{3}, \frac{2}{9}, \frac{2}{27}, \ldots$ is _____.

80. (estimate) $2.1^6 =$ _____.

Sprint Round
12220

 Place ID Sticker
Inside This Box

Name _____

Grade _____

School _____

1. (A) (B) (C) (D) (E)   11. (A) (B) (C) (D) (E)   21. (A) (B) (C) (D) (E)

2. (A) (B) (C) (D) (E)   12. (A) (B) (C) (D) (E)   22. (A) (B) (C) (D) (E)

3. (A) (B) (C) (D) (E)   13. (A) (B) (C) (D) (E)   23. (A) (B) (C) (D) (E)

4. (A) (B) (C) (D) (E)   14. (A) (B) (C) (D) (E)   24. (A) (B) (C) (D) (E)

5. (A) (B) (C) (D) (E)   15. (A) (B) (C) (D) (E)   25. (A) (B) (C) (D) (E)

6. (A) (B) (C) (D) (E)   16. (A) (B) (C) (D) (E)   26. (A) (B) (C) (D) (E)

7. (A) (B) (C) (D) (E)   17. (A) (B) (C) (D) (E)   27. (A) (B) (C) (D) (E)

8. (A) (B) (C) (D) (E)   18. (A) (B) (C) (D) (E)   28. (A) (B) (C) (D) (E)

9. (A) (B) (C) (D) (E)   19. (A) (B) (C) (D) (E)   29. (A) (B) (C) (D) (E)

10. (A) (B) (C) (D) (E)   20. (A) (B) (C) (D) (E)   30. (A) (B) (C) (D) (E)

1. In the cafeteria, drinks cost $1 each, and lunches cost $2 each. Samantha purchases three drinks and two lunches for herself and a friend. What is the total cost, in dollars, of Samantha's purchase?

   (A) $7   (B) $4   (C) $8   (D) $6   (E) $5

2. What is the value of $1 + 3 + 5 + 7 + 9 + 11 + 13 + 15 + 17 + 19$?

   (A) 125   (B) 144   (C) 120   (D) 64   (E) 100

3. Maxim bent a wire of length 42 inches into a triangle. One side of the triangle had length 13 inches. Another side of the triangle had length 15 inches. What was the length of the third side of Maxim's triangle, in inches?

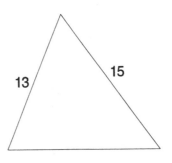

   (A) 13   (B) 14   (C) 12   (D) 10   (E) 11

4. Daniel is doing a trade with a merchant, where for every 5 gold blocks Daniel gives, the merchant will give 2 diamond blocks to Daniel. Daniel has 45 gold blocks. If he trades all of them to the merchant, how many diamond blocks will Daniel receive from the merchant?

   (A) 18   (B) 10   (C) 15   (D) 9   (E) 12

5. Jeremiah spends $2.50 to play five rounds of an arcade game. At the same price per arcade round, how much would seven rounds cost?

   (A) $3.50   (B) $4.20   (C) $2.50   (D) $2.10   (E) $0.50

6. April calculated the value of 36 divided by 3, and Melcka calculated the value of 39 divided by 13. What is the product of April's result and Melcka's result?

   (A) 28   (B) 36   (C) 32   (D) 40   (E) 24

7. This past week, Ellen spent 15 minutes starting an essay on Monday. Each day after Monday, she spent 15 more minutes working on the essay than she did the day before. After she finished her essay on Thursday, how many total minutes had she spent doing the essay?

   (A) 225   (B) 60   (C) 120   (D) 135   (E) 150

8. What is the hundreds digit of 56×99?

   (A) 7   (B) 5   (C) 4   (D) 8   (E) 6

9. A whole number greater than 680 and less than 687 is a multiple of 4. What is the units digit of that number?

   (A) 8   (B) 0   (C) 4   (D) 6   (E) 2

10. As shown below, a square of side length 10 is split into four rectangles by three line segments parallel to two sides of the square. What is the total length of all the segments in the figure?

   (A) 80   (B) 100   (C) 110   (D) 70   (E) 60

11. Juliet prepared a pancake and decided to cut some slices. She cut one piece that was 25% and two slices that were each 20% of the pancake. The final piece was the remainder of the pancake. What fraction of the pancake was the final piece?

(A) $\frac{3}{14}$ (B) $\frac{7}{20}$ (C) $\frac{13}{20}$ (D) $\frac{11}{20}$ (E) $\frac{11}{14}$

12. How many minutes pass from noon on December 6th until noon on December 14th?

(A) 11340   (B) 11520   (C) 11400   (D) 11280   (E) 11640

13. A rectangle with whole number side lengths has the same area as a square with a perimeter of 48. If the shorter side of the rectangle has a length that differs by 4 from the side length of the square, then what is the perimeter of the rectangle?

(A) 50   (B) 52   (C) 56   (D) 54   (E) 58

14. Justin writes all possible arrangements of four letters that contain the letters *M*, *E*, *T*, and *A* exactly once. For example, two of the possible arrangements are *META* and *TEAM*. How many arrangements that Justin wrote do not have the *M* and *T* next to each other?

(A) 2   (B) 6   (C) 12   (D) 4   (E) 8

15. Charlotte is managing a factory that produces boots. The factory produces boots 10 at a time and finishes all of them at the same time, and it takes 15 minutes to finish all 10 boots. However, every 30 minutes, one boot has to get discarded. How long, in minutes, will it take Charlotte to have 190 boots available?

(A) 285   (B) 150   (C) 200   (D) 300   (E) 225

16. The right triangle shown below has legs of length 16 and 30. The smaller gray triangle is formed by connecting the midpoints of the right triangle. What fraction of the total area is not gray?

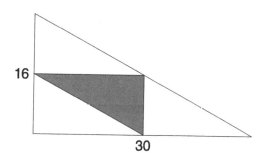

(A) $\frac{1}{4}$ (B) $\frac{1}{2}$ (C) $\frac{3}{4}$ (D) $\frac{2}{3}$ (E) $\frac{1}{3}$

17. Charlie averaged a score of 95 on three quizzes. On two of the quizzes, he had the same score. On the third quiz, he scored a 91. What was the range of Charlie's scores on the three quizzes?

(A) 7 (B) 6 (C) 4 (D) 5 (E) 3

18. Daisy calculated the value of $\frac{1}{0.1} + \frac{11}{0.01} + \frac{10}{0.001}$ and then summed the digits of her result. What was Daisy's sum?

(A) 4 (B) 3 (C) 6 (D) 5 (E) 7

19. How many positive whole numbers evenly divide 72 but do not evenly divide 80?

(A) 8 (B) 4 (C) 6 (D) 2 (E) 3

20. If $a \heartsuit b = a^2 - 2ab + b^2$, then what is the value of $(66 \heartsuit 12) - (36 \heartsuit 12)$?

(A) 2370 (B) 2280 (C) 2400 (D) 2340 (E) 2310

21. Christine has at least 3 each of jump stickers, hammer stickers, and flower stickers. Stickers of the same type are considered the same, but stickers of different types are considered different. She wants to select 5 stickers (without regard to order) such that she selects at least 1 jump sticker, 1 hammer sticker, and 1 flower sticker. How many different ways can Christine select 5 stickers? For example, one such possibility is 2 jump stickers, 2 hammer stickers, and 1 flower sticker.

(A) 8   (B) 7   (C) 9   (D) 6   (E) 5

22. A rectangular piece of paper measures 10 inches on the shorter side and 25 inches on the longer side. Opposite corners of the piece of paper are folded until they meet at opposite edges, and the folded over portions are then cut off and removed. To the nearest whole number, in inches, what is the perimeter of the resulting piece of paper?

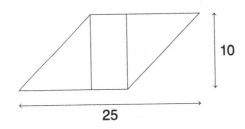

10

25

(A) 56   (B) 62   (C) 64   (D) 58   (E) 60

23. Mabel and Ann each chose a positive whole number. Twice Mabel's number plus Ann's number summed to 110. Twice Ann's number plus Mabel's number summed to 115. What is the product of Mabel's number and Ann's number?

(A) 1400   (B) 1575   (C) 1200   (D) 1050   (E) 1800

24. Ashley is observing some bugs in one area of the laboratory. In the area, every bug is either a stag beetle or a single-horned beetle, and every bug is either shiny or not shiny. There are 69 bugs in the area. There are 15 more single-horned beetles than there are stag beetles, and there are 55 more non-shiny bugs than there are shiny bugs. Ashley observes that there are 25 non-shiny stag beetles in the area. How many shiny single-horned beetles are in the area?

(A) 37   (B) 42   (C) 27   (D) 5   (E) 2

25. Emma's team took part in a soccer league along with three other teams. During the season, every team played every other team in the league twice, and none of the games ended in a tie. The standings of teams in the league are calculated using a point system where a win is worth 2 points and a loss is worth 0 points. At the end of the season, Emma's team got first place while the other three teams got 4 points each. How many points did Emma's team get?

(A) 10   (B) 14   (C) 6   (D) 8   (E) 12

26. From least to greatest, what is the order of 5^{21}, 2^{42}, and 11^{14}?

(A) $5^{21} < 11^{14} < 2^{42}$ (B) $2^{42} < 5^{21} < 11^{14}$ (C) $11^{14} < 2^{42} < 5^{21}$ (D) $2^{42} < 11^{14} < 5^{21}$ (E) $5^{21} < 2^{42} < 11^{14}$

27. How many positive even whole numbers divide 10!?

(A) 240   (B) 64   (C) 128   (D) 120   (E) 270

28. Farmer John has a field with some grass, and the grass grows at a constant rate. He wants to feed some of his cows on this field. All of his cows consume the same amount of grass per day. If Farmer John places 180 cows in the field, the field will be bare in twelve weeks. If Farmer John places 200 cows in the field, the field will be bare in ten weeks. If Farmer John only needs to feed cows in the field for four weeks, then what is the greatest number of cows he can place in the field?

(A) 380   (B) 300   (C) 375   (D) 400   (E) 305

29. A 6×4 checkerboard is shown below. A number of rectangles exist on this board, with boundaries of each rectangle that are boundaries of the small squares or boundaries of the board. A single small square is one such rectangle, and the entire board is another such rectangle. One of these rectangles is randomly chosen. The probability that it is a square can be expressed as a common fraction. What is the sum of the numerator and denominator of that fraction?

(A) 253   (B) 6   (C) 49   (D) 87   (E) 26

30. In equilateral triangle *ABC*, shown below, points *X* and *Y* are the midpoints of sides *AB* and *BC*, respectively. Additionally, point *Z* lies on side *AC* such that the length of *AZ* is three times the length of *CZ*. What is the ratio of the area of triangle *XYZ* to the area of triangle *ABC*?

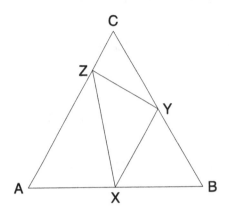

(A) $\frac{\sqrt{3}}{6}$ (B) $\frac{1}{2}$ (C) $\frac{1}{3}$ (D) $\frac{1}{4}$ (E) $\frac{7}{24}$

Target Round
12220

Name _____

Grade _____

School _____

Problems 1 & 2

1. Paige summed all of the whole numbers greater than 5 and less than 25 that are not even and also do not have a units digit of five. What is the value of Paige's sum?

1.

2. A four-digit number is odd, a multiple of 5, and a multiple of 11. The hundreds digit of the number is a 3, and the thousands digit is the same value as the tens digit. What is the four-digit number?

2.

Place ID Sticker
Inside This Box

Name _____

Grade _____

School _____

Problems 3 & 4

3. Marian's birthday is March 15th. In the year 2022, the month of January has 31 days, and the month of February has 28 days. How many days in 2022 occur before Marian's birthday (not including the exact day itself)?

3.

4. Silver studs are worth 10 points and gold studs are worth 100 points. Chase has 5 more silver studs than gold studs, and the total value of Chase's silver and gold studs is 1700 points. What is the total number of silver and gold studs that Chase has?

4.

Place ID Sticker
Inside This Box

Name _____

Grade _____

School _____

Problems 5 & 6

---

5. Jeff does roll call by counting all the positive whole numbers from 1 to 30 inclusive, but any time a number is a multiple of 7 or has a digit that is equal to 7, Jeff says "buzz" instead. How many times does Jeff say "buzz" in the count?

5.

6. In the figure below, dots are in a square grid so that each dot has a horizontal and vertical distance of 1 unit from neighboring dots, and the area of the entire grid is $5 \times 5 = 25$. What is the area of the quadrilateral shown?

6.

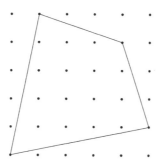

  Place ID Sticker
Inside This Box

Name _____

Grade _____

School _____

Problems 7 & 8

7. Becca cuts out the figure below and folds it into a cube, with the squares shown becoming faces of the cube. Becca writes down the number on the side opposite the face numbered 0, and she writes down the number on the face opposite the face numbered 1. What is the product of the two numbers Becca wrote down?

7.

		7
3	3	5

0	1

8. Lindsey has three fair dice. Each die is a cube that has either red or blue faces. One cube has exactly 1 face that is red, one cube has exactly 3 faces that are red, and one cube has exactly 5 faces that are red. Lindsey rolls all three dice. What is the probability that exactly one die shows a red face? Express your answer as a common fraction.

8.

School or Team

Name _____

Name _____

Name _____

Name _____

Place ID Sticker
Inside This Box

Place ID Sticker
Inside This Box

Place ID Sticker
Inside This Box

Place ID Sticker
Inside This Box

1.

2.

3.

4.

5.

6.

7.

8.

9.

10.

1. Patrick started watching a TV episode about a yellow sponge. The episode started at 1:46 PM and finished at 2:00 PM. How many minutes long was the episode?

2. At an amusement park, tickets cost $60 for children who are under 13 years old and $75 for everyone else. Andrew, Reagan, and Brandon are planning on attending the theme park. Andrew is 14 years old, Reagan is 13 years old, and Brandon is 11 years old. How many dollars do the three of them have to pay for all of them to attend the amusement park?

3. The figure below shows a rhombus partitioned into smaller identical equilateral triangles. How many equilateral triangles, of any size, exist in the figure?

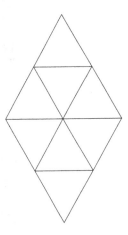

4. In the stock market, the Sigma stock falls by 15 points every month, while the X stock increases by 12 points every month. This month, the Sigma stock and X stock each have 120 points. Three months ago, what was the sum of the point values of the Sigma stock and the X stock?

5. When Nariyaki measured his height on his 8th birthday, he was 51 inches tall. When Nariyaki measured his height on his 12th birthday, he was 62 inches tall. On average, how many inches per year did Nariyaki grow between these two measurements? Express your answer as a mixed number.

6. In the figure below, all angles are right angles, and side lengths are as shown. What is the total area enclosed by the figure?

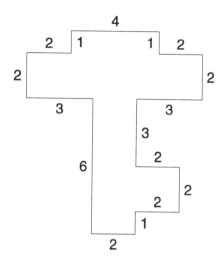

7. Three bells on a clocktower ring at precise times. The north bell rings every four hours. The east bell rings every six hours. The south bell rings every eight hours. If all three bells ring at the same time at 12 : 00 PM on a Monday, then how many times over the next 42 hours will exactly two of the bells ring at the same time?

8. Manuel and Eric live three miles away from each other. Eric leaves his house walking towards Manuel's house at a speed of 3 miles per hour. Manuel leaves his house for Eric's house at the same time, but he is riding his skateboard at a speed that is three times as fast as Eric's walking speed. When Manuel and Eric meet, how many miles more has Manuel travelled than Eric walked? Express your answer as a mixed number.

9. Tomi prepared a number of chemical solutions that were a mixture of hydrochloric acid and distilled water. Each solution measured 25 milliliters. One particular solution used $\frac{1}{4}$ of the total hydrochloric acid she used for all solutions and $\frac{1}{6}$ of the total distilled water she used for all solutions. How many solutions did Tomi prepare?

10. A rectangular piece of paper measuring 70 by 98 is folded along its diagonal. After folding, what is the area of the region where the paper has double its original thickness?

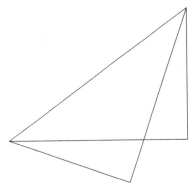

Sprint Round

1. A	11. B	21. D	
2. E	12. B	22. D	
3. B	13. B	23. A	
4. A	14. C	24. D	
5. A	15. D	25. E	
6. B	16. C	26. D	
7. E	17. B	27. A	
8. B	18. A	28. A	
9. C	19. A	29. E	
10. D	20. D	30. D	

Target Round

1. 120
2. 4345
3. 73
4. 35
5. 6
6. 16
7. 21
8. $\frac{31}{72}$

Team Round

1. 14
2. ($)210
3. 10
4. 249
5. $2\frac{3}{4}$
6. 36
7. 6
8. $1\frac{1}{2}$
9. 5
10. 2590

Number Sense

1. 24	21. 700	41. 1	61. $\frac{1}{18}$
2. 7	22. 2	42. 160	62. $30\frac{1}{4}$
3. 421	23. 3	43. 112	63. 22977
4. 32	24. 9	44. 1536	64. $\frac{2}{3}$
5. 196	25. 484	45. 40	65. 144
6. 260	26. 31	46. 720	66. 24
7. 3	27. $\frac{5}{8}$	47. 2121	67. 9801
8. 120	28. 150	48. 243	68. 6241
9. 5	29. $\frac{3}{7}$	49. 57	69. 1002
10. [599, 661]	30. [25622, 28318]	50. [170513, 188461]	70. [79345, 87697]
11. 99	31. 50	51. $\frac{1}{12}$	71. 31
12. 144	32. 1584	52. 10815	72. 1005006
13. 8	33. 28	53. 220	73. 8
14. 374	34. 12	54. 61	74. 16
15. 280	35. 2025	55. 729	75. 12
16. 256	36. 10	56. 60	76. 92
17. 396	37. 1224	57. 46	77. 21600
18. 130	38. 72	58. 3	78. 10
19. 630	39. 3	59. 2125	79. 1
20. [28974, 32022]	40. [199, 219]	60. [1899999, 2099997]	80. [82, 90]

Sprint Round Solutions

1. The total cost of 3 drinks is $3 \cdot \$1 = \$3$, and the total cost of 2 lunches is $2 \cdot \$2 = \$4$, so the total cost of Samantha's purchase is $\$3 + \$4 = \boxed{\$7}$.

2. This can be rewritten as $(1 + 19) + (3 + 17) + (5 + 15) + (7 + 13) + (9 + 11)$, which is $20 \times 5 = \boxed{100}$.

3. The sum of the lengths of the three sides of the triangle must be 42 inches. The two given sides have a total length of $13 + 15 = 28$ inches, so the length of the third side, in inches, is $42 - 28 = \boxed{14}$.

4. Daniel gives the merchant $45 \div 5 = 9$ groups of 5 gold blocks, so Daniel will receive 9 groups of 2 diamond blocks, for a total of $9 \cdot 2 = \boxed{18}$.

5. One round of an arcade game costs $\$2.50 \div 5 = \$0.50$, so 7 rounds of the arcade game would cost $7 \cdot \$0.50 = \boxed{\$3.50}$.

6. The two values are $36 \div 3 = 12$ and $39 \div 13 = 3$, and $12 \cdot 3 = \boxed{36}$.

7. Ellen spent 15 minutes on Monday, 30 minutes on Tuesday, 45 minutes on Wednesday, and 60 minutes on Thursday. Altogether, the number of minutes Ellen spent doing the essay was $15 + 30 + 45 + 60 = \boxed{150}$.

8. This is $56 \times 100 - 56 \times 1$, which is $5600 - 56$. Since 56 is less than 100, the hundreds digit of the result will be $6 - 1 = \boxed{5}$.

9. The number 600 is a multiple of 4, so the number between 80 and 87 (exclusive) that is 600 less than the original number must also be a multiple of 4. The only multiple of 4 in that range is 84, which has a units digit of $\boxed{4}$.

10. The perimeter of the square is $4 \times 10 = 40$. Each segment creates 1 side of length 10. There are 3 such segments, so the total length of all the segments exceeds the perimeter of the square by $3 \times 1 \times 10 = 30$. Thus, the total length of all the segments is $40 + 30 = \boxed{70}$.

11. As a fraction, 25% equals $\frac{1}{4}$, and 20% equals $\frac{1}{5}$. The pieces that were cut totaled $\frac{1}{4} + \frac{1}{5} + \frac{1}{5} = \frac{5}{20} + \frac{4}{20} + \frac{4}{20} = \frac{13}{20}$ of the pancake, so as a fraction of the pancake, the final piece was $1 - \frac{13}{20} = \boxed{\frac{7}{20}}$.

12. This is a period of $14 - 6 = 8$ days. There are 24 hours in 1 day, so this is $8 \times 24 = 192$ hours. There are 60 minutes in 1 hour, so the number of minutes is $192 \times 60 = \boxed{11520}$.

13. The side length of the square is $48 \div 4 = 12$, so the area of the square is $12 \cdot 12 = 144$. The shorter side of the rectangle must have a length less than 12, so it has length $12 - 4 = 8$. Then the other side of the rectangle has length $144 \div 8 = 18$. The perimeter of the rectangle is $2 \cdot (8 + 18) = \boxed{52}$.

14. If the arrangement starts with the letter M or the letter T, then the other letter, M or T, must be in the third or fourth position, yielding *META*, *MATE*, *MAET*, *MEAT*, *TEMA*, *TAME*, *TAEM*, and *TEAM*. If the arrangement starts with the letter E or A, then the letters M and T must be in the second and fourth positions, yielding *ETAM*, *EMAT*, *ATEM*, and *AMET*. Altogether, the number of arrangements with the M and T not next to each other is $\boxed{12}$.

15. Every 15 minutes, Charlotte has 10 boots available, so every 30 minutes, there are 20 boots available. But also every 30 minutes, one boot gets discarded, so the total change in 30 minutes is gaining $20 - 1 = 19$ boots. Thus, the number of minutes required to have a total of 190 boots is $\frac{190}{19} \cdot 30 = \boxed{300}$.

16. The area of the entire right triangle is $\frac{1}{2} \cdot 30 \cdot 16 = 240$. The grey triangle formed by connecting the midpoints is also a right triangle, with legs that are half the length of the legs of the larger triangle, so its area is $\frac{1}{2} \cdot 15 \cdot 8 = 60$. The fraction of the total area of the right triangle that is not gray is $\frac{240 - 60}{240} = \boxed{\frac{3}{4}}$.

17. The sum of Charlie's scores on the 3 quizzes is 3 times his average score, or $3 \cdot 95 = 285$. Because the third quiz had a score of 91, the other two quizzes had scores summing to $285 - 91 = 194$. As the scores on these two quizzes were equal, they were each $\frac{194}{2} = 97$, so the range of Charlie's scores is $97 - 91 = \boxed{6}$.

18. Multiplying the first fraction by 10, the second by 100, and the third by 1000 yields $\frac{10}{1} + \frac{1100}{1} + \frac{10000}{1}$. This is 11110, and the sum of the digits of this number is $\boxed{4}$.

19. One way is to manually count and list factors, but another way is to observe the prime factorization of 72 and 80. The prime factorization of 72 is $2^3 \cdot 3^2$, and the prime factorization of 80 is $2^4 \cdot 5$. Since 2^3 evenly divides 80, any number that divides 72 but does not divide 80 must be a multiple of 3. These numbers are 3, 6, 9, 12, 18, 24, 36, and 72, for a total of $\boxed{8}$.

20. The given expression can be rewritten as $a^2 - 2ab + b^2 = (a - b)^2$, so $66 \heartsuit 12 = (66 - 12)^2$, and $36 \heartsuit 12 = (36 - 12)^2$. Finally, $(66 - 12)^2 - (36 - 12)^2$ is $54^2 - 24^2$. By difference of squares, this is $(54 + 24)(54 - 24) = 78 \cdot 30$, or $\boxed{2340}$.

21. We know that there is at least 1 jump sticker, at least 1 hammer sticker, and at least 1 flower sticker used, meaning that Christine can then select any two stickers to finish off the selection. If the two stickers are the same type, then Christine has 3 ways. If the two stickers are different type, then Christine also has 3 ways. The total number of possible sticker selections is $3 + 3 = \boxed{6}$.

22. After the pieces are removed, the paper is a parallelogram. The remaining edges of the original piece of paper are 2 segments of length 15 inches, for a combined length of $2 \cdot 15 = 30$ inches. The additional 2 edges are hypotenuses of isosceles right triangles with legs of length 10. Each has a length of $10\sqrt{2}$, and their combined length is $20\sqrt{2}$. The total perimeter is $30 + 20\sqrt{2}$ inches, and since $\sqrt{2} \approx 1.41$, the whole number nearest to $30 + 20\sqrt{2}$ is $\boxed{58}$.

23. Let Mabel's number be M and Ann's number be A. Then $2M + A = 110$ and $M + 2A = 115$. Subtract the first equation from the second equation to get $A - M = 5$. Add this to the second equation to get $3A = 120$, so $A = 40$. Then $M = 35$, and $A \cdot M = \boxed{1400}$.

24. Of the 69 bugs, 27 are stag beetles and 42 are single-horned beetles. Additionally, 62 are non-shiny and 7 are shiny. Since 25 bugs are non-shiny stag beetles, $27 - 25 = 2$ bugs are shiny stag beetles. Since 7 bugs are shiny, the number of shiny single-horned beetles must be $7 - 2 = \boxed{5}$.

25. Each team plays each of the other three teams twice, so each team plays $3 \cdot 2 = 6$ games. For each of the four teams to play 6 games, there must be a total of $\frac{1}{2} \cdot 4 \cdot 6 = 12$ games, since each game always involves two teams. In each of the 12 games, exactly 2 total points are always awarded. Therefore, the total number of points in the league standings must equal $12 \cdot 2 = 24$. The three known point totals sum to $4 \cdot 3 = 12$, so the number of points earned by Emma's team is $24 - 12 = \boxed{12}$.

26. Each exponent is a multiple of 7, so raising each number to the $\frac{1}{7}$ power yields 5^3, 2^6, and 11^2. These can now be compared. Since $5^3 = 125$, $2^6 = 64$, and $11^2 = 121$, the numbers can be ordered as $\boxed{2^{42} < 11^{14} < 5^{21}}$.

27. The prime factorization of 10! is $2^8 \cdot 3^4 \cdot 5^2 \cdot 7$. When an even divisor is prime factored, it will have at least 1 power of 2. Then there are 8 possibilities for the exponent of 2 in such a prime factorization, $4 + 1 = 5$ possibilities for the exponent of 3 (as 0 is a possible exponent), $2 + 1 = 3$ possibilities for the exponent of 5, and $1 + 1 = 2$ possibilities for the exponent of 7. Therefore, the number of even divisors is $8 \cdot 5 \cdot 3 \cdot 2 = \boxed{240}$.

28. To support 180 cows for 12 weeks, the field must supply $12 \cdot 180 = 2160$ cow-weeks of grass. To support 200 cows for 10 weeks, the field must supply $10 \cdot 200 = 2000$ cow-weeks of grass. The additional $2160 - 2000 = 160$ cow-weeks of grass means the grass in the field grows at a rate of $\frac{160}{12-10} = 80$ cow-weeks per week. At the start of the 10 week period, the field has $2000 - 10 \cdot 80 = 1200$ cow-weeks of grass, so at the end of a four week period, the field would be able to provide a total of $1200 + 4 \cdot 80 = 1520$ cow-weeks of grass, which is enough to supply a number of cows equal to $\frac{1520}{4} = \boxed{380}$.

29. Including the boundaries of the board, there are $6 + 1 = 7$ possible vertical boundaries and $4 + 1 = 5$ possible horizontal boundaries. A rectangle can be formed by choosing any 2 of the 7 vertical boundaries and any 2 of the 5 horizontal boundaries, for a total of $\binom{7}{2} \cdot \binom{5}{2} = 210$ possible rectangles. There are $4 \cdot 6 = 24$ squares that are 1×1. For a 2×2 square, there are 3 horizontal possibilities for the lower left corner, and 5 vertical possibilities for the same lower left corner, for a total of $3 \cdot 5 = 15$ squares that are 2×2. For 3×3, the number is $2 \cdot 4 = 8$, and for 4×4, the number is $1 \cdot 3 = 3$. The total number of squares is $24 + 15 + 8 + 3 = 50$. The probability that a randomly chosen rectangle is a square is $\frac{50}{210} = \frac{5}{21}$, and $5 + 21 = \boxed{26}$.

30. Since X and Y are the midpoints of sides AB and BC, respectively, the length of XY is half that of AC. Moreover, the length of a perpendicular line segment from any point on AC to XY is half that of the altitude from B to AC because XY and AC are parallel. In other words, the base and altitude lengths of triangle XYZ are both half those of triangle ABC. Since the area of a triangle scales with the base and altitude lengths, the ratio of the area of triangle XYZ to that of triangle ABC is $\frac{1}{2} \cdot \frac{1}{2} = \boxed{\frac{1}{4}}$.

Target Round Solutions

1. The sum of the odd whole numbers from 6 through 24, inclusive, is $7 + 9 + 11 + 13 + 15 + 17 + 19 + 21 + 23 = 135$. But 15 has a units digit of 5 and must be removed, so the final value of the sum is $135 - 15 = \boxed{120}$.

2. For a four-digit number to be divisible by 11, the sum of the tens and thousands digits must differ from the sum of the units and hundreds digits by a value that is a multiple of 11. Since the number is also a multiple of 5, the units digit is 0 or 5, and it cannot be 0 since the number must be odd, so the units digit is 5. The sum of the hundreds and units digits is $3 + 5 = 8$. Therefore, the sum of the tens and thousands digits must be 8, as $8 - 8 = 0$ and any larger sums are not possible for two digits. Therefore, the tens and thousands digit must both be $8 \div 2 = 4$, and the number is $\boxed{4345}$.

3. In the first two months of the year, $31 + 28 = 59$ days occur. In March, $15 - 1 = 14$ days occur before Marian's birthday. The number of days in 2022 that occur before Marian's birthday is $59 + 14 = \boxed{73}$.

4. Without the five extra silver studs, Chase's coins are worth $1700 - 5 \cdot 10 = 1650$ points. The remaining studs can be grouped into pairs of 1 silver stud and 1 gold stud, with each pair worth $100 + 10 = 110$ points. There are $1650 \div 110 = 15$ such pairs, which are comprised of $2 \cdot 15 = 30$ studs. Including the five extra silver studs, the total number of studs is $30 + 5 = \boxed{35}$.

5. The numbers less than 30 that are multiples of 7 are 7, 14, 21, and 28, for a total of 4. The numbers less than 30 that have a digit that is 7 are 7, 17, and 27, for a total of 3. However, the number 7 appears in both lists, so the total number of numbers that appear in at least one of the lists is $4 + 3 - 1 = \boxed{6}$.

6. The entire grid has an area of 25. The area of the quadrilateral can be calculated by removing the regions of the grid that are outside the quadrilateral. The area of the triangle in the upper left is $\frac{1}{2} \cdot 5 \cdot 1 = \frac{5}{2}$. The area of the triangle in the lower right is also $\frac{1}{2} \cdot 5 \cdot 1 = \frac{5}{2}$. The upper region can be partitioned into three regions. In the upper left, there is a triangle with base 3 and height 1, and an area of $\frac{1}{2} \cdot 3 \cdot 1 = \frac{3}{2}$. In the upper right, there is a square that has area $1 \cdot 1 = 1$. Finally, below the rectangle there is a triangle with base 1 and height 3, and an area of $\frac{1}{2} \cdot 1 \cdot 3 = \frac{3}{2}$. The area of the quadrilateral is $25 - \frac{5}{2} - \frac{5}{2} - \frac{3}{2} - 1 - \frac{3}{2} = \boxed{16}$.

7. When folded, the face opposite the face numbered 0 has the number 3, and the face opposite the face numbered 1 has the number 7. The product of 3 and 7 is $\boxed{21}$.

8. As a cube has 6 faces, the probabilities that each die shows a red face are $\frac{1}{6}$, $\frac{1}{2}$, and $\frac{5}{6}$. The probabilities that each die does not show a red face is $\frac{5}{6}$, $\frac{1}{2}$, and $\frac{1}{6}$. The probability that only the first die shows a red face is $\frac{1}{6} \cdot \frac{1}{2} \cdot \frac{1}{6} = \frac{1}{72}$. The probability that only the second die shows a red face is $\frac{5}{6} \cdot \frac{1}{2} \cdot \frac{1}{6} = \frac{5}{72}$. The probability that only the third die shows a red face is $\frac{5}{6} \cdot \frac{1}{2} \cdot \frac{5}{6} = \frac{25}{72}$. The probability that exactly one die shows a red face is $\frac{1}{72} + \frac{5}{72} + \frac{25}{72} = \boxed{\frac{31}{72}}$.

Team Round Solutions

1. There are 60 minutes in an hour. The time 1:46 PM is 46 minutes after 1 PM, while 2:00 PM is 60 minutes after 1 PM. Therefore, the length of the episode, in minutes, was $60 - 46 = \boxed{14}$.

2. Among the three people, two of them (Andrew and Reagan) have to pay $75 each, and one of them (Brandon) only has to pay $60. The total amount that the three have to pay is $\$75 + \$75 + \$60 = \boxed{\$210}$.

3. There are a total of 8 small equilateral triangles. However, we can put four small equilateral triangles together to form one large equilateral triangle, and there are 2 such triangles – one facing up and one facing down. Altogether, the total number of equilateral triangles is $8 + 2 = \boxed{10}$.

4. The Sigma stock falls by 15 points every month, so three months ago, the Sigma stock had $120 + 3 \cdot 15 = 165$ points. The X stock increases by 12 points each month, so three months ago, the X stock had $120 - 3 \cdot 12 = 84$ points. The sum of the point values of the two stocks three months ago is $165 + 84 = \boxed{249}$.

5. The total height Nariyaki gained was $62 - 51 = 11$ inches. The time between the measurements was $12 - 8 = 4$ years. Therefore, the average increase in inches per year for Nariyaki is $\frac{11}{4} = \boxed{2\frac{3}{4}}$.

6. There are many ways to partition the figure into rectangles. One way is shown below. This creates a 4×1 rectangle, an 8×2 rectangle, a 6×2 rectangle, and a square of side length 2. The total area is $4 \cdot 1 + 8 \cdot 2 + 6 \cdot 2 + 2 \cdot 2 = \boxed{36}$.

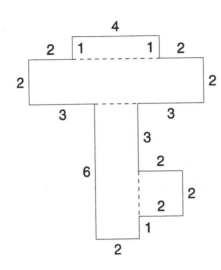

7. We check each case where a pair of bells ring at the same time. The north and east bells ring at the same time every 12 hours, the east and south bells ring at the same time every 24 hours, the south and north bells ring at the same time every 8 hours, and all three bells ring at the same time every 24 hours. So exactly two bells ring at the same time when the number of hours that pass is a multiple of 8 or 12 but not a multiple of 24. The multiples of 8 under 42 that are not multiples of 24 are 8, 16, 32, and 40, and the multiples of 12 under 42 that are not multiples of 24 are 12 and 36, so the number of times exactly two bells ring at the same time over the next 42 hours is $\boxed{6}$.

8. The absolute speed each travels at does not matter. Since they have both traveled for the same amount of time, Manuel has traveled 3 times as far as Eric. Therefore, Manuel has traveled $\frac{3}{3+1} = \frac{3}{4}$ of the total distance, while Eric has traveled $\frac{1}{3+1} = \frac{1}{4}$ of the total distance. The difference in between the two distances each travels is $\frac{3}{4} - \frac{1}{4} = \frac{1}{2}$ of 3 miles, or $\boxed{1\frac{1}{2}}$ miles.

9. Let w be the total number of milliliters of water that Tomi used in preparing the solutions, a be the total number of mliliters of acid that Tomi used, and n be the number of solutions she prepared. From the total volume, $w + a = 25n$. Additionally, from the known solution, $\frac{a}{4} + \frac{w}{6} = 25$. Substituting the second equation into the first, $w + a = \left(\frac{a}{4} + \frac{w}{6}\right) \cdot n$. Simplifying, $24w + 24a = 6an + 4wn$, and $24w - 4wn = 6an - 24a$. Factoring, $4w \cdot (6 - n) = 6a \cdot (n - 4)$. Both $4w$ and $6a$ are positive, and n must also be positive. The only whole number value of n for which both sides of the equation produce a positive value is $\boxed{5}$.

10. Let the distance from an unfolded corner to the the point where the overlapped paper begins be x. This is the shorter leg of a right triangle where the other leg has length 70, and the hypotenuse has length $98 - x$. By the Pythagorean Theorem, $x^2 + 70^2 = (98 - x)^2$, or $x^2 + 4900 = x^2 - 196x + 9604$. Solving this equation, $x = 24$, so the hypotenuse of this triangle has length $98 - 24 = 74$. The region where the paper has double its original thickness is half of the rectangle minus a 24-70-74 right triangle. This is also be viewed as an obtuse triangle with a base of 74 and a height of 70, which has area $\frac{1}{2} \cdot 74 \cdot 70 = \boxed{2590}$.

Number Sense
12221

Place ID Sticker
Inside This Box

Name _____

Grade _____

School _____

1. $122 + 22 =$ _____.

2. $479 + 342 =$ _____.

3. The hundreds digit of 58934 is _____.

4. $5 + 8 \times 5 =$ _____.

5. $712 - 389 =$ _____.

6. The remainder of $87 \div 5$ is _____.

7. $17 + 41 + 39 + 13 =$ _____.

8. $72 \div 12 =$ _____.

9. The product of 14 and 3 is _____.

10. (estimate) $258 + 473 + 559 =$ _____.

11. $42 \times 11 =$ _____.

12. $517 - 289 - 122 =$ _____.

13. $13^2 =$ _____.

14. The remainder of $107 \div 9$ is _____.

15. $15 \times 26 =$ _____.

16. $6 \times 9 \times 5 =$ _____.

17. $21 \times 19 =$ _____.

18. *CXXXIV* in Arabic numerals is _____.

19. $1.4 \times 0.9 =$ _____ (decimal).

20. (estimate) $199 \times 203 =$ _____.

21. The GCD of 12 and 20 is _____.

22. $38 \times 25 =$ _____.

23. $15 \times 8 \div 10 =$ _____.

24. If 1 mile is equal to 5280 feet, then $\frac{1}{10}$ mile is equal to _____ feet.

25. $273 \div 13 =$ _____.

26. The greater of $\frac{2}{3}$ and $\frac{5}{7}$ is _____ (fraction).

27. $27^2 =$ _____.

28. $\frac{2}{7} + \frac{1}{21} =$ _____ (fraction).

29. $14 + 17 + 20 + 23 + 26 =$ _____.

30. (estimate) $234567 \div 117 =$ _____.

31. $99 \times 13 =$ _____.

32. $\frac{1}{4} =$ _____ %.

33. The area of a square with perimeter 32 is _____.

34. $35^2 =$ _____.

35. The number of even whole numbers between 11 and 41 is _____.

36. $27 \times 23 =$ _____.

37. The LCM of 12 and 20 is _____.

38. 20% of 60 is _____.

39. 42 days is _____ weeks.

40. (estimate) $667 \times 180 =$ _____.

41. $14 \times 4 + 8 \times 13 = $ _____.

42. The remainder of $474 \div 11$ is _____.

43. $87 \times 27 = $ _____.

44. The area of a right triangle with legs of length 12 and 9 is _____.

45. $54 \times 101 = $ _____.

46. The tenth term in the arithmetic sequence $3, 7, 11, \ldots$ is _____.

47. $22^2 - 12^2 = $ _____.

48. 45_6 in base 10 is _____.

49. $\sqrt{1156} = $ _____.

50. (estimate) $12 \times 142857 = $ _____.

51. $104 \times 107 = $ _____.

52. $12\frac{1}{2}\% = $ _____ (fraction).

53. 21_4 in base 2 is _____ $_2$.

54. $2^7 = $ _____.

55. The sum of the terms of the arithmetic sequence $5, 10, 15, \ldots, 100$ is _____.

56. $98 \times 95 = $ _____.

57. The measure of an interior angle in a regular quadrilateral is _____ $^\circ$.

58. $31 \times 111 = $ _____.

59. The median of the list $5, 11, 4, 13, 1$ is _____.

60. (estimate) $\sqrt{202222} = $ _____.

61. $4\frac{1}{3} \times 4\frac{2}{3} = $ _____ (mixed number).

62. Two fair coins are flipped. The probability that both show the same result is _____ (fraction).

63. $0.\overline{18} = $ _____ (fraction).

64. The number 56 written in base 5 is _____ $_5$.

65. $74 \times 125 = $ _____.

66. $63^2 = $ _____.

67. The perimeter of a right triangle with legs of length 8 and 15 is _____.

68. $15 \times 35 \times 21 = $ _____.

69. If $w = 7$, then $w^2 + 6w + 9 = $ _____.

70. (estimate) $51^3 = $ _____.

71. $988 \times 989 = $ _____.

72. The number of subsets of $\{L, E, T, S, G, O\}$ is __.

73. $\sqrt[3]{636056} = $ _____.

74. The number of positive whole number divisors of 28 is _____.

75. If $3^x = \frac{1}{3}$, then $3^{2-x} = $ _____.

76. $\sqrt{8} \times \sqrt{98} = $ _____.

77. The sum of the terms of the infinite geometric sequence $1, \frac{1}{2}, \frac{1}{4}, \ldots$ is _____.

78. $75 \times 92 \times 9 = $ _____.

79. The surface area of a cube with an edge of length 8 is _____.

80. (estimate) $\sqrt{21 \times 22 \times 23} = $ _____.

Place ID Sticker
Inside This Box

Name _____

Grade _____

School _____

1. Ⓐ Ⓑ Ⓒ Ⓓ Ⓔ   11. Ⓐ Ⓑ Ⓒ Ⓓ Ⓔ   21. Ⓐ Ⓑ Ⓒ Ⓓ Ⓔ

2. Ⓐ Ⓑ Ⓒ Ⓓ Ⓔ   12. Ⓐ Ⓑ Ⓒ Ⓓ Ⓔ   22. Ⓐ Ⓑ Ⓒ Ⓓ Ⓔ

3. Ⓐ Ⓑ Ⓒ Ⓓ Ⓔ   13. Ⓐ Ⓑ Ⓒ Ⓓ Ⓔ   23. Ⓐ Ⓑ Ⓒ Ⓓ Ⓔ

4. Ⓐ Ⓑ Ⓒ Ⓓ Ⓔ   14. Ⓐ Ⓑ Ⓒ Ⓓ Ⓔ   24. Ⓐ Ⓑ Ⓒ Ⓓ Ⓔ

5. Ⓐ Ⓑ Ⓒ Ⓓ Ⓔ   15. Ⓐ Ⓑ Ⓒ Ⓓ Ⓔ   25. Ⓐ Ⓑ Ⓒ Ⓓ Ⓔ

6. Ⓐ Ⓑ Ⓒ Ⓓ Ⓔ   16. Ⓐ Ⓑ Ⓒ Ⓓ Ⓔ   26. Ⓐ Ⓑ Ⓒ Ⓓ Ⓔ

7. Ⓐ Ⓑ Ⓒ Ⓓ Ⓔ   17. Ⓐ Ⓑ Ⓒ Ⓓ Ⓔ   27. Ⓐ Ⓑ Ⓒ Ⓓ Ⓔ

8. Ⓐ Ⓑ Ⓒ Ⓓ Ⓔ   18. Ⓐ Ⓑ Ⓒ Ⓓ Ⓔ   28. Ⓐ Ⓑ Ⓒ Ⓓ Ⓔ

9. Ⓐ Ⓑ Ⓒ Ⓓ Ⓔ   19. Ⓐ Ⓑ Ⓒ Ⓓ Ⓔ   29. Ⓐ Ⓑ Ⓒ Ⓓ Ⓔ

10. Ⓐ Ⓑ Ⓒ Ⓓ Ⓔ   20. Ⓐ Ⓑ Ⓒ Ⓓ Ⓔ   30. Ⓐ Ⓑ Ⓒ Ⓓ Ⓔ

1. Which of the following expressions has the greatest value?

(A) 6×9 (B) 2×29 (C) 3×19 (D) 12×5 (E) 4×14

2. At the theater concession stand, a large bucket of popcorn is sold for $5, and a regular bucket of popcorn is sold for $3. A group celebrating a birthday purchased three large buckets of popcorn and two regular buckets of popcorn. How many dollars did the group spend on popcorn?

(A) $22   (B) $20   (C) $21   (D) $18   (E) $19

3. Mackenzie started watching the most recent episode of *The Mandalorian* at 7:48 PM. The episode was 44 minutes long, and Mackenzie watched it from start to finish without taking any breaks. What time was it when Mackenzie finished watching the episode?

(A) 8:24 PM   (B) 8:22 PM   (C) 8:34 PM   (D) 8:32 PM   (E) 8:28 PM

4. The *T*-shaped figure below is formed by two identical rectangles, each with a width of 9 and a length of 4. What is the perimeter of the *T*-shaped figure?

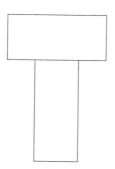

(A) 48   (B) 44   (C) 52   (D) 40   (E) 42

5. If the day before yesterday was a Tuesday, then what day of the week will it be two days after tomorrow?

(A) Thursday   (B) Monday   (C) Saturday   (D) Sunday   (E) Friday

6. Britney handed the cashier at the arcade three $20 bills and asked to be paid back the same amount using only bills worth less than $20. The cashier handed Britney three $10 bills, four $5 bills, and two rare $2 bills. The remaining bills were all $1 bills. How many $1 bills did Britney receive from the cashier?

(A) 11   (B) 6   (C) 1   (D) 4   (E) 9

7. How many positive whole numbers greater than 1 and less than 10 evenly divide 168?

(A) 7   (B) 5   (C) 6   (D) 4   (E) 3

8. A regular pentagon is shown below, with one diagonal drawn. When all of the possible diagonals of the pentagon are drawn, at how many different points inside the pentagon do two or more diagonals intersect, or cross another diagonal?

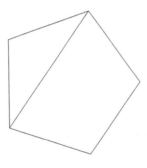

(A) 10   (B) 6   (C) 5   (D) 4   (E) 8

9. Five friends enjoyed a dinner together at a restaurant, and planned to split the bill evenly. Unfortunately, Thomas forgot his money. The other four guests paid an extra $6 each to cover Thomas' share of the bill. What was the total bill for the meal for all five friends?

(A) $120   (B) $100   (C) $150   (D) $90   (E) $140

10. The first mathleague.org Elementary National Championship was held in 2014, and the championship has been held every year since. Jake turned eleven years old the same year he competed in the eighth mathleague.org Elementary National Championship. What year was Jake born?

(A) 2009   (B) 2013   (C) 2012   (D) 2010   (E) 2011

11. The sum of three different prime numbers is 32. What is the greatest possible value for the product of the three numbers?

(A) 322　　　　(B) 418　　　　(C) 504　　　　(D) 442　　　　(E) 546

12. The figure below shows a square, with one diagonal of the square drawn. A second square is formed by connected the midpoints of the sides of the original square, with both diagonals of that smaller square drawn as well. If the area of the original square is 24, then what is the total area of the shaded regions?

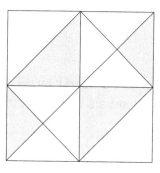

(A) 8　　　　(B) 12　　　　(C) 6　　　　(D) 10　　　　(E) 9

13. Four soccer players are choosing an order to try penalty kicks, but Alejandro refuses to be first or last, and Scott refuses to be first. How many ways can the four soccer players be placed in an order to try penalty kicks?

(A) 12　　　　(B) 8　　　　(C) 9　　　　(D) 6　　　　(E) 4

14. A number is twice as far from 51 on the number line as it is from 75. What is the sum of all possible values of the number?

(A) 142　　　　(B) 99　　　　(C) 67　　　　(D) 166　　　　(E) 190

15. Raymond averaged a score of 27 on his four quizzes. Raymond's scores on the first two quizzes were equal, and his score on the third quiz was six points less than his score on the fourth quiz. Raymond scored a 29 on his fourth quiz. What was Raymond's score on each of the first two quizzes?

(A) 28　　　　(B) 29　　　　(C) 25　　　　(D) 26　　　　(E) 27

16. The right triangle below has one leg of length 16 and an area of 56. What is the least positive whole number that is greater than the length of the hypotenuse of the triangle?

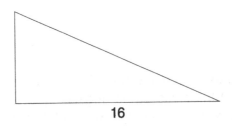

16

(A) 21   (B) 20   (C) 19   (D) 17   (E) 18

17. Shana chose a positive whole number and divided it by 65. Her result was greater than $\frac{1}{8}$ but less than $\frac{1}{3}$. How many different positive whole numbers could Shana have chosen?

(A) 10   (B) 12   (C) 14   (D) 13   (E) 11

18. The factorial of a positive whole number is marked by a ! after the number, and the value of the factorial of a positive whole number is the product of all of the positive whole numbers less than or equal to the number. For example, $5! = 5 \cdot 4 \cdot 3 \cdot 2 \cdot 1$, which is 120. What is the value of $\frac{11!-10!-9!}{8!}$?

(A) 861   (B) 891   (C) 899   (D) 900   (E) 810

19. The Little Six basketball league has six teams. Each team in the league plays four games against teams from other leagues. Then each team in the league plays every other team in the league twice. How many total games are played where at least one of the teams playing is from The Little Six basketball league?

(A) 60   (B) 72   (C) 84   (D) 64   (E) 54

20. If $A \heartsuit B = \frac{A+2B}{2}$, then for what number k is $10 \heartsuit (6 \heartsuit k)$ equal to 19?

(A) 15   (B) 13   (C) 12   (D) 14   (E) 11

21. A bag contains only red, blue, and green marbles. The ratio of red marbles to blue marbles is 15 : 16. The ratio of green marbles to blue marbles is 5 : 4. After one dozen blue marbles are added to the bag, the ratio of red marbles to blue marbles is 5 : 6, and the ratio of green marbles to blue marbles is 10 : 9. What is the total number of red and green marbles in the bag?

    (A) 190   (B) 210   (C) 180   (D) 200   (E) 195

22. Which of the following is greater than 20?

    (A) $8\sqrt{6}$ (B) $9\sqrt{5}$ (C) $4\sqrt{23}$ (D) $6\sqrt{11}$ (E) $14\sqrt{2}$

23. At Pete's Pastel Pizzeria, an extra large pizza is 21 inches in diameter. The pizza is sliced into six equal pieces by making three cuts along diameters of the pizza, as shown below. To the nearest whole number of inches, what is the perimeter of one of these six pieces of pizza?

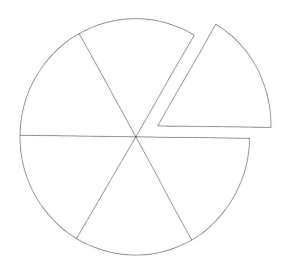

    (A) 36   (B) 31   (C) 35   (D) 33   (E) 32

24. The value of the decimal product $2 \cdot 2 \cdot 2 \cdot 2 \cdot 3 \cdot 3 \cdot 3 \cdot 7$ is written in base 5. The result has how many more digits that are 4 than digits that are 0?

    (A) 1   (B) 2   (C) 3   (D) 0   (E) 5

25. On Monday, Travis averaged 45 miles per hour on his roundtrip journey from home to work and then back home. On Tuesday, Travis averaged 40 miles per hour on the same roundtrip journey, and his roundtip journey took 12 minutes longer than it did on Monday. How far, in miles, is Travis' home from his work?

(A) 72   (B) 45   (C) 54   (D) 36   (E) 48

26. In the figure below, segments *AE*, *ED*, and *DB* have equal length, and segments *CE*, *CD*, and *CB* have equal length. Additionally, points *A*, *E*, and *C* are collinear, and points *A*, *D*, and *B* are collinear. What is the sum of the digits of the angle measure, in degrees, of angle *EAD*?

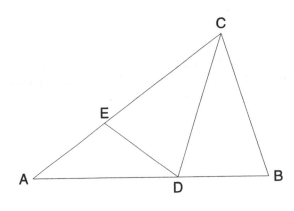

(A) 3   (B) 6   (C) 8   (D) 12   (E) 9

27. Rudy enters the number 1892 into his calculator and presses the square root button. He then adds 1892 to the result, and presses the square root button again. He repeats the process a dozen more times, always adding 1892 to the result of the square root and then pressing the square root button. The final number displayed on Rudy's calculator is nearest to what positive whole number?

(A) 44   (B) 47   (C) 46   (D) 43   (E) 45

28. What is the sum of the digits of the greatest four-digit positive whole number that has a remainder of 4 when divided by 7, a remainder of 5 when divided by 9, and a remainder of 6 when divided by 11?

(A) 21   (B) 25   (C) 20   (D) 24   (E) 23

29. A dodecagon is formed by removing four squares of side length 60 from a square of side length 289, as shown below. What is the side length of the largest possible square that lies entirely on or in this dodecagon?

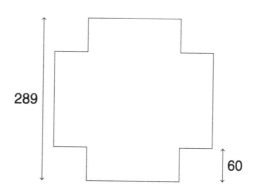

289

60

(A) 216　　　　　(B) 225　　　　　(C) 220　　　　　(D) 221　　　　　(E) 224

30. Three points are chosen at random on a circle. What is the probability that the triangle formed by the three points is acute?

(A) $\frac{1}{8}$　　　　　(B) $\frac{1}{3}$　　　　　(C) $\frac{1}{2}$　　　　　(D) $\frac{1}{6}$　　　　　(E) $\frac{1}{4}$

Name _____

Grade _____

School _____

Problems 1 & 2

1. On Monday, Kenneth's walk to school was twelve minutes. On Tuesday, his walk to school was eleven minutes. On Wednesday, his walk to school was thirteen minutes. On Thursday, his walk to school was one minute longer than his walk on Wednesday, and on Friday his walk to school was two minutes shorter than his walk on Monday. Altogether, from Monday through Friday, how many minutes did Kenneth spend walking to school?

1.

2. A rectangular piece of paper on a table is divided into three identical squares, as shown below. Each of the squares is then colored either red or blue. If rotations of the same coloring are considered to be identical, then how many different ways are there to color the three squares?

2.

Place ID Sticker
Inside This Box

Name _____

Grade _____

School _____

Problems 3 & 4

3. Quarters are coins worth 25 cents, and dimes are coins worth 10 cents. Vai has a collection of seven quarters and six dimes. What is the fewest number of additional coins, all quarters or dimes, that Vai needs so that her quarters and dimes are worth a total of exactly 400 cents?

3. _____

4. Jamie runs 18 meters in the same time Jessica runs 15 meters. Jamie and Jessica are standing next to each other on a circular running track that is 360 meters in length, and both start running at the same time and in the same direction. If Jamie and Jessica each run at an unchanging pace, how many laps will Jamie have completed around the track when she passes Jessica for the first time?

4. _____

Place ID Sticker
Inside This Box

Name _____

Grade _____

School _____

Problems 5 & 6

5. A number is called a *perfect square* if it is the result of a whole number multiplied by itself. For example, since $5 \times 5 = 25$, the number 25 is a perfect square. What is the four-digit perfect square that has a thousands digit less than its hundreds digit, a hundreds digit less than its tens digit, and a tens digit less than its ones digit?

5.

6. A regular nonagon is shown below. How many different triangles have vertices that are also vertices of the nonagon, and share at least one side with the nonagon?

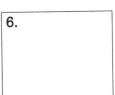

6.

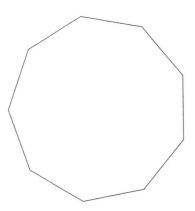

Place ID Sticker
Inside This Box

Name _____

Grade _____

School _____

Problems 7 & 8

7. Emily needed to read a book over the weekend. On Friday after school, she started reading the book from the beginning. That evening she read half the pages of the book plus an additional twelve pages. On Saturday morning, she read half the remaining pages plus an additional nine pages. On Sunday, she read the final forty-seven pages of the book. How many pages long was the book?

7.

8. An ant travels along the surface of a $17 \times 25 \times 40$ right rectangular prism, starting at one corner of the prism and ending at the corner that is farthest away from the starting corner. What is the shortest possible distance the ant traveled? Express your answer to the nearest whole number.

8.

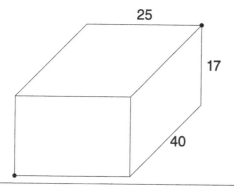

School or Team

Name _____

Name _____

Name _____

Name _____

Place ID Sticker
Inside This Box

Place ID Sticker
Inside This Box

Place ID Sticker
Inside This Box

Place ID Sticker
Inside This Box

1.	2.	3.	4.	5.
6.	7.	8.	9.	10.

1. What is the sum of all of the positive whole numbers less than 31 that are even but not multiples of 3?

2. Marlee has a collection of memes saved on her smartphone. If Marlee had one more meme, the memes could be displayed in a gallery with seven memes per row and no incomplete rows. If Marlee had four fewer memes, the memes could be displayed in a gallery with six memes per row and no incomplete rows. What is the least possible number of memes that Marlee could have on her smartphone?

3. A twelve-hour analog clock rings its chimes every hour, and the chimes ring a number of times equal to the number of the hour. For example, at both seven o'clock in the morning and seven o'clock in the evening, the chimes ring seven times. This is true for all hours except midnight. At midnight, to signal the start of a new day, the chimes ring two dozen times. How many total times do the chimes ring in the month of October?

4. Using only segments in the figure below as sides of the triangle, how many different triangles can be formed?

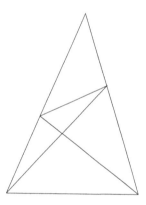

5. Each of the digits 2, 4, 7, and 9 is used exactly once to replace a □ in the expression $(□ + □) \times (□ + □)$. For example, one possible value of the expression is $(2 + 7) \times (4 + 9) = 117$. What is the value of the greatest possible value of the expression minus the least possible value of the expression?

6. A jar of salad dressing is filled with a mix of 80% oil and the rest is vinegar. A second jar of salad dressing, half the size of the first jar, is filled with a mix of 90% oil and the rest is vinegar. The contents of both jars are mixed in a larger jar. To the nearest whole number, what percent of the resulting mixture is vinegar?

7. A palindrome is a number that is unchanged when the order of its digits is reversed. For example, 1221 and 6556 are both palindromes. How many four-digit positive whole numbers are palindromes and multiples of 99?

8. Six students are going to be seated around a circular table. Andre insists on sitting next to Bryce, but Bryce refuses to sit next to Charlotte. If seating arrangements are considered different only if a student has someone different seated beside them on their left, then how many different ways can the students be seated around the table?

9. In a trapezoid, a leg of length 600 is perpendicular to both bases. Two circles are each tangent to three sides of the trapezoid as shown. The radius of the larger circle is 200. To the nearest whole number, what is the radius of the smaller circle?

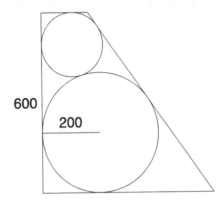

600

200

10. Leland has a large collection of identical Lego bricks that are each 1 unit tall, and a large collection of identical Lego bricks that are each 2 units tall. Using these bricks, how many different ways can Leland assemble a tower that is fifteen units tall?

Answers
12221

Sprint Round

1. D	11. D	21. B
2. C	12. E	22. B
3. D	13. B	23. E
4. B	14. D	24. C
5. D	15. A	25. D
6. B	16. E	26. E
7. C	17. D	27. A
8. C	18. B	28. E
9. A	19. E	29. D
10. D	20. E	30. E

Target Round

1. 60
2. 6
3. 9
4. 6
5. 1369
6. 54
7. 248
8. 58

Team Round

1. 150
2. 34
3. 5208
4. 12
5. 25
6. 17(%)
7. 10
8. 36
9. 107
10. 987

Number Sense

1. 144	21. 4
2. 821	22. 950
3. 9	23. 12
4. 45	24. 528
5. 323	25. 21
6. 2	26. $\frac{5}{7}$
7. 110	27. 729
8. 6	28. $\frac{1}{3}$
9. 42	29. 100
10. [1226, 1354]	30. [1905, 2105]
11. 462	31. 1287
12. 106	32. 25
13. 169	33. 64
14. 8	34. 1225
15. 390	35. 15
16. 270	36. 621
17. 399	37. 60
18. 134	38. 12
19. 1.26	39. 6
20. [38378, 42416]	40. [114057, 126063]

41. 160	61. $20\frac{2}{9}$
42. 1	62. $\frac{1}{2}$
43. 2349	63. $\frac{2}{11}$
44. 54	64. 211
45. 5454	65. 9250
46. 39	66. 3969
47. 340	67. 40
48. 29	68. 11025
49. 34	69. 100
50. [1628570, 1799998]	70. [126019, 139283]
51. 11128	71. 977132
52. $\frac{1}{8}$	72. 64
53. 1001	73. 86
54. 128	74. 6
55. 1050	75. 27
56. 9310	76. 28
57. 90	77. 2
58. 3441	78. 62100
59. 5	79. 384
60. [428, 472]	80. [98, 108]

Sprint Round Solutions

1. Evaluating each, $6 \times 9 = 54$, $4 \times 14 = 56$, $3 \times 19 = 57$, $2 \times 29 = 58$, and $12 \times 5 = 60$. The greatest value among these is $\boxed{60}$.

2. The large buckets of popcorn totaled $3 \times \$5 = \$15$, and the regular buckets of popcorn totaled $2 \times \$3 = \$6$. The total price of the popcorn was $\$15 + \$6 = \boxed{\$21}$.

3. After 12 minutes have passed, it will be 8:00 PM, and there will be $44 - 12 = 32$ minutes left of the episode. After those 32 minutes elapse, the time will be $\boxed{\text{8:32 PM}}$.

4. The perimeter of each individual rectangle is $4 + 4 + 9 + 9 = 26$. If the two rectangles were separate, their total perimeter would be $26 + 26 = 52$. But when the *T*-shaped figure is formed, the segments of length 4 where the rectangles meet are removed from the figure. The perimeter of the *T*-shaped figure is therefore $52 - 4 - 4 = \boxed{44}$.

5. If the day before yesterday was a Tuesday, then yesterday was a Wednesday, and today is a Thursday. Tomorrow is a Friday. One day after tomorrow is a Saturday, and two days after tomorrow is a $\boxed{\text{Sunday}}$.

6. The total amount of money Britney gave the cashier was $3 \times \$20 = \$60$. The amount of money Britney received from the cashier in bills other than \$1 bills was $3 \times \$10 + 4 \times \$5 + 2 \times \$2 = \$54$. Therefore, Britney received $60 - 54 = \boxed{6}$ \$1 bills.

7. The number 168 can be expressed as 21×8. Since it is divisible by 8, it is also divisible by 2 and 4. Since it is divisible by 21, it is divisible by 3 and 7. Since it is divisible by 2 and 3, it is also divisible by 6. It is not divisible by 5, and since $1 + 6 + 8 = 15$ is not a multiple of 9, it is not divisible by 9. The whole numbers greater than 1 and less than 10 that evenly divide 168 are 2, 3, 4, 6, 7, and 8, for a total of $\boxed{6}$ divisors.

8. When all of the 5 diagonals are drawn, a five-pointed star is formed, and each diagonal intersects exactly 2 other diagonals. This is $5 \times 2 = 10$ intersections, but it double counts each intersection, so the number of points of intersection is $10 \div 2 = \boxed{5}$.

9. The other four friends contributed a total of $\$6 \times 4 = \$24$ for Thomas, which was his portion of the bill. Therefore, the total bill for all five friends was $5 \times \$24 = \boxed{\$120}$.

10. The first championship was held in 2014, so the eighth championship was held in $2014 + (8-1) = 2021$. Since Jake turned 11 years old in 2021, he was born in $2021 - 11 = \boxed{2010}$.

11. The sum of three odd numbers is an odd number, but since 32 is even, at least one of the primes must be even. The only even prime is 2, so the other two primes are odd and sum to $32 - 2 = 30$. The possible prime pairs that sum to 30 are 7 and 23, 11 and 19, and 13 and 17. The products of each pair are 161, 209, and 221, so the greatest possible value for the product of the three numbers is $2 \cdot 221 = \boxed{442}$.

12. The two large triangular regions are each $\frac{1}{8}$ of the original square, and the two small triangular regions are each $\frac{1}{16}$ of the original square. Altogether, the shaded regions total $\frac{1}{8} + \frac{1}{8} + \frac{1}{16} + \frac{1}{16} = \frac{3}{8}$ of the square, and have an area of $\frac{3}{8} \cdot 24 = \boxed{9}$.

13. Since neither Alejandro or Scott wants to be first, there are only 2 possibilities for the player that goes first. After selecting this player, because Alejandro does not want to be last, there are only 2 possibilities for the player that goes last. After the first and last player are selected, there are 2 possibilities for the player that goes second, as Alejandro is now a possibility, and then, after all of these players are selected, only 1 possibility for the player that goes third. The total number of possible orderings of the players is $2 \times 2 \times 2 \times 1 = \boxed{8}$.

14. There are two possibilities for the location of the number on the number line. The first possibility is that the number is between 51 and 75. The distance from 75 to 51, which is $75 - 51 = 24$, would need to be split into two pieces, one twice the other. Since $\frac{2}{3}$ of 24 is 16, the number could be $51 + 16 = 67$. The second possibility is that the number is greater than 75, and the distance from the number to 51 would always be 24 more than the distance from the number to 75, so for that distance to be double the distance from 75, the distance from 75 would also be 24, and the number could be 99. Therefore, the sum of all possible values of the number is $67 + 99 = \boxed{166}$.

15. The total points Raymond scored on the four quizzes was $27 \times 4 = 108$. Raymond scored a 29 on the fourth quiz and a $29 - 6 = 23$ on the third quiz. Therefore the sum of Raymond's scores on his first two quizzes was $108 - 29 - 23 = 56$, and since both scores were equal, each was $56 \div 2 = \boxed{28}$.

16. Because the area of the triangle is 56, the product of the lengths of the legs is $2 \cdot 56 = 112$, so the length of the other leg is $\frac{112}{16} = 7$. By the Pythagorean Theorem, the square of the length of the hypotenuse is $16^2 + 7^2 = 305$. Since $17^2 = 289$ and $18^2 = 324$, the least positive whole number that is greater than the length of the hypotenuse is $\boxed{18}$.

17. If the number divided by 65 was greater than $\frac{1}{8}$, then 8 times the number must be greater than 65. This is true for all numbers greater than or equal to 9. Similarly, if the number divided by 65 was less than $\frac{1}{3}$, then 3 times the number must be less than 65. This is true for all numbers less than or equal to 21. Therefore Shana could have chosen any positive whole number from 9 through 21, so the number of possibilities is $21 - 9 + 1 = \boxed{13}$.

18. The number 11! can be expressed as $11 \cdot 10 \cdot 9 \cdot 8!$. Similarly, the number 10! can be expressed as $10 \cdot 9 \cdot 8!$, and 9! as $9 \cdot 8!$. Then $\frac{11! - 10! - 9!}{8!} = \frac{11 \cdot 10 \cdot 9 \cdot 8! - 10 \cdot 9 \cdot 8! - 9 \cdot 8!}{8!}$, which is $11 \cdot 10 \cdot 9 - 10 \cdot 9 - 9$. Factoring yields $9 \cdot (11 \cdot 10 - 10 - 1)$, or $9 \cdot 99$, which is $\boxed{891}$.

19. The number of games played against teams in other leagues is $6 \times 4 = 24$. Now suppose that of the two games between any two teams in the league, each team is designated as the home team for exactly one of the games. Then each team will have exactly $6 - 1 = 5$ games as the home team. Therefore there are $6 \cdot 5 = 30$ games played between two teams in the league, and the total number of games played by teams in the Little Six is $24 + 30 = \boxed{54}$.

20. The expression $A\heartsuit B$ can be simplified to $\frac{A}{2} + B$. So if $10\heartsuit m = 19$, then $5 + m = 19$, and $m = 14$. Then $6\heartsuit k = 14$, so $3 + k = 14$, and $k = \boxed{11}$.

21. Let the number of blue marbles be $16b$. Then the number of red marbles is $15b$, and the number of green marbles is $20b$. After adding 12 blue marbles to the bag, the ratio of red marbles to blue marbles is $\frac{15b}{16b+12}$, which is $\frac{5}{6}$. Setting these quantities equal and simplifying, $90b = 80b + 60$, so $10b = 60$ and $b = 6$. Then the number of red marbles if $15 \cdot 6 = 90$, the number of green marbles is $20 \cdot 6 = 120$, and the total number of red and green marbles is $90 + 120 = \boxed{210}$.

22. The square of 20 is $20^2 = 400$. Squaring each answer choice yields $4^2 \cdot 23 = 368$, $8^2 \cdot 6 = 384$, $14^2 \cdot 2 = 392$, $6^2 \cdot 11 = 396$, and $9^2 \cdot 5 = 405$. The only answer choice that is greater than 400 when squared, and therefore greater than 20, is $\boxed{9\sqrt{5}}$.

23. The perimeter of a pizza slice is composed of two straight edges, each with a length equal to the radius of the pizza, and a curved portion that is equal to $\frac{1}{6}$ of the circumference of the pizza. The two radii sum to the diameter of the pizza, which is 21. Using $\frac{22}{7}$ as an approximation for π, the curved portion has length of very nearly $\frac{1}{6} \cdot \frac{22}{7} \cdot 21 = 11$. To the nearest whole number of inches, the total perimeter is $21 + 11 = \boxed{32}$.

24. The product can be grouped as $(2 \cdot 2 \cdot 2 \cdot 3) \cdot (2 \cdot 3 \cdot 3 \cdot 7)$, or $24 \cdot 126$. Converting each to base 5 yields $44_5 \cdot 1001_5$. This is $44_5 \cdot 1000_5 + 44_5 \cdot 1$, or $44000_5 + 44_5 = 44044_5$. The number of digits that are 4 exceeds the number of digits that are 0 by $\boxed{3}$.

25. Let D be the distance, in miles, from Travis' home to his work. Then his roundtrip journey is distance $2D$. Let T be the time, in hours, of Travis' roundtrip on Monday. Then $T + \frac{12}{60}$, or $T + \frac{1}{5}$, is the time, in hours, of Travis' roundtrip on Tuesday. Since rate is equal to distance divided by time, $\frac{2D}{T} = 45$, and $\frac{2D}{T + \frac{1}{5}} = 40$. Simplifying both equations, $2D = 45T$, and $2D = 40T + 8$. Therefore, $45T = 40T + 8$, and $T = \frac{8}{5}$. Then $2D = \frac{8}{5} \cdot 45$, so $2D = 72$, and D is $\boxed{36}$.

26. Triangles *ECD* and *DCB* are isosceles and congruent, and triangle *AED* is isosceles. Let the degree measure of angle *CDB* be x. Then the degree measure of angle *EDC* is also x, and the degree measure of angle *ADE* is $180° - 2x$. But angle *CED* is also x, so angle *AED* is $180° - x$, and because triangle *AED* is isosceles, the degree measure of angle *ADE* is $\frac{180° - (180° - x)}{2}$. Setting these two values for the measure of angle *ADE* equal, $180° - 2x = \frac{180° - (180° - x)}{2}$, so $360° - 4x = x$, and $x = 72°$. Then the measure of angle *EAD*, which is equal to the measure of angle *ADE*, is $180° - 2 \cdot 72° = 36°$, and $3 + 6 = \boxed{9}$.

27. Suppose there is a number k to which this operation converges. That is, a number that the results on Rudy's calculator approach more and more closely the more he performs the operation. Then $\sqrt{1892 + k} = k$. Squaring both sides of this equation, $1892 + k = k^2$, and $k^2 - k - 1892 = 0$. This quadratic can be factored as $(k - 44)(k + 43)$. Since the value of k is the result of a square root, k must be positive, so k is 44. A dozen applications of the operation are far more than enough to get very close to this value, so the positive whole number nearest to Rudy's result is $\boxed{44}$.

28. Considering the first two conditions, the smallest number that has a remainder of 4 when divided by 7 and a remainder of 5 when divided by 9 is 32. Since the least common multiple of 7 and 9 is 63, any positive whole number that meets these two conditions is of the form $32 + 63k$, where k is a non-negative whole number. For $32 + 63k$ to be 6 more than a multiple of 11, $26 + 63k$ must be a multiple of 11, and since $22 + 55k$ is always a multiple of 11, $4 + 8k$ must be a multiple of 11. This first occurs when k is 5. Therefore the smallest number that meets all three conditions is $5 \cdot 63 + 32 = 347$. Since $11 \cdot 63 = 693$ is the least common multiple of 7, 9, and 11, any number that meets all three conditions is of the form $347 + 693k$. The greatest possible value of k for which this is a four-digit number is $k = 13$, yielding $347 + 693 \cdot 13 = 9356$, and $9 + 3 + 5 + 6 = \boxed{23}$.

29. The longer side length of the dodecagon is $289 - 2 \cdot 60 = 169$. The largest possible square has one vertex on each of the four sides of length 169, and sides of the square that just touch the vertices of the dodecagon where two side lengths of 60 meet. Now partition the dodecagon into a central square of side length 169 and four congruent rectangles, each on a side of this central square, that are 60×169. The sides of the largest possible square partition each of these 60×169 rectangles into three right triangles. The largest of these triangles is half of the rectangle, and has a hypotenuse of length 169 and an altitude to the hypotenuse of length 60. The side of the square is equal to the sum of the lengths of the legs of this right triangle. Let the lengths of these two legs be x and y. By the Pythagorean Theorem, $x^2 + y^2 = 169^2$. By the area of the triangle, $xy = 60 \cdot 169$. Then $x^2 + 2xy + y^2 = 169^2 + 2 \cdot 60 \cdot 169$, or $289 \cdot 169$. Therefore, $x + y$, which, again, is the side length of the square, is $\sqrt{289 \cdot 169} = 17 \cdot 13$, or $\boxed{221}$.

30. The triangle is acute only if all three points do not lie on the same semicircle. Any two points will lie on a semicircle with probability 1. If the two points are the endpoints of a minor arc of 180°, then the third point will lie on a semicircle with the other two with probability 1. If the two points are the endpoints of a minor arc of $k°$, any point in the $k°$ minor arc will lie in the same semicircle, as will any point in the $180° - k°$ arc on either end of the minor arc. This probability is $\frac{k° + 180° - k° + 180° - k°}{360°} = \frac{360° - k°}{360°}$. Since $k°$ varies from 0° to 180°, the probability all three points lie on a semicircle varies linearly from 1 to $\frac{1}{2}$, and the average probability is $\frac{1 + \frac{1}{2}}{2} = \frac{3}{4}$. This is the probability the three points lie on a semicircle and form an obtuse triangle, so the probability the three points do not lie on a semicircle and form an acute triangle is $1 - \frac{3}{4} = \boxed{\dfrac{1}{4}}$.

Target Round Solutions

1. The Monday walk was 12 minutes, Tuesday was 11, and Wednesday was 13. Thursday was $13 + 1 = 14$ minutes, and Friday was $12 - 2 = 10$ minutes. Altogether, the total number of minutes was $12 + 11 + 13 + 14 + 10 = \boxed{60}$.

2. The squares could be colored all red, or all blue, for 2 colorings. The only other possibility is for two of the squares to be colored red or two to be colored blue. If two are colored red, then the blue square can either be in the middle or on the end, for 2 colorings. Similarly, if two are colored blue, then the red square can either be in the middle or on the end, for another 2 colorings. Altogether, the total number of possible colorings is $2 + 2 + 2 = \boxed{6}$.

3. Vai's quarters are worth $7 \times 25 = 175$ cents, and her dimes are worth $6 \times 10 = 60$ cents. Vai has a total of $175 + 60 = 235$ cents, and needs $400 - 235 = 165$ cents more. The fewest number of coins is accomplished by maximizing the number of quarters used. While 6 quarters are worth 150 cents, the remaining $165 - 150 = 15$ cents cannot be formed using quarters and dimes. But 5 quarters are worth 125 cents, and the remaining $165 - 125 = 40$ cents can be formed with 4 dimes. The total number of additional coins needed is $5 + 4 = \boxed{9}$.

4. Regardless of the distance run, Jamie will always run $\frac{18}{15} = \frac{6}{5}$ as far as Jessica can in the same amount of time. When Jessica runs 1 lap, Jamie will have run $\frac{6}{5}$ of a lap. When Jessica runs 5 laps, Jamie will pass her for the first time, and her number of laps run will be $\boxed{6}$.

5. The units digit of a perfect square can only be a 1, 4, 5, 6, or 9, and if the units digit of a perfect square is 5, then the tens digit must be 2. Based on the inequality conditions for digits, we find that the units digit can not equal 1 or 5 because there is no way to select the hundreds and thousands digits. Additionally, the only number that ends in 4 that satisfies the inequality condition for digits is 1234, but that is not a perfect square. If the units digit is a 6, then the number has to be less than 3000 because 3456 is not a perfect square, but $34^2 = 1156$, $36^2 = 1296$, $44^2 = 1936$, $46^2 = 2116$, $54^2 = 2916$, and $56^2 = 3136$ fail the digit condition, so the units digit cannot be a 6. If the units digit is a 9, the number must be less than 6000 because 6789 is not a perfect square. Checking squares with a units digit of 9, $33^2 = 1089$, and $37^2 = 1369$. All of 43^2, 47^2, 53^2, 57^2, 63^2, 67^2, 73^2, 77^2, and 83^2 fail the digit condition, so the only such four-digit perfect square is $\boxed{1369}$.

6. As no triangle can share all three sides with the nonagon, there are two remaining possibilities to consider. The first is that the triangle shares exactly 2 sides with the nonagon. These two sides of the nonagon must be adjacent, so there are 9 such triangles. The second possibility is that the triangle shares exactly 1 side with the nonagon. Once one of the 9 sides of the nonagon is selected for the triangle, the third vertex must be one of the 5 vertices that is not adjacent to the selected side, so there are $9 \cdot 5 = 45$ such triangles. Altogether, the total number of possible triangles is $9 + 45 = \boxed{54}$.

7. We find the answer by working backwards. After Emily read half the remaining pages on Saturday morning, there were $47 + 9 = 56$ pages remaining, so when she woke up on Saturday there were $2 \times 56 = 112$ pages remaining. Similarly, after she read half of the pages on Friday evening, there were $112 + 12 = 124$ pages remaining. Therefore, the total number of pages in the book was $2 \times 124 = \boxed{248}$.

8. The ant could take a path that travels along the 40×17 face, crosses an edge of length 17, and then travels along the 17×25 face. This is the hypotenuse of a right triangle with legs of length $25 + 40 = 65$ and 17, and would result in a path length of $\sqrt{65^2 + 17^2} = \sqrt{4514}$. Alternatively, the ant could take a path that travels along the 40×25 face, crosses an edge of length 25, and then travels along the 25×17 face. This is the hypotenuse of a right triangle with legs of length $17 + 40 = 57$ and 25. This is slightly better, resulting in a path of length $\sqrt{57^2 + 25^2} = \sqrt{3874}$. Finally, the ant could take a path that travels along the 25×40 face, crosses an edge of length 40, and then travels along the 40×17 face. This is the hypotenuse of a right triangle with legs of length $17 + 25 = 42$ and 40. This is best, resulting in a path of length $\sqrt{42^2 + 40^2} = \sqrt{3364}$, which is exactly $\boxed{58}$.

Team Round Solutions

1. The sum of the numbers that are even is $2+4+6+8+10+12+14+16+18+20+22+24+26+28+30 = 240$. However, the numbers that are multiples of 3, which are all of the multiples of $2 \times 3 = 6$, must be removed. The sum of those numbers is $6 + 12 + 18 + 24 + 30 = 90$. Therefore, the desired sum is $240 - 90 = \boxed{150}$.

2. The number must be 4 more than a multiple of 6 and 1 less than a multiple of 7. So there must be a multiple of 7 that is $4 + 1 = 5$ more than a multiple of 6. Since 7 is one more than 6, this first occurs at $7 \times 5 = 35$ and $6 \times 5 = 30$. Therefore, the least possible number of memes that Marlee could have is $35 - 1 = \boxed{34}$.

3. In a twelve-hour period, not including midnight, the chimes ring $1+2+3+4+5+6+7+8+9+10+11+12 = 78$ times. Since each twelve-hour period including midnight adds an additional $24 - 12 = 12$ rings, there are $78 \times 2 + 12 = 168$ rings each day. There are 31 days in October, so the total number of rings in October is $31 \times 168 = \boxed{5208}$.

4. The figure is divided into 5 regions. Using exactly one region per triangle, there are 5 triangles. Using exactly two regions per triangle, there are 4 triangles. Using exactly three regions per triangle, there are 2 triangles. There are no triangles that use exactly four regions, and only 1 triangle that uses all five regions. Altogether, the number of triangles in the figure is $5 + 4 + 2 + 0 + 1 = \boxed{12}$.

5. The four digits sum to $2 + 4 + 7 + 9 = 22$. The greatest possible product occurs when 22 is split into two equal sums, one inside each set of parentheses. Thus, 4 must be paired with 7, and 2 with 9, for a product of $11 \times 11 = 121$. The least possible product occurs when 22 is split into the two most unequal sums. Thus 2 must be paired with 4, and 7 with 9, for a product of $6 \times 16 = 96$. The difference between the greatest and least possible products is $121 - 96 = \boxed{25}$.

6. Suppose the original jar has a volume of 200 milliliters. Then, of that 200 milliliters, $100\% - 80\% = 20\%$, or $200 \cdot 0.20 = 40$ milliliters are vinegar. Since the second jar is half the size of the first jar, it would have a volume of $200 \div 2 = 100$ milliliters, and $100\% - 90\% = 10\%$, or $100 \cdot 0.10 = 10$ milliliters are vinegar. The resulting mixture would have a volume of $200 + 100 = 300$ milliliters, of which $40 + 10 = 50$ milliliters would be vinegar. This is $\frac{50}{300}$, which to the nearest whole number percent is $\boxed{17\%}$.

7. A four-digit palindrome can be expressed as $ABBA$, where A and B are digits. For a number to be a multiple of 99, it must be a multiple of both 9 and 11. A four-digit number $WXYZ$ is divisible by 11 when $(W + Y) - (X + Z)$ is a multiple of 11. Because $(A + B) - (B + A) = 0$, every four-digit palindrome is a multiple of 11. A number is a multiple of 9 if the sum of its digits is a multiple of 9. The sum of the digits of $ABBA$ is $2 \cdot (A + B)$. Thus, for $ABBA$ to be a multiple of 9, A and B must sum to a multiple of 9. As A cannot be 0, this only happens when AB is a two-digit multiple of 9. Therefore, the total number of four-digit palindromes that are multiples of 99 is $\boxed{10}$.

8. Consider the arrangements where Andre is seated next to Bryce. The two can be regarded as one student, so it would be as if 5 students are seated around the circular table. If the students were seated in a line there would be $5! = 120$ ways. But since the table is a circle and rotations about the table are indistinguishable, there are only $\frac{5!}{5} = 24$ possible ways. Additionally, since Andre could be on either the left or right or Bryce, there are 2 possibilities for each of these 24 ways, for a total of $2 \cdot 24 = 48$. Some of these have Charlotte on the other side of Bryce, however. Now suppose the Andre, Bryce, Charlotte trio is considered as one person. There would be $\frac{4!}{4} = 6$ ways to seat the students around the table. But the Andre, Bryce, Charlotte trio could be seated as Andre on the left of Bryce and Charlotte on the right, or Andre on the right of Bryce and Charlotte on the left, so there are $2 \cdot 6 = 12$ arrangements that have Bryce between Andre and Charlotte. Thus the number of arrangements that have Andre next to Bryce and Charlotte not next to Bryce is $48 - 12 = \boxed{36}$.

9. Let the radius of the smaller circle be r. Construct a right triangle with endpoints of the hypotenuse at centers of the circles, and one leg parallel to the bases of the trapezoid and another leg parallel to the segment of length 600. Then the shorter leg of this right triangle has a length of $200 - r$, the longer leg is has a length of $600 - 200 - r = 400 - r$, and the hypotenuse has a length of $200 + r$. By the Pythagorean Theorem, $(200 - r)^2 + (400 - r)^2 = (200 + r)^2$. This simplifies to $r^2 - 1600r + 160000 = 0$. Completing the square, $r^2 - 1600r + 640000 = 480000$, so $r - 800 = \pm 400\sqrt{3}$, and $r = 800 \pm 400\sqrt{3}$. Since r must be less than 200, $r = 800 - 400\sqrt{3}$, which to the nearest whole number is $\boxed{107}$.

10. There is 1 way for Leland to assemble a tower that is 1 unit tall. There are 2 ways for Leland to assemble a tower that is 2 units tall. Now consider a tower that is 3 units tall. If the bottom brick is 1 unit tall, the remainder of the tower can be completed in the number of ways to assemble a 2 unit tall tower, which is 2. If the bottom brick is 2 units tall, the remainder of the tower can be completed in the number of ways to assemble a 1 unit tall tower, which is 1. Therefore, the total number of ways to assemble a tower that is 3 units tall is $2 + 1 = 3$. For a tower 4 units tall, if the bottom brick is 2 units tall, there are 2 ways to assemble the remainder of the tower, and if the bottom brick is 1 unit tall, there are 3 ways to assemble the remainder of the tower, for a total of $2 + 3 = 5$. The pattern continues, so that a tower 5 units tall can be assembled in $5 + 3 = 8$ ways, a tower 6 units tall can be assembled in $8 + 5 = 13$ ways, and so on. These are Fibonacci numbers, and the sequence in this instance is $1, 2, 3, 5, 8, 13, 21, 34, 55, 89, 144, 233, 377, 610, 987$, so the number of ways to assemble a tower that is fifteen units tall is $\boxed{987}$.

Number Sense
12222

Place ID Sticker
Inside This Box

Name _____

Grade _____

School _____

1. $221 + 12 =$ _____.

2. The hundreds digit of 67345 is _____.

3. $439 + 198 =$ _____.

4. The remainder of $79 \div 4$ is _____.

5. $544 - 288 =$ _____.

6. $7 + 7 \times 7 =$ _____.

7. $98 \div 14 =$ _____.

8. $19 + 31 + 41 + 38 =$ _____.

9. $30 \times 21 =$ _____.

10. (estimate) $507 + 234 + 429 =$ _____.

11. $11 \times 53 =$ _____.

12. $514 - 228 - 126 =$ _____.

13. The remainder of $173 \div 3$ is _____.

14. $26 \times 35 =$ _____.

15. $17^2 =$ _____.

16. $12 \times 9 \times 5 =$ _____.

17. *CXCVI* in Arabic numerals is _____.

18. $1.28 \div 0.16 =$ _____.

19. $31 \times 29 =$ _____.

20. (estimate) $301 \times 298 =$ _____.

21. $15 \times 18 \div 45 =$ _____.

22. $43 \times 25 =$ _____.

23. If 1 yard is equal to 36 inches, then 108 inches is equal to _____ yards.

24. $24^2 =$ _____.

25. The GCD of 28 and 49 is _____.

26. $448 \div 14 =$ _____.

27. The lesser of $\frac{5}{11}$ and $\frac{9}{20}$ is _____ (fraction).

28. $\frac{3}{4} + \frac{1}{20} =$ _____ (fraction).

29. $15 + 19 + 23 + 27 + 31 + 35 =$ _____.

30. (estimate) $41 \times 40 \times 49 =$ _____.

31. The perimeter of a square with area 121 is _____.

32. $59 \times 51 =$ _____.

33. The number of odd whole numbers between 12 and 60 is _____.

34. $\frac{3}{5} =$ _____ %.

35. $42 \times 99 =$ _____.

36. 75% of 36 is _____.

37. The LCM of 28 and 49 is _____.

38. $65^2 =$ _____.

39. 6 days is _____ hours.

40. (estimate) $48602 \div 247 =$ _____.

41. The area of a rectangle with width 8 and perimeter 20 is _____.

42. $18 \times 8 + 4 \times 9 = $ _____.

43. The remainder of $1853 \div 11$ is _____.

44. $62 \times 42 = $ _____.

45. The fifteenth term in the arithmetic sequence $13, 25, 37, \ldots$ is _____.

46. $86 \times 101 = $ _____.

47. $2^3 \times 3^2 = $ _____.

48. 66_7 in base 10 is _____.

49. $63^2 - 33^2 = $ _____.

50. (estimate) $\sqrt{654321} = $ _____.

51. $6\frac{1}{4}\% = $ _____ (fraction).

52. 101101_2 in base 4 is _____ $_4$.

53. The sum of the terms of the arithmetic sequence $6, 12, 18, \ldots 66$ is _____.

54. $112 \times 104 = $ _____.

55. The mean of the list $7, 17, 45, 13, 3$ is _____.

56. $97 \times 87 = $ _____.

57. $34 \times 125 = $ _____.

58. The measure of an interior angle in a regular pentagon is _____ $^\circ$.

59. $\sqrt{5929} = $ _____.

60. (estimate) $285714 \times 11 = $ _____.

61. The number of ways to choose 2 books from a set of 4 different books is _____.

62. $134 \times 111 = $ _____.

63. The area of an isosceles right triangle with a hypotenuse of length $6\sqrt{2}$ is _____.

64. $0.1\overline{6} = $ _____ (fraction).

65. The number 49 written in base 6 is _____ $_6$.

66. $81^2 = $ _____.

67. $32 \times 12 \times 24 = $ _____.

68. If $w = 16$, then $w^2 - 2w + 1 = $ _____.

69. $4\frac{1}{3} \times 2\frac{1}{3} = $ _____ (mixed number).

70. (estimate) The area of a circle with diameter 28 is _____.

71. $1014 \times 1011 = $ _____.

72. The sum of the terms of the infinite geometric sequence $\frac{2}{5}, \frac{4}{25}, \frac{8}{125}, \ldots$ is _____ (fraction).

73. $\frac{3}{5}$ of 24 is $\frac{8}{15}$ of _____.

74. $11^3 = $ _____.

75. If $5^y = \frac{1}{25}$ then $5^{3-y} = $ _____.

76. The volume of a cube that has a surface area of 384 is _____.

77. $\sqrt{128} \div \sqrt{8} = $ _____.

78. The sum of the prime divisors of 130 is _____.

79. $75 \times 92 \times 61 = $ _____.

80. (estimate) $2.41^3 \times 3.74^3 = $ _____.

 Place ID Sticker
Inside This Box

Name _____

Grade _____

School _____

1. Ⓐ Ⓑ Ⓒ Ⓓ Ⓔ   11. Ⓐ Ⓑ Ⓒ Ⓓ Ⓔ   21. Ⓐ Ⓑ Ⓒ Ⓓ Ⓔ

2. Ⓐ Ⓑ Ⓒ Ⓓ Ⓔ   12. Ⓐ Ⓑ Ⓒ Ⓓ Ⓔ   22. Ⓐ Ⓑ Ⓒ Ⓓ Ⓔ

3. Ⓐ Ⓑ Ⓒ Ⓓ Ⓔ   13. Ⓐ Ⓑ Ⓒ Ⓓ Ⓔ   23. Ⓐ Ⓑ Ⓒ Ⓓ Ⓔ

4. Ⓐ Ⓑ Ⓒ Ⓓ Ⓔ   14. Ⓐ Ⓑ Ⓒ Ⓓ Ⓔ   24. Ⓐ Ⓑ Ⓒ Ⓓ Ⓔ

5. Ⓐ Ⓑ Ⓒ Ⓓ Ⓔ   15. Ⓐ Ⓑ Ⓒ Ⓓ Ⓔ   25. Ⓐ Ⓑ Ⓒ Ⓓ Ⓔ

6. Ⓐ Ⓑ Ⓒ Ⓓ Ⓔ   16. Ⓐ Ⓑ Ⓒ Ⓓ Ⓔ   26. Ⓐ Ⓑ Ⓒ Ⓓ Ⓔ

7. Ⓐ Ⓑ Ⓒ Ⓓ Ⓔ   17. Ⓐ Ⓑ Ⓒ Ⓓ Ⓔ   27. Ⓐ Ⓑ Ⓒ Ⓓ Ⓔ

8. Ⓐ Ⓑ Ⓒ Ⓓ Ⓔ   18. Ⓐ Ⓑ Ⓒ Ⓓ Ⓔ   28. Ⓐ Ⓑ Ⓒ Ⓓ Ⓔ

9. Ⓐ Ⓑ Ⓒ Ⓓ Ⓔ   19. Ⓐ Ⓑ Ⓒ Ⓓ Ⓔ   29. Ⓐ Ⓑ Ⓒ Ⓓ Ⓔ

10. Ⓐ Ⓑ Ⓒ Ⓓ Ⓔ   20. Ⓐ Ⓑ Ⓒ Ⓓ Ⓔ   30. Ⓐ Ⓑ Ⓒ Ⓓ Ⓔ

1. What is the value of $1 + 3 + 6 + 10 + 15 + 21 + 28$?

   (A) 82   (B) 85   (C) 83   (D) 84   (E) 81

2. On a number line, Lina drew a line from 2 to 21. She then drew a line from 21 to 13. Finally, she drew a line from 13 to 34. What was the total length of the lines that Lina drew?

   (A) 32   (B) 40   (C) 44   (D) 48   (E) 36

3. Anna chose a number. When Anna doubled the number and then added seven, Anna's result was seventy-seven. What number did Anna choose?

   (A) 42   (B) 37   (C) 35   (D) 39   (E) 40

4. At the movie theater, a candy bar costs $3, a soda costs $2, and a bucket of popcorn costs $4. Alan purchases three candy bars, three sodas, and a bucket of popcorn for himself and his two friends. How many dollars does Alan spend?

   (A) $14   (B) $16   (C) $17   (D) $20   (E) $19

5. How many two-digit positive whole numbers have a tens digit and units digit that differ by five? For example, two such numbers are 83 and 38, since $8 - 3 = 5$.

   (A) 10   (B) 4   (C) 5   (D) 9   (E) 8

6. Collin cut a rectangular piece of paper measuring 10 inches wide and 18 inches long into two identical smaller rectangular pieces of paper, each with a width of 10 inches. What is the total perimeter, in inches, of the two smaller pieces of paper?

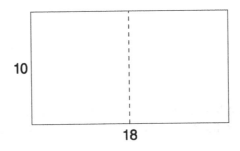

(A) 66   (B) 56   (C) 76   (D) 72   (E) 64

7. The year 2021 has 365 days. The month of December has 31 days, and the month of November has 30 days. If December 31st is day 365 of the year 2021, then what day of the year 2021 is November 7th?

(A) 310   (B) 313   (C) 314   (D) 311   (E) 312

8. How many positive whole numbers less than 10 evenly divide 840?

(A) 7   (B) 8   (C) 9   (D) 5   (E) 6

9. Two squares with side length 12 are placed so that the squares overlap, forming a rectangle with a height of 12 and a width of 20. What is the area of the region common to both squares?

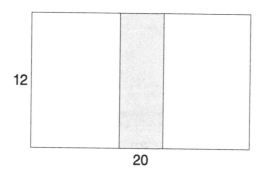

(A) 32   (B) 72   (C) 48   (D) 60   (E) 40

10. Jill, Bill, Gil, and Will are friends lining up to buy ice cream. Jill insists on being in front of Gil in line, but Gil does not want to be right behind Jill in line. How many different ways can the four friends line up to buy ice cream?

(A) 6   (B) 2   (C) 4   (D) 12   (E) 8

11. What is the remainder when $11 \times 12 \times 13 \times 14 \times 16 \times 17 \times 18 \times 19$ is divided by 5?

(A) 1   (B) 4   (C) 3   (D) 0   (E) 2

12. Jalen gets paid for helping his family with housework. On Friday, Jalen helped for half an hour. On Saturday, Jalen helped for 40 minutes. On Sunday, Jalen helped from 8:50 AM until 9:28 AM. Jalen is paid per minute at a rate of $5 per hour. How much money, in dollars, did Jalen earn for his help on Friday, Saturday, and Sunday?

(A) $12   (B) $10   (C) $8   (D) $9   (E) $11

13. A right triangle has an area of 12 and one leg that has a length of 3. A second right triangle has one leg that is three times as long as one leg of the first triangle, and a second leg that is half as long as another leg of the first triangle. What is the area of the second triangle?

(A) 12　　　　(B) 18　　　　(C) 15　　　　(D) 24　　　　(E) 16

14. Sally has 400 milliliters of a solution that is 20% acid, and the rest of the solution is water. Sally also has 100 milliliters of a solution that is 10% acid, and the rest of the solution is water. Sally pours both of the solutions into larger container. What percent of the resulting solution is water?

(A) 80%　　　　(B) 85%　　　　(C) 82%　　　　(D) 86%　　　　(E) 84%

15. The reciprocal of a number is the value of 1 divided by the number. For example, the reciprocal of 2 is $1 \div 2 = \frac{1}{2}$. The harmonic mean of a list of numbers is the reciprocal of the average, or arithmetic mean, of the reciprocals of the numbers. What is the harmonic mean of 2, 4, and 12?

(A) 3　　　　(B) $\frac{6}{5}$　　　　(C) 6　　　　(D) $\frac{18}{5}$　　　　(E) $\frac{12}{5}$

16. How many positive whole numbers are greater than $\sqrt{120}$ but less than $\sqrt{1200}$?

(A) 24　　　　(B) 11　　　　(C) 22　　　　(D) 23　　　　(E) 34

17. A large circle has a diameter of 18. A small circle within the large circle has a diameter of 6. The area inside the small circle is painted dark gray, and the area between the two circles is painted light gray. What is the value of the area of the light gray region divided by the area of the dark gray region?

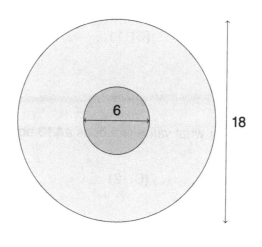

(A) 6   (B) 3   (C) 12   (D) 9   (E) 8

18. Carmen's new car has four wheels. Each wheel has a tire, and the car also has a spare tire that is identical to each of the other tires. By occasionally swapping the spare tire with one of the other four tires so that each tire is used the same amount, Carmen wants to drive 40,000 miles on each of the five tires before buying a new set of five tires. What is the greatest distance, in miles, that Carmen can drive in her new car before purchasing a new set of five tires?

(A) 50,000   (B) 40,000   (C) 54,000   (D) 48,000   (E) 45,000

19. How many diagonals of a regular octagon are not parallel to a side of the octagon?

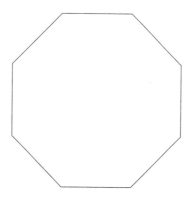

(A) 20   (B) 16   (C) 10   (D) 12   (E) 8

20. A mathleague.org Sprint Round has thirty questions. Each correct answer is worth 4 points, each incorrect answer is worth -1 point, and each question not answered is worth 0 points. Ahmed scored a 61 on the Sprint Round at a recent mathleague.org contest. What is the greatest number of questions Ahmed could have answered incorrectly?

(A) 12　　　　(B) 14　　　　(C) 11　　　　(D) 13　　　　(E) 10

21. If $a \clubsuit b = ab - 2a - 2b + 3$, then for what value of a does $a \clubsuit 13$ equal 208?

(A) 19　　　　(B) 18　　　　(C) 21　　　　(D) 20　　　　(E) 22

22. Among the numbers in the answer choices, which is prime?

(A) 7131　　　　(B) 6319　　　　(C) 6743　　　　(D) 5779　　　　(E) 9793

23. A rhombus has a diagonal of length 14 and an area of 336. What is the perimeter of the rhombus?

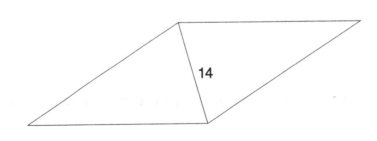

(A) $40\sqrt{7}$　　　　(B) 100　　　　(C) $40\sqrt{6}$　　　　(D) 96　　　　(E) 120

24. Mr. Diaz has two fair six-sided dice. The numbers on the six sides of the first die are 2, 3, 4, 5, 6, and 7. The numbers on the six sides of the second die are 1, 2, 3, 4, 5, and 6. Mr. Diaz rolls the first die and then rolls the second die. What is the probability that the number shown on the first die is greater than the number shown on the second die?

(A) $\frac{2}{3}$　　　　(B) $\frac{1}{2}$　　　　(C) $\frac{11}{18}$　　　　(D) $\frac{7}{12}$　　　　(E) $\frac{5}{9}$

25. Lisa wrote down a list of consecutive positive whole numbers. The sum of the numbers in Lisa's list was 161. If Lisa's list included more than one number, then what is the sum of all possible lengths for Lisa's list?

(A) 16   (B) 23   (C) 7   (D) 30   (E) 9

26. The figure below shows sixteen dots arranged into four rows and four columns. In each row, the dots are one unit apart horizontally, and in each column, the dots are one unit apart vertically. Two different dots are selected at random from the sixteen dots. What is the probability the distance between the two dots is one unit?

(A) $\frac{1}{8}$ (B) $\frac{1}{5}$ (C) $\frac{2}{5}$ (D) $\frac{1}{6}$ (E) $\frac{1}{4}$

27. Among the numbers in the answer choices, which is the second greatest?

(A) 5^{30} (B) 3^{42} (C) 10^{21} (D) 2^{70} (E) 11^{20}

28. Walter walked $1\frac{1}{2}$ miles to school in the morning exactly one mile per hour faster than he walked the same distance home in the afternoon. The total time for Walter's walks to and from school was $52\frac{1}{2}$ minutes. How many minutes longer was Walter's walk home from school than his walk to school?

(A) 10   (B) $7\frac{1}{2}$ (C) $4\frac{1}{2}$ (D) $10\frac{1}{2}$ (E) 5

29. A circle with center O has radius 6. Quadrilateral $COAX$ is a square of side length 3. Points B and D are on the circle, and B, X, and A are collinear, while D, X and C are also collinear. What is the area of the region bounded by segment BX, segment DX, and arc BD?

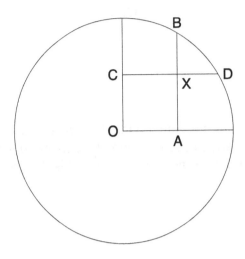

(A) $4\pi - 6\sqrt{3}$ (B) $3\pi + 6 - 6\sqrt{3}$ (C) $3\pi + 6 - 9\sqrt{3}$ (D) $3\pi + 12 - 6\sqrt{3}$ (E) $3\pi + 9 - 9\sqrt{3}$

30. How many positive whole number divisors of the square of $43^{23} \cdot 47^{21}$ are less than $43^{23} \cdot 47^{21}$ but do not divide $43^{23} \cdot 47^{21}$?

(A) 505   (B) 483   (C) 528   (D) 1010   (E) 527

Target Round
12222

Name _____

Grade _____

School _____

Problems 1 & 2

---

1. Seth has a history test on Friday. On Monday, Seth studies for the test for twenty minutes. On each of Tuesday, Wednesday, and Thursday, he studies five more minutes than he did the day before. From Monday through Thursday, how many total minutes does Seth study for his history test?

1.

2. The figure below consists of five identical squares. The total area of the figure is 45. What is the perimeter of the figure?

2.

Place ID Sticker
Inside This Box

Name _____

Grade _____

School _____

Problems 3 & 4

3. Mrs. Watson's fifth grade class has nineteen students. Four of the students do not have either a dog or a cat. Ten students have a dog. If seven students have a cat, then how many students have both a dog and a cat?

3.

4. The mean, or average, of a list of five different positive whole numbers is also a whole number. If four of the numbers are 5, 9, 17, and 20, then what is the sum of all possible values of the median, or middle number, of the list?

4.

Target Round
12222

Name _____

Grade _____

School _____

Problems 5 & 6

5. Pierre chose a three-digit positive whole number. The product of the digits of Pierre's number was 36. For example, since $2 \times 3 \times 6 = 36$, one number that Pierre could have chosen is 236. How many different numbers could Pierre have chosen?

5.

6. When Joanna runs, she runs at a constant speed of of 10 kilometers per hour. When Joanna walks, she walks at a constant speed of 6 kilometers per hour. Joanna is participating in a race that is 15 kilometers in length. If Joanna wants to finish the race in no more than one hour and forty minutes, then what is the greatest whole number of minutes that Joanna could walk during the race?

6.

Place ID Sticker
Inside This Box

Name _____

Grade _____

School _____

Problems 7 & 8

7. An ant starts at the circle marked *A* in the grid shown below and attempts to reach the circle marked *B*. The ant can only travel either up or to the right along the lines of the grid. But the black circle contains a poison that will kill the ant. How many different paths can the ant take to successfully travel from *A* to *B*?

7.

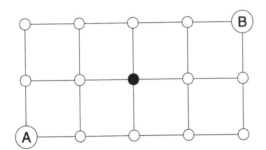

8. Mr. Goodbar is giving five different candy bars to Amy, Ben, and Carly. However, he wants to give Amy at least two candy bars, and he wants to give Ben at least one candy bar. It is possible that Carly receives no candy bars. How many different ways can Mr. Goodbar give the candy bars to Amy, Ben, and Carly?

8.

Team Round
12222

School or Team

Name _____

Name _____

Name _____

Name _____

Place ID Sticker
Inside This Box

Place ID Sticker
Inside This Box

Place ID Sticker
Inside This Box

Place ID Sticker
Inside This Box

1.	2.	3.	4.	5.
6.	7.	8.	9.	10.

1. What is the sum of the odd whole numbers that are greater than 20 and less than 40?

2. Sondra can purchase twelve cans of soda for $4, or thirty-six cans of soda for $11. Sondra is hosting a party where she will need 132 cans of soda for her guests. What is the fewest number of dollars that Sondra will need to spend on sodas for her party?

3. Emilio has a box of oranges, a box of apples, and a box of bananas. Unfortunately, Emilio can only weigh amounts between twenty and forty pounds on his scale, so he decides to weigh two of the boxes at the same time. Together, the box of oranges and the box of apples weigh thirty-five pounds. Together, the box of apples and the box of bananas weigh thirty-three pounds. And together, the box of oranges and the box of bananas weighs thirty-two pounds. How many pounds do Emilio's three boxes of fruit weigh, in total?

4. The month of December has 31 days. In a certain year, December has the same number of Fridays as it has Sundays. In that same year, how many different days of the week are possible for December 1st?

5. In the figure below, each number in a box is the product of the numbers in the two boxes that touch it in the row above, and the number in each box is a positive whole number. For example, if the number in the box labeled a was 2 and the number in the box labeled b was 5, then the number in the box labeled d would be $2 \times 5 = 10$. If the number in the lowermost box is 100, as shown, then how many different values are possible for the box labeled b?

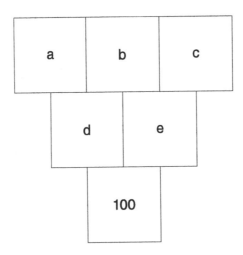

6. On the latest math assessment for fifth grade students at Statstown Elementary, 15% of the students scored 80 points, 25% scored 85 points, 35% scored 90 points, 10% scored 100 points, and the remaining students scored 95 points. What is the positive difference between the mean and median score on the assessment?

7. Dan can run at a constant pace of 8 minutes per mile, and Dave can run at a constant pace of 9 minutes per mile. Dan and Dave decide to run a 15 mile race as a relay, so that each runs only part of the 15 miles, but together they run the complete distance. Dan and Dave decide to plan their relay so that each runs for the same amount of time. To the nearest whole number of minutes, what is the total time Dan and Dave will run to complete the 15 mile relay?

8. The number 112 has 10 positive whole number divisors: 1, 2, 4, 7, 8, 14, 16, 28, 56, and 112. How many different three-digit positive whole numbers have exactly ten positive whole number divisors?

9. A bag contains a number of tokens. The bag has one token labeled with a 1, two tokens labeled with a 2, three tokens labeled with a 3, four tokens labeled with a 4, five tokens labeled with a 5, and six tokens labeled with a 6. The bag contains no other tokens. Mr. Tolkien selects two different tokens from the bag. What is the probability that the sum of the numbers shown on Mr. Tolkien's tokens is a prime number? Express your answer as a common fraction.

10. The figure below shows a small circle of radius 5 tangent to a larger circle of radius 20. Segment *AB* is tangent to the smaller circle at *A* as well as the larger circle. Segment *DC* has the same length as *AB* and is tangent to the smaller circle at *D* as well as the larger circle. Segment *BC* passes through the center of the larger circle. What is the area of quadrilateral *ABCD*?

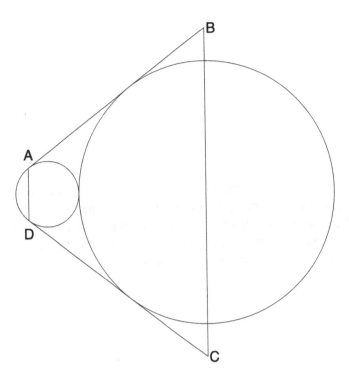

Sprint Round

1. D	11. A	21. C
2. D	12. D	22. D
3. C	13. B	23. B
4. E	14. C	24. D
5. D	15. D	25. B
6. C	16. A	26. B
7. D	17. E	27. C
8. B	18. A	28. B
9. C	19. D	29. E
10. A	20. C	30. B

Target Round

1. 110
2. 36
3. 2
4. 40
5. 21
6. 25
7. 6
8. 105

Team Round

1. 300
2. ($)41
3. 50
4. 3
5. 4
6. 1
7. 127
8. 20
9. $\frac{1}{3}$
10. 812

Number Sense

1. 233	21. 6	41. 16	61. 6
2. 3	22. 1075	42. 180	62. 14874
3. 637	23. 3	43. 5	63. 18
4. 3	24. 576	44. 2604	64. $\frac{1}{6}$
5. 256	25. 7	45. 181	65. 121
6. 56	26. 32	46. 8686	66. 6561
7. 7	27. $\frac{9}{20}$	47. 72	67. 9216
8. 129	28. $\frac{4}{5}$	48. 48	68. 225
9. 630	29. 150	49. 2880	69. $10\frac{1}{9}$
10. [1112, 1228]	30. [76342, 84378]	50. [769, 849]	70. [585, 646]
11. 583	31. 44	51. $\frac{1}{16}$	71. 1025154
12. 160	32. 3009	52. 231	72. $\frac{2}{3}$
13. 2	33. 24	53. 396	73. 27
14. 910	34. 60	54. 11648	74. 1331
15. 289	35. 4158	55. 17	75. 3125
16. 540	36. 27	56. 8439	76. 512
17. 196	37. 196	57. 4250	77. 4
18. 8	38. 4225	58. 108	78. 20
19. 899	39. 144	59. 77	79. 420900
20. [85214, 94182]	40. [187, 206]	60. [2985712, 3299996]	80. [696, 768]

Sprint Round Solutions

1. The sum of the first three terms is 10. The sum of the last two terms is 49. Therefore the sum is $10 + 10 + 15 + 49$, or $10 + 10 + 15 + 50 - 1$, which is $85 - 1 = \boxed{84}$.

2. The length of the line from 2 to 21 is $21 - 2 = 19$. The length of the line from 21 to 13 is $21 - 13 = 8$. Finally, the length of the line from 13 to 34 is $34 - 13 = 21$. Altogether, the total length of the lines is $19 + 8 + 21 = \boxed{48}$.

3. Before adding 7, Anna's result was $77 - 7 = 70$. Before doubling, Anna's number was $70 \div 2 = \boxed{35}$.

4. Each set of candy bars and sodas costs $\$3 + \$2 = \$5$, so three sets costs $3 \times \$5 = \$15$. The bucket of popcorn brings the total to $\$15 + \$4 = \boxed{\$19}$.

5. If the tens digit is greater than the units digit, then the possible numbers are 94, 83, 72, 61, and 50, for 5 possibilities. If the tens digit is less than the units digit, then the possible numbers are 16, 27, 38, and 49, for 4 possibilities. Altogether, the total count is $5 + 4 = \boxed{9}$.

6. The perimeter of the original rectangle is $10 + 10 + 18 + 18 = 56$ inches. The cut adds 2 sides, each of length 10 inches, for an increase of $2 \times 10 = 20$ inches, so the total perimeter of the two rectangles, in inches, is $56 + 20 = \boxed{76}$.

7. November 30th is day $365 - 31 = 334$, and November 7th is $30 - 7 = 23$ days before November 30th, so in the year 2021, November 7th is day $334 - 23 = \boxed{311}$.

8. The number 840 is a multiple of 10, so it is a multiple of both 2 and 5. The number 84 is a multiple of 4 and 21, so it must be multiple of 3 and 7. Additionally, because 84 is even and a multiple of 3, it must also be a multiple of 6. Finally, because 84 is a multiple of 4 and 10 is a multiple of 2, 840 must be a multiple of 8. Therefore 840 is divisible by 1, 2, 3, 4, 5, 6, 7, and 8, and the total number of divisors less than 10 is $\boxed{8}$.

9. The area of the region common to both squares is a rectangle with a height of 12, as it is equal to the side length of the square. The total width of both squares is $12 + 12 = 24$, but the width of the entire rectangle is only 20, so the width of the region common to both squares is $24 - 20 = 4$. The area of this region is $12 \times 4 = \boxed{48}$.

10. If Jill is in the first position in line, then Gil can be in either the third or fourth position. If Jill is in the second position in line, then Gil can only be in the fourth position. Jill cannot be in the third or fourth position in line. For any any of the 3 positionings of Jill and Gil, there are 2 ways to place Will and Bill, so the total number of ways the four can line up is $3 \times 2 = \boxed{6}$.

11. The remainder when a number is divided by 5 is determined by the units digit of the number. The units digit of $11 \times 12 \times 13 \times 14$ is 4, and the units digit of $16 \times 17 \times 18 \times 19$ is also 4. The units digit of 4×4 is 6, and when a number with a units digit of 6 is divided by 5, the remainder is $\boxed{1}$.

12. On Friday, Jalen helped for $\frac{1}{2} \cdot 60 = 30$ minutes, on Saturday he helped for 40 minutes, and on Sunday he helped for 38 minutes. Altogether, he helped for $30 + 40 + 38 = 108$ minutes. This is $\frac{108}{60} = \frac{9}{5}$ hours, so the number of dollars Jalen earned is $\frac{9}{5} \cdot \$5 = \boxed{\$9}$.

13. The product of the leg lengths of the first triangle is $2 \cdot 12 = 24$, so the second leg of the first triangle is $\frac{24}{3} = 8$. In the second triangle, one leg could be $3 \cdot 3 = 9$, and the other could be $\frac{1}{2} \cdot 8 = 4$. Alternatively, one leg could be $3 \cdot 8 = 24$ and the other could be $\frac{1}{2} \cdot 3 = \frac{3}{2}$. In either case, the product of the leg lengths is 36, and the area of the second triangle is $\frac{36}{2} = 18$. In general, halving one leg length would half the original area of 12, for an area of 6, and tripling the other leg length would triple that area of 6, for an area of $\boxed{18}$.

14. In the 400 milliliter solution, $20\% \cdot 400 = 80$ milliliters is acid. In the 100 milliliter solution, $10\% \cdot 100 = 10$ milliliters is acid. In the mixed solution, $80 + 10 = 90$ milliliters is acid, out of a total of 500 milliliters, so $\frac{90}{500} \cdot 100\% = 18\%$ is acid, and the percent that is water is $100\% - 18\% = \boxed{82\%}$.

15. The reciprocals of 2, 4, and 12 are $\frac{1}{2}$, $\frac{1}{4}$, and $\frac{1}{12}$. The sum of these reciprocals is $\frac{5}{6}$, so the arithmetic mean of these reciprocals is $\frac{1}{3} \times \frac{5}{6} = \frac{5}{18}$. The reciprocal of this number is the harmonic mean of the three numbers, and the reciprocal of $\frac{5}{18}$ is $\boxed{\dfrac{18}{5}}$.

16. Since $10^2 = 100$ and $11^2 = 121$, the least positive whole number that is greater than $\sqrt{120}$ is 11. Since $34^2 = 1156$ and $35^2 = 1225$, the greatest positive whole number that is less than $\sqrt{1200}$ is 34. The number of positive whole numbers greater than or equal to 11 and less than or equal to 34 is $34 - 11 + 1 = \boxed{24}$.

17. The radius of the large circle is $\frac{18}{2} = 9$, and the radius of the small circle is $\frac{6}{2} = 3$. The area of the large circle is $9^2 \cdot \pi = 81\pi$, and the area of the small circle, which is also the dark gray region, is $3^2 \cdot \pi = 9\pi$. The area of the light gray region is $81\pi - 9\pi = 72\pi$, so the value of the area of the light gray region divided by the area of the dark gray region is $\frac{72\pi}{9\pi} = \boxed{8}$.

18. The total number of miles that can be accumulated on all 5 tires is $40,000 \times 5 = 200,000$. But since the spare tire is not in use, each mile the car travels only accumates 4 total miles on the tires. Therefore the number of miles that the car can travel is $200,000 \div 4 = \boxed{50,000}$.

19. From each vertex of a regular octagon, diagonals can be drawn to $8-3=5$ other vertices, as diagonals cannot be drawn to the vertex itself or either of the adjacent vertices. This would lead to $8 \cdot 5 = 40$ diagonals. But this counts each diagonal twice, once for one vertex of the diagonal and again for another vertex of the diagonal. So the total number of diagonals is $\frac{40}{2} = 20$. The diagonals parallel to sides of the octagon are those that connect two vertices which are separated by either 3 or 5 sides of the octagon, or are perpendicular to opposite sides of the octagagon. There are 8 such diagonals. Therefore the total number of diagonals not parallel to a side of the octagon is $20-8 = \boxed{12}$.

20. The number of questions answered incorrectly can be added to 61. That result is the total points earned for correct answers, and therefore must be a multiple of 4. Furthermore, the number of questions answered incorrectly and correctly must sum to no more than 30. If 3 is added to 61, then Ahmed answered $64 \div 3 = 16$ questions correctly and 3 incorrectly. If 7 is added to 61, then Ahmed answered $68 \div 4 = 17$ questions correctly and 7 incorrectly. If 11 is added to 61, then Ahmed answered $72 \div 4 = 18$ questions correctly and 11 incorrectly. Any larger possibilities would require more than 30 questions, so the greatest possible number of incorrect answered is $\boxed{11}$.

21. If $a\clubsuit 13 = 208$, then $13a - 2a - 2\cdot 13 + 3 = 208$, or $11a = 231$, so a is $\frac{231}{11} = \boxed{21}$.

22. The sum of the digits of 7131 is a multiple of 3, so 7131 is divisible by 3 and is therefore not prime. The sum of the thousands and tens digits of 6743 is equal to the sum of the hundreds and units digits, so 6743 is divisible by 11 and is therefore not prime. The number 9793 is 7 less than 9800, which is a multiple of 7, so 9793 is divisible by 7 and is therefore not prime. Finally, the number 6319 can be expressed as a difference of squares, $80^2 - 9^2$, and can be factored as $(80+9)(80-9)$, or $89 \cdot 71$. Therefore 6319 is not prime, and the prime number must be $\boxed{5779}$.

23. The area of a rhombus is half the product of the diagonals of the rhombus, so the second diagonal of the rhombus has length $\frac{2\cdot 336}{14} = 48$. Additionally, the diagonals of a rhombus are perpendicular and bisect one another. Thus the diagonals partition the rhombus into four congruent right triangles, with legs of length $\frac{14}{2} = 7$ and $\frac{48}{2} = 24$. By the Pythagorean Theorem, the length of the hypotenuse of one of these right triangles, which is also the length of a side of the rhombus, is $\sqrt{7^2 + 24^2} = 25$, so the perimeter of the rhombus is $4 \cdot 25 = \boxed{100}$.

24. There are $6 \cdot 6 = 36$ total possible outcomes. If the first die shows a 7, then there are 6 outcomes where it is greater than the number shown on the second die. If the first die shows a 6, then there are 5 outcomes where it is greater than the number shown on the second die. If the first shows a 5, there are 4 outcomes. If the first shows a 4, there are 3 outcomes. If the first shows a 3, there are 2 outcomes. If the first shows a 2, there is only 1 outcome. Altogether, there are $6+5+4+3+2+1 = 21$ outcomes where the first die shows a number greater than the second die, for a probability of $\frac{21}{36} = \boxed{\frac{7}{12}}$.

25. If the number of consecutive positive whole numbers Lisa wrote down was odd, then the middle number, or average value, in Lisa's list must be a whole number that divides 161. The prime factorization of 161 is $7 \cdot 23$, so either Lisa wrote down 7 numbers with a middle number of 23, or 23 numbers with a middle number of 7. But all of the whole numbers were positive, so the only possibility is 7 numbers with a middle number of 23. If the number of consecutive positive whole numbers Lisa wrote down was even, then the middle number, or average value, in Lisa's list must be $\frac{1}{2}$ more than a whole number. This is equivalent to the number of consecutive whole numbers being an even divisor of $2 \cdot 161 = 322$. This yields possibilities of 2 numbers with an average value of 80.5 or 14 numbers with an average value of 11.5. A list of 46 numbers with an average value of 3.5 is not possible since it would include negative numbers. Thus the sum of all possible values for the number of whole numbers in Lisa's list is $7 + 2 + 14 = \boxed{23}$.

26. There are $\binom{16}{2} = \frac{16 \cdot 15}{2}$, or 120 possible pairs of dots. Dots can only be one unit apart either horizontally or vertically. For dots that are one unit apart horizontally, there are 12 possible selections for the leftmost dot in the pair. Similarly, for dots that are one unit apart vertically, there are 12 possible selections for the topmost dot in the pair. Thus, the total number of pairs of dots that are seperated by a distance of one unit is $12 + 12 = 24$, for a probability of $\frac{12+12}{120} = \boxed{\frac{1}{5}}$.

27. Because $2^{10} > 10^3$, $2^{70} > 10^{21}$. Because $2^7 > 5^3$, $2^{70} > 5^{30}$. Because $2^{10} > 3^6$, $2^{70} > 3^{42}$. Because $2^7 > 11^2$, $2^{70} > 11^{20}$. Therefore 2^{70} is the greatest number. Because $10 > 3^2$, $10^{21} > 3^{42}$, and the second greatest number cannot be 3^{42}. Because $5^5 = 3125$, $5^{10} < 10^7$, so $5^{30} < 10^{21}$, and the second greatest greatest number cannot be 5^{30}. Now compare 11^{20} and 10^{21}. If the value of $\frac{10^{21}}{11^{20}} = 10 \cdot \left(\frac{10}{11}\right)^{20}$ is greater than 1, then 10^{21} is greater. This is equivalent to showing that $\left(\frac{10}{11}\right)^{20}$ is greater than $\frac{1}{10}$. The value of $\left(\frac{10}{11}\right)^4 = \frac{10000}{14641}$, which is greater than $\frac{2}{3}$. The value of $\left(\frac{2}{3}\right)^5 = \frac{32}{243}$, which is greater than $\frac{1}{10}$. Therefore $\left(\frac{10}{11}\right)^{20} > \left(\frac{2}{3}\right)^5 > \frac{1}{10}$, so $10^{21} > 11^{20}$, and the second greatest number is $\boxed{10^{21}}$.

28. Let the speed, in miles per hour, Walter walked in the morning be r. Then the time Walter walked in the morning, in hours, is $\frac{\frac{3}{2}}{r}$, and the time Walter walked in the afternoon, in hours, is $\frac{\frac{3}{2}}{r+1}$. Together these sum to Walter's total time, which is $\frac{52\frac{1}{2}}{60} = \frac{7}{8}$ hours. So $\frac{\frac{3}{2}}{r} + \frac{\frac{3}{2}}{r+1} = \frac{7}{8}$. Simplifying, $\frac{12}{r} + \frac{12}{r+1} = 7$, and $12(r+1) + 12r = 7r(r+1)$. Therefore $7r^2 - 17r - 12 = 0$, or $(7r+4)(r-3) = 0$. Since r must be positive, r is 3. The time Walter spent walking in the morning was $\frac{\frac{3}{2}}{3} = \frac{1}{2}$ hours, and the time Walter spent walking in the evening was $\frac{\frac{3}{2}}{4} = \frac{3}{8}$ hours, for a difference of $\frac{1}{2} - \frac{3}{8} = \frac{1}{8}$ hours. In minutes, this is $\frac{60}{8} = \boxed{7\frac{1}{2}}$.

29. Drop a perpendicular from D to the radius that includes A, forming a right triangle with a hypotenuse of length 6 and one leg of length 3. This is a $30-60-90$ right triangle, so the length of the perpendicular is $3\sqrt{3}$ and the length of XD is $3\sqrt{3}-3$. Similarly, the length of BX is also $3\sqrt{3}-3$. Now consider the sector bounded by arc BD and radii OB and OD. Because the triangles identified previously are $30-60-90$, the central angle of this sector is $90° - 30° - 30° = 30°$, so the area of the sector is $\frac{30°}{360°} \cdot 6^2 \cdot \pi = 3\pi$. Finally, triangles OXB and OXD are congruent, with bases DX and BX of length $3\sqrt{3}-3$, and altitudes of 3. Their combined area is $2 \cdot \frac{1}{2} \cdot 3 \cdot (3\sqrt{3}-3) = 9\sqrt{3}-9$. When this area is subtracted from the area of the sector, only the desired area remains, so the area of the region is $3\pi - (9\sqrt{3}-9) = \boxed{3\pi + 9 - 9\sqrt{3}}$.

30. The square of $43^{23} \cdot 47^{21}$ is $43^{46} \cdot 47^{42}$. This number has $(46+1)(42+1) = 2021$ positive whole number divisors. Of these 1 is equal to $43^{23} \cdot 47^{21}$, and, since each factor pair includes one number greater than the square root of a number and one number less than the square root of a number, $\frac{2021-1}{2} = 1010$ are less than $43^{23} \cdot 47^{21}$. The number $43^{23} \cdot 47^{21}$ has $(23+1)(21+1) = 528$ positive whole number divisors, and 527 of these are less than $43^{23} \cdot 47^{21}$. Therefore the number of divisors of the square of $43^{23} \cdot 47^{21}$ that are less than $43^{23} \cdot 47^{21}$ but which do not divide $43^{23} \cdot 47^{21}$ is $1010 - 527 = \boxed{483}$.

Target Round Solutions

1. On Tuesday, Seth studies for $20 + 5 = 25$ minutes. On Wednesday, he studies $25 + 5 = 30$ minutes, and on Thursday he studies $30 + 5 = 35$ minutes. The total number of minutes Seth studies for the test is $20 + 25 + 30 + 35 = \boxed{110}$.

2. Each square has an area of $45 \div 5 = 9$, so the side length of each square is $\sqrt{9} = 3$. Two of the squares have 3 sides that are part of the perimeter of the figure, and three of the squares have 2 sides that are part of the perimeter of the figure. Altogether there are $2 \times 3 + 3 \times 2 = 12$ segments that are sides of squares and part of the perimeter of the figure. Therefore the total perimeter of the figure is $3 \times 12 = \boxed{36}$.

3. There are $19 - 4 = 15$ students that have either a dog, a cat, or both. But the total number of students that own a dog or a cat is $10 + 7 = 17$. This counts twice the students that own both a dog and a cat, so the number of students that own both a dog and a cat is $17 - 15 = \boxed{2}$.

4. The sum of four numbers in the list is $5 + 9 + 17 + 20 = 51$. Additionally, since the mean is a whole number, the sum of all five numbers must be a multiple of 5. There are three possibilities for the median. If the fifth number is less than 9, then the median is 9. This occurs when the fifth number is 4 and the sum is 55. If the fifth number is greater than 17, then the median is 17. This occurs when the fifth number is 19 or a multiple of 5 more than 19. But if the fifth number is between 9 and 17, then the median is the fifth number. The only number between 9 and 17 that can be added to 51 to produce a multiple of 5 is 14. The sum of all possible values of the median is $9 + 14 + 17 = \boxed{40}$.

5. If the smallest digit is 1, then the other two digits must have a product of 36. There are two possibilities: either the other two digits are both 6, in which case the collection of digits 1, 6, and 6 can be used to form 3 different three-digit positive whole numbers, or the other two digits are 4 and 9, in which case the collection of digits 1, 4, and 9 can be used to form 6 different three-digit positive whole numbers. If the smallest digits is 2, then the other two digits could be 3 and 6, for another 6 numbers, or 2 and 9, for another 3 numbers. If the smallest digit is 3, then the other two digits could only be 3 and 4, for another 3 numbers. Altogether, the total number of possibilities is $3 + 6 + 6 + 3 + 3 = \boxed{21}$.

6. Let R be the number of hours Joanna runs and W be the number of hours Joanna walks. Then since the race is 15 kilometers in length, $6W + 10R = 15$. The total time Joanna has to complete the race is 1 hour and 40 minutes, or $\frac{5}{3}$ hours, so $W + R = \frac{5}{3}$. Multiplying the second equation by -6 yields $-6W - 6R = -10$, and adding it to the first equation produces $4R = 5$. Then $R = \frac{5}{4}$ hours, and $W = \frac{5}{3} - \frac{5}{4}$, or $\frac{5}{12}$ hours, which to the nearest minute is $\frac{5}{12} \cdot 60 = \boxed{25}$.

7. If the first move of the ant is up, then there are only 2 paths for the ant to take to reach B. If the first two moves of the ant are right and up, there is only 1 path for the ant to take to reach B. Otherwise the first three moves must be to the right. If the first four moves are to the right, there is only 1 path for the ant to take to reach B. If the first three moves are to the right and the fourth move is up, then there are 2 paths for the ant to take to reach B. Altogether, the total number of paths the ant can take is $2 + 1 + 1 + 2 = \boxed{6}$.

8. Consider casework based on the number of candy bars that Amy receives. Amy can receive exactly 2 candy bars in $\binom{5}{2} = 10$ ways. If Amy receives exactly two candy bars, then Ben can receive exactly 3, exactly 2, or exactly 1. In each case, once Ben has his candy bars, the candy bars for Carly are determined. There are $\binom{3}{3} = 1$ ways for Ben to receive exactly 3, $\binom{3}{2} = 3$ ways for Ben to receive exactly 2, and $\binom{3}{1} = 3$ ways for Ben to receive exactly 1. So for each of the 10 ways Amy receives 2 candy bars, there are $1 + 3 + 3 = 7$ ways for Ben to receive his candy bars, for $10 \cdot 7 = 70$ possibilities. Amy can also receive exactly 3 candy bars in $\binom{5}{3} = 10$ ways. Then Ben can receive exactly 2 or exactly 1. There are $\binom{2}{2} = 1$ way for Ben to receive exactly 2, and $\binom{2}{1} = 2$ ways for Ben to receive exactly 1. So for each of the 10 ways Amy receives 3 candy bars, there are $1 + 2 = 3$ ways for Ben to receive his candy bars, for $10 \cdot 3 = 30$ possibilities. Finally, if Amy receives exactly 4 candy bars, then the fifth candy bar must go to Ben. This can be done in $\binom{5}{4} = 5$ ways. Altogether, the total number of ways to distribute the candy bars is $70 + 30 + 5 = \boxed{105}$.

Team Round Solutions

1. This sum is $21 + 23 + 25 + 27 + 29 + 31 + 33 + 35 + 37 + 39$. This is also $(39 + 21) + (37 + 23) + (35 + 25) + (33 + 27) + (31 + 29)$, or $60 + 60 + 60 + 60 + 60$, which is $5 \times 60 = \boxed{300}$.

2. The unit price per can is lower for the thirty-six pack rather than the twelve pack. Now note that $132 \div 36$ is 3 with a remainder of 24. The cost of 3 thirty-six packs of soda is $3 \cdot \$11 = \$33$, and Sondra still has 24 cans left to purchase. She could get another thirty-six pack for \$11, or she can get 2 twelve packs for $2 \cdot \$4 = \$8$. The cheaper option is getting 2 twelve packs, and her total cost is $\$33 + \$8 = \boxed{\$41}$.

3. The total amount weighed is $35 + 33 + 32 = 100$ pounds. In this total, each box of fruit is weighed exactly twice. Therefore if each box of fruit is weighed exactly once, the total weight, in pounds, would be $100 \div 2 = \boxed{50}$.

4. The day that is December 1 occurs five times, as it also appears on day 8, 15, 22, and 29. Similarly, the days that are December 2 and 3 also occur five times. All other days occur only four times. If December 1 is a Monday, then Monday, Tuesday, and Wednesday occur 5 times, and Sunday and Friday occur four times, so December 1 could be a Monday. Similarly, December 1 could be a Tuesday. But if December 1 is a Wednesday or Thursday, then a Friday would occur five times and a Sunday would only occur four times, so December 1 could not be a Wednesday or a Thursday. If December 1 is a Friday, then both Friday and Sunday would occur five times, so December 1 could be a Friday. But if December 1 is a Saturday or Sunday, then a Sunday would occur five times and a Friday would only occur four times. Therefore December 1 could only be a Monday, Tuesday, or Friday, and the total number of possibilities is $\boxed{3}$.

5. The number in the box labeled d is the product of the boxes a and b, and can be thought of as $a \times b$. The number in the box labeled e is the product of the boxes b and c, and can be thought of as $b \times c$. Then the number 100 is the product of the boxes labeled d and e, or $a \times b \times b \times c$. Therefore b must be a number with a square that evenly divides 100. The only numbers with squares that evenly divide 100 are 1, 2, 5, and 10, so the total number of possible values for b is $\boxed{4}$.

6. The percentages given sum to $15\% + 25\% + 35\% + 10\% = 85\%$, so the percentage of students that scored 95 is $100\% - 85\% = 15\%$. Now suppose that exactly 100 students took the assessment. Then the lowest 15 scores were 80, the next 25 were 85, and the next 35, which includes the median score, were 90. Therefore the median score is 90. The mean score is $\frac{15 \cdot 80 + 25 \cdot 85 + 35 \cdot 90 + 10 \cdot 100 + 15 \cdot 95}{100} = 89$, and the positive difference between the median and mean is $90 - 89 = \boxed{1}$.

7. The speed of Dan is $\frac{60}{8} = \frac{15}{2}$ miles per hour, and the speed of Dave is $\frac{60}{9} = \frac{20}{3}$ miles per hour. Since each runs for the same time in hours, h, the total distance run is equal to $\frac{15}{2}h + \frac{20}{3}h$. Setting this equal to 15 and solving, $h = \frac{18}{17}$, so the total time to complete the race is $2 \cdot \frac{18}{17} = \frac{36}{17}$ hours, or $60 \cdot \frac{36}{17} = \frac{2160}{17}$ minutes, which to the nearest whole number is $\boxed{127}$.

8. For a number to have exactly 10 positive whole number divisors, the prime factorization of the number must be $p^4 \cdot q$, where p and q are distinct primes, or p^9. In the second case, the only possibility is $2^9 = 512$, which is 1 such number. In the first case, if p is 2, then $p^4 = 16$, and q can be any of $7, 11, 13, 17, 19, 23, 29, 31, 37, 41, 43, 47, 53, 59, 61$, for 15 such numbers. If p is 3, then $p^4 = 81$, and q can be any of $2, 5, 7, 11$, for four such numbers. No larger values of p are possible. Altogether, the total number of three-digit positive whole numbers that have exactly ten positive whole number divisors is $1 + 15 + 4 = \boxed{20}$.

9. There are $6 + 5 + 4 + 3 + 2 + 1 = 21$ tokens in the bag, so there are $\binom{21}{2} = 210$ possible pairs of tokens. Now consider the prime numbers. Because there is only one token with the number 1, there are no pairs of tokens that will sum to 2. The only way to have a sum of 3 is to select one of the tokens with a 2 and the token with a 1. This can occur in $\binom{2}{1} \cdot \binom{1}{1} = 2$ ways. For a sum of 5, one of the tokens with the number 4 could be selected along with the token with the number 1. This can occur in $\binom{4}{1} \cdot \binom{1}{1} = 4$ ways. Additionally, one of the tokens with the number 3 could be selected along with one of the tokens with the number 2. This can occur in $\binom{3}{1} \cdot \binom{2}{1} = 6$ ways. For a 7, the token pairs could be a 6 and a 1, a 5 and a 2, or a 4 and a 3. This can occur in a total of $6 \cdot 1 + 5 \cdot 2 + 4 \cdot 3 = 28$ ways. For an 11, the token pairs could only be a 6 and a 5. This can occur in $6 \cdot 5 = 30$ ways. No two tokens have a sum that is any greater prime. Altogether, the total number of pairs of tokens that with a sum that is a prime number is $2 + 4 + 6 + 28 + 30 = 70$, for a probability of $\frac{70}{210} = \boxed{\frac{1}{3}}$.

10. As shown below, let point E be the point on the larger circle where segment AB is tangent, let O and P be the centers of the circles, let Q be the point on AD so that points P, O, and Q are collinear, and let F be on EP so that OF is parallel to AE. Then quadrilateral $AOFE$ is a rectangle, and the length of FP is $20 - 5 = 15$. The length of OP is $5 + 20 = 25$. By the Pythagorean Theorem, the length of OF is $\sqrt{25^2 - 15^2} = 20$. Note from symmetry that $\angle OPB = \angle OPC = 90°$, and so angles OPF and FPB are complementary. Then from some angle chasing, we find that $\triangle EPB$ and $\triangle QAO$ are both similar to $\triangle FOP$. As such, $\frac{OF}{OP} = \frac{PE}{PB}$, or $\frac{20}{25} = \frac{20}{PB}$, and $PB = 25$. Additionally, $\frac{OF}{OP} = \frac{AQ}{AO}$, or $\frac{20}{25} = \frac{AQ}{5}$, and $QA = 4$. By the Pythagorean Theorem, $QO = 3$. Quadrilateral $AQPB$ is a trapezoid with bases of length 4 and 25 and an altitude of $3 + 25 = 28$, so its area is $\frac{1}{2} \cdot 28 \cdot (4 + 25) = 406$. Quadrilateral $DQPC$ is congruent to trapezoid $AQPB$, so the entire area of quadrilateral $ABCD$ is $2 \cdot 406 = \boxed{812}$.

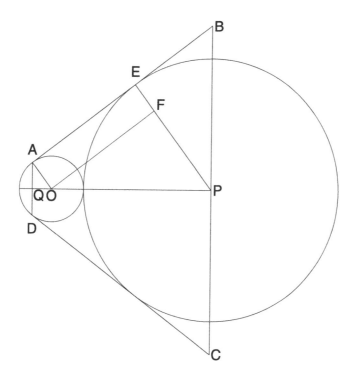

Number Sense
12223

Place ID Sticker
Inside This Box

Name _____

Grade _____

School _____

1. $21 + 21 + 21 =$ _____.

2. $192 + 361 =$ _____.

3. The thousands digit of 424264 is _____.

4. $6 + 6 \times 11 =$ _____.

5. $713 - 379 =$ _____.

6. $13 \times 40 =$ _____.

7. $18 + 41 + 29 + 53 =$ _____.

8. The remainder of $86 \div 3$ is _____.

9. $156 \div 12 =$ _____.

10. (estimate) $426 + 781 + 923 =$ _____.

11. $542 - 127 - 216 =$ _____.

12. $15^2 =$ _____.

13. $11 \times 48 =$ _____.

14. The remainder of $93 \div 6$ is _____.

15. $42 \times 15 =$ _____.

16. $14 \times 17 \times 5 =$ _____.

17. *MDXXIII* in Arabic numerals is _____.

18. $0.6 \times 1.9 =$ _____ (decimal).

19. $26 \times 14 =$ _____.

20. (estimate) $211 \times 401 =$ _____.

21. If 1 mile is equal to 1760 yards, then $\frac{1}{5}$ mile is equal to _____ yards.

22. $65 \times 25 =$ _____.

23. $12 \times 35 \div 15 =$ _____.

24. The greater of $\frac{3}{11}$ and $\frac{4}{15}$ is _____ (fraction).

25. $28^2 =$ _____.

26. The GCD of 24 and 44 is _____.

27. $19 + 22 + 25 + 28 + 31 + 34 =$ _____.

28. $798 \div 21 =$ _____.

29. $\frac{3}{4} - \frac{1}{6} - \frac{1}{12} =$ _____ (fraction).

30. (estimate) $41 \times 39 \times 15 =$ _____.

31. $75^2 =$ _____.

32. The perimeter of a rectangle with width 18 and length 13 is _____.

33. $74 \times 99 =$ _____.

34. The LCM of 24 and 44 is _____.

35. $\frac{3}{4} =$ _____ %.

36. 1020 seconds is _____ minutes.

37. $69 \times 61 =$ _____.

38. 30% of 120 is _____.

39. The number of even whole numbers between 27 and 79 is _____.

40. (estimate) $167 \times 479 =$ _____.

41. $71 \times 31 =$ _____.

42. The sixteenth term in the arithmetic sequence $9, 15, 21, \ldots$ is _____.

43. $5 \times 12 + 8 \times 15 =$ _____.

44. The remainder of $2712 \div 11$ is _____.

45. $43^2 - 32^2 =$ _____.

46. $101 \times 57 =$ _____.

47. The side length of an octagon with perimeter 184 is _____.

48. $12^3 =$ _____.

49. 132_5 in base 10 is _____.

50. (estimate) $777777 \div 192 =$ _____.

51. The median of the list $14, -5, 7, 9, -4, 16$ is ___.

52. $121 \times 104 =$ _____.

53. $14\frac{2}{7}\%$ of 133 is _____.

54. The sum of the terms of the arithmetic sequence $9, 14, 19, \ldots, 59$ is _____.

55. $\sqrt{8836} =$ _____.

56. The measure of an interior angle in a regular hexagon is _____°.

57. $94 \times 85 =$ _____.

58. 172_8 in base 2 is _____$_2$.

59. $375 \times 24 =$ _____.

60. (estimate) $\sqrt{469534} =$ _____.

61. $8\frac{1}{3} \times 10\frac{1}{3} =$ _____ (mixed number)

62. The number of different ways to order the letters *SENSE* is _____.

63. $222 \times 23 =$ _____.

64. The number 62 written in base 8 is _____$_8$.

65. $0.0\overline{63} =$ _____.

66. $18 \times 48 \times 13 =$ _____.

67. The area of a right triangle with a leg of length 21 and a hypotenuse of length 29 is _____.

68. $68^2 =$ _____.

69. If $z = 18$, then $z^2 + 4z =$ _____.

70. (estimate) $857142 \times 8 =$ _____.

71. The number of positive whole number divisors of 90 is _____.

72. $988 \times 987 =$ _____.

73. The number of proper subsets of $\{S, T, N, I, C, K\}$ is _____.

74. $\sqrt{3} \times \sqrt{96} \times \sqrt{2} =$ _____.

75. $24 \times 15 \times 34 =$ _____.

76. If $4^{3-k} = 32$, then $4^{k+1} =$ _____.

77. The sum of the terms of the infinite geometric series $12, 4, \frac{4}{3}, \ldots$ is _____.

78. $625^{\frac{3}{4}} =$ _____.

79. The surface area of a $5 \times 6 \times 6$ right rectangular prism is _____.

80. (estimate) The radius of a circle with area 6543 is _____.

Sprint Round
12223

Place ID Sticker
Inside This Box

Name _____

Grade _____

School _____

1. (A) (B) (C) (D) (E)   11. (A) (B) (C) (D) (E)   21. (A) (B) (C) (D) (E)

2. (A) (B) (C) (D) (E)   12. (A) (B) (C) (D) (E)   22. (A) (B) (C) (D) (E)

3. (A) (B) (C) (D) (E)   13. (A) (B) (C) (D) (E)   23. (A) (B) (C) (D) (E)

4. (A) (B) (C) (D) (E)   14. (A) (B) (C) (D) (E)   24. (A) (B) (C) (D) (E)

5. (A) (B) (C) (D) (E)   15. (A) (B) (C) (D) (E)   25. (A) (B) (C) (D) (E)

6. (A) (B) (C) (D) (E)   16. (A) (B) (C) (D) (E)   26. (A) (B) (C) (D) (E)

7. (A) (B) (C) (D) (E)   17. (A) (B) (C) (D) (E)   27. (A) (B) (C) (D) (E)

8. (A) (B) (C) (D) (E)   18. (A) (B) (C) (D) (E)   28. (A) (B) (C) (D) (E)

9. (A) (B) (C) (D) (E)   19. (A) (B) (C) (D) (E)   29. (A) (B) (C) (D) (E)

10. (A) (B) (C) (D) (E)   20. (A) (B) (C) (D) (E)   30. (A) (B) (C) (D) (E)

1. Which of the following sums is even?

   (A) $13 + 7 + 2$ (B) $9 + 5 + 11$ (C) $7 + 14 + 6$ (D) $4 + 12 + 3$ (E) $8 + 15 + 6$

2. At the grocery store, three apples can be purchased for \$2, or a single apple can be purchased for \$1. What is the greatest number of apples that can be purchased for \$9?

   (A) 9   (B) 10   (C) 13   (D) 11   (E) 12

3. A fortnight is two weeks. How many total days are in one fortnight, one week, and one day?

   (A) 22   (B) 16   (C) 15   (D) 21   (E) 29

4. Nickels are coins worth 5 cents and dimes are coins worth 10 cents. Pete has five dimes and three nickels. Ricky has as many dimes as Pete has nickels, and as many nickels as Pete has dimes. Counting only their dimes and nickels, how many more cents than Ricky does Pete have?

   (A) 10   (B) 25   (C) 15   (D) 20   (E) 5

5. From a square piece of paper measuring four inches on each side, a square is cut out from the interior. The square that is cut out measures one inch on each side. After the square is cut out, what is sum of the lengths of all edges of the piece of paper, in inches?

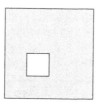

   (A) 12   (B) 18   (C) 20   (D) 16   (E) 24

6. Andre multiplied 12 by 14. Bethany multiplied a number by 8 and had the same result as Andre. What number did Bethany multiply by 8?

   (A) 28   (B) 16   (C) 18   (D) 24   (E) 21

7. On December 1st, Zach vacuumed his apartment and washed a load of laundry. If Zach vacuums his apartment every fifth day and washes a load of laundry every second day, then on what day of December will Zach do both on the same day for the third time that month?

(A) 20th   (B) 10th   (C) 31st   (D) 21st   (E) 11th

8. Penny can paint four figurines in one hour. If Penny always takes the same amount of time to paint a figurine, then how long, in minutes, will it take Penny to paint seven figurines?

(A) 90   (B) 96   (C) 105   (D) 120   (E) 108

9. Priyana wrote down a list of positive whole numbers. The numbers in Priyana's list were 57, 87, 91, 97, 111, and 143. A prime number is a number that is only evenly divisible by itself and 1. How many numbers in Priyana's list were prime?

(A) 3   (B) 1   (C) 0   (D) 4   (E) 2

10. A rectangle has a width of 12 and a height of 8. As shown below, a triangle is shaded in the rectangle, and the corners of the triangle are a corner of the rectangle and the middle points of two sides of the rectangle. What is the area of the shaded triangle?

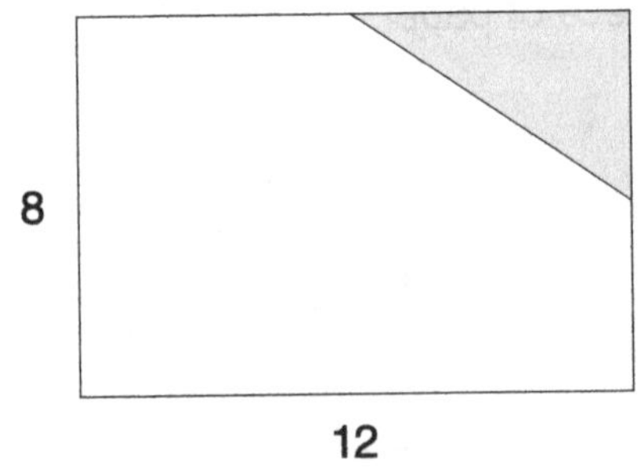

(A) 16   (B) 18   (C) 20   (D) 24   (E) 12

11. What is the remainder when $5 \times 15 \times 25 \times 35$ is divided by 11?

(A) 1   (B) 5   (C) 10   (D) 8   (E) 3

12. Once every four years in the Mushroom Kingdom, a President is chosen to serve for the next four years. If each chosen President must complete their full four years as President, what is the greatest number of people who could serve between March 10, 1985 and March 10, 2000?

(A) 3   (B) 6   (C) 5   (D) 4   (E) 2

13. A picture measuring 6 inches wide and 8 inches high is placed in a frame. The frame has a width of 2 inches on all sides, as shown below. What is the area of the frame, in square inches?

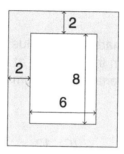

(A) 80   (B) 60   (C) 54   (D) 72   (E) 64

14. After basketball practice, Samantha attempted fifty free throws and made exactly 70%. She then attempted a number of additional free throws and made them all, so that the percentage made of all free throws she shot after practice was exactly 75%. How many additional free throws did Samantha attempt?

(A) 11   (B) 10   (C) 8   (D) 7   (E) 9

15. Which of the following fractions is greater than $\frac{2}{3}$ and less than $\frac{7}{10}$?

(A) $\frac{17}{26}$ (B) $\frac{9}{13}$ (C) $\frac{13}{20}$ (D) $\frac{12}{17}$ (E) $\frac{17}{24}$

16. The right triangle below has two legs of length 15. What is the greatest whole number that is less than the perimeter of this triangle?

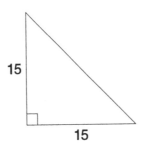

(A) 54   (B) 53   (C) 52   (D) 50   (E) 51

17. A bag of marbles contains three red marbles, four blue marbles, five green marbles, and six yellow marbles. Selena removes marbles from the bag one at a time, but does not look at the marbles she removes. How many marbles must Selena remove from the bag in order to guarantee that she has at least one marble of each color?

(A) 16   (B) 14   (C) 13   (D) 15   (E) 17

18. In a list of four numbers, the unique mode is 9, the mean, or average, is 12, and the range is 10. What is the greatest number in the list?

(A) 18   (B) 16   (C) 17   (D) 20   (E) 19

19. A regular hexagon is shown below. One pair of sides that is parallel, or positioned in the same direction, is highlighted. How many different pairs of sides of the hexagon are not parallel?

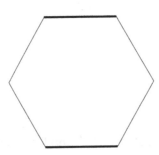

(A) 8   (B) 15   (C) 10   (D) 12   (E) 18

20. If $x \clubsuit y = x^2 - y^2$, then what is the value of $(28 \clubsuit 26) \clubsuit (24 \clubsuit 22)$?

(A) 4000   (B) 3000   (C) 2800   (D) 3600   (E) 3200

21. Of the values 8^{2021}, 3^{2022}, 25^{2023}, 12^{2024}, and 15^{2025}, how many are perfect squares?

(A) 5   (B) 1   (C) 4   (D) 3   (E) 2

22. Mika wrote down every six-digit binary, or base-two, number that has exactly one 0. One of the numbers Mika wrote down was 110111_2. Mika then summed all of the numbers she wrote down and converted the sum to base ten. What was Mika's sum?

(A) 280   (B) 284   (C) 296   (D) 292   (E) 288

23. The isosceles triangle shown below has an area of 1260, and the unequal side has a length of 56. What is the perimeter of the triangle?

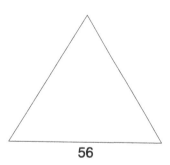

56

(A) 162   (B) 168   (C) 172   (D) 176   (E) 156

24. Max can run one mile in six minutes, Nate can run one mile in seven minutes, and Phil can run one mile in eight minutes. Max, Nate, and Phil all start running at the same time. To the nearest whole number of minutes, after how many minutes will Max, Nate, and Phil run a total distance of ten miles?

(A) 25   (B) 30   (C) 23   (D) 27   (E) 21

25. How many different arrangements of the letters *KAPPA* have at least one instance of the letter *A* between the two instances of the letter *P*?

(A) 10   (B) 12   (C) 16   (D) 15   (E) 18

26. Anna, Brian, and Cameron volunteer in the community. Anna volunteers at the library every third day. Brian volunteers at the animal shelter every fifth day, and Cameron volunteers at the food bank every seventh day. All three did volunteer work on December 31, 2020. How many days during the year 2021 did none of Anna, Brian, and Cameron volunteer?

(A) 174   (B) 184   (C) 188   (D) 170   (E) 167

27. In the figure below, the vertices of a rectangle lie on a circle of radius 10. Additionally, the center of the circle and two of the vertices of the rectangle are vertices of an equilateral triangle. To the nearest whole number, what is the area of the region that lies inside the circle but outside the rectangle?

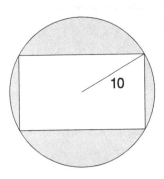

(A) 101   (B) 181   (C) 121   (D) 141   (E) 161

28. Emily and her five friends are riding rollercoasters at Seven Flags amusement park. On a rollercoaster, any of the friends may decide to ride alone, or paired with one of the others. If an arrangement is only considered different if the number of paired riders are different or a friend has a different friend sitting next to them, then how many different ways can the members of the group arrange themselves to ride a rollercoaster?

(A) 98   (B) 76   (C) 116   (D) 56   (E) 196

29. Sabrina is walking from home to school. While walking to school, Sabrina stops and realizes that if she walked home and then rode her bike to school, it would take the same amount of time as if she continued walking to school. If Sabrina always walks at a constant rate and rides her bike three times as fast as she walks, then what is the ratio of the distance from Sabrina's current location to home to the distance from Sabrina's current location to school?

(A) $\frac{2}{5}$ (B) $\frac{1}{3}$ (C) $\frac{1}{2}$ (D) $\frac{1}{4}$ (E) $\frac{2}{3}$

30. What is the sum of the digits of the value of $\dfrac{1}{\sqrt{1+\frac{1}{21^2}+\frac{1}{22^2}}-1}$?

(A) 12   (B) 14   (C) 11   (D) 13   (E) 15

Place ID Sticker
Inside This Box

Name _____

Grade _____

School _____

Problems 1 & 2

1. Hayden chose a two-digit positive whole number. The sum of the units digit and tens digit of Hayden's number was 8, and the product of the units digit and tens digit of Hayden's number was 12. If the tens digit was greater than the units digit, then what was Hayden's number?

1.

2. The figure below is made up of six identical squares. Each square has a side length of 6. What is the perimeter of the figure?

2.

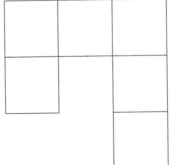

Place ID Sticker
Inside This Box

Name _____

Grade _____

School _____

Problems 3 & 4

3. Ritvik has a number of $5 bills, $10 bills, and $20 bills. The total value of his bills is $200. If Ritvik has six $20 bills and five $10 bills, then how many $5 bills does Ritvik have?

3.

4. Mrs. Moreau is the math team coach at Jamison Middle Schoool. The average age of the five fifth graders on the team is 10, and the average age of the seven sixth graders on the team is 11. The average age of all of the team's fifth graders, sixth graders, and Mrs. Moreau is 13. What is Mrs. Moreau's age?

4.

Place ID Sticker
Inside This Box

Name _____

Grade _____

School _____

Problems 5 & 6

5. The magic square shown below is a 3×3 grid of smaller squares. The sum of the three numbers in any row, column, and diagonal of the grid is the same. What number must go in the smaller square that is in the upper right corner of the magic square?

5.

8		
1		
		2

6. Chip has three identical red chips, two identical blue chips, and one white chip. How many different ways can Chip arrange his chips in a line so that either the first or last chip in the line is red?

6.

Place ID Sticker
Inside This Box

Name _____

Grade _____

School _____

Problems 7 & 8

---

7. Tamara was practicing geometry problems and word problems for the up-coming mathleague.org contest. No problem is considered both a geometry problem and a word problem. She completed each geometry problem in nine minutes, and she completed each word problem in seven minutes. Tamara completed all of the problems in 110 minutes. How many problems did Tamara complete?

7.

8. The figure below is a grid of evenly spaced dots. Each dot has a vertical distance of one unit from the dots above or below, and a horizontal distance of one unit from the dots to either side. Additionally, the line segment shown has endpoints that are dots. What is the shortest distance from the circled dot to the line segment? Express your answer as a common fraction.

8.

Team Round
12223

School or Team

Name _____

Name _____

Name _____

Name _____

Place ID Sticker
Inside This Box

Place ID Sticker
Inside This Box

Place ID Sticker
Inside This Box

Place ID Sticker
Inside This Box

1.

2.

3.

4.

5.

6.

7.

8.

9.

10.

1. Sammy summed all of the positive whole numbers less than 41 that are multiples of 5 but not multiples of 3. What was the value of Sammy's sum?

2. Armondo has a bag of marbles. Armando gave half of the marbles to Bianca. He then gave seven marbles to Cindy. Armando gave half of the remaining marbles to Daniel, and then he gave six marbles to Emily. Armando kept the remaining five marbles for himself. Before Armando gave any marbles away, how many marbles were in Armando's bag?

3. Colin has a number of stamps in his stamp collection. Colin can evenly divide his stamps into three equal groups, and he can also divide his stamps into four equal groups. However, Colin cannot divide his stamps into fifteen, sixteen, or eighteen equal groups. If Colin has more than thirty stamps, then what is the fewest number of stamps that he could have?

4. In a 2×3 grid of identical squares, exactly four squares are shaded gray. How many different ways can the squares be shaded? If a shading can be flipped or spun to match another shading, the shadings are not different. For example, the three shadings shown below are all the same.

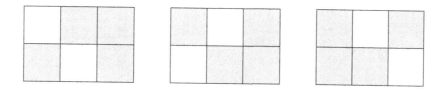

5. How many positive whole numbers have a square root that, when rounded to the nearest whole number, is equal to 99? For example, one such whole number is 9876, since the square root of 9876 is approximately 99.378, and 99.378 rounded to the nearest whole number is 99.

6. Dale and Jeff raced their cars in a 200 mile race. Both drivers started the race at the same time. Jeff finished the race with an average speed of 87 miles per hour, and he finished the race exactly 10 minutes and 13 seconds before Dale. To the nearest whole number, what was Dale's average speed for the race, in miles per hour?

7. A secret code is three-letter sequence, with letters selected from a limited alphabet that only has twelve different letters. One of the possible letters is X, but no codes may have more than one use of the letter X. All other codes are permitted. How many different secret codes are possible?

8. How many positive whole numbers less than 100 have five or fewer positive whole number divisors?

9. Right triangle *ABC*, with right angle at *B*, is shown below. Point *X* lies on segment *AB* so that the length of *AX* is 9 and the length of *XB* is 27. Additionally, point *Y* lies on segment *BC* so that the length of *BY* is 12 and the length of *YC* is 36. Finally, point *Z* lies on segment *AC* so that the length of *AZ* is 45. What is the area of triangle *XYZ*?

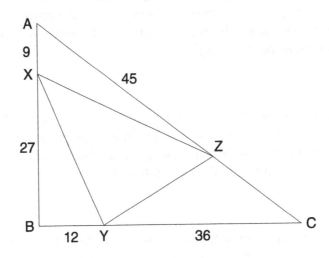

10. Two lists of positive whole numbers have different first terms. In both lists, the second term is greater than or equal to the first term. Additionally, in both lists, all terms after the second term are equal to the sum of the previous two terms in the list. However, the eighth term in both lists is the same. What is the least possible value for the eighth term in both lists?

Sprint Round

1. A	11. C	21. D
2. C	12. C	22. B
3. A	13. D	23. A
4. A	14. B	24. C
5. C	15. B	25. D
6. E	16. E	26. E
7. D	17. A	27. D
8. C	18. E	28. B
9. B	19. D	29. C
10. E	20. E	30. A

Target Round

1. 62
2. 84
3. 6
4. 42
5. 4
6. 48
7. 14
8. $\frac{17}{5}$

Team Round

1. 135
2. 58
3. 84
4. 6
5. 198
6. 81
7. 1694
8. 64
9. 378
10. 294

Number Sense

1. 63	21. 352	41. 2201	61. $86\frac{1}{9}$
2. 553	22. 1625	42. 99	62. 30
3. 4	23. 28	43. 180	63. 5106
4. 72	24. $\frac{3}{11}$	44. 6	64. 76
5. 334	25. 784	45. 825	65. $\frac{7}{110}$
6. 520	26. 4	46. 5757	66. 11232
7. 141	27. 159	47. 23	67. 210
8. 2	28. 38	48. 1728	68. 4624
9. 13	29. $\frac{1}{2}$	49. 42	69. 396
10. [2024, 2236]	30. [22786, 25184]	50. [3849, 4253]	70. [6514280, 7199992]
11. 199	31. 5625	51. 8	71. 12
12. 225	32. 62	52. 12584	72. 975156
13. 528	33. 7326	53. 19	73. 63
14. 3	34. 264	54. 374	74. 24
15. 630	35. 75	55. 94	75. 12240
16. 1190	36. 17	56. 120	76. 8
17. 1523	37. 4209	57. 7990	77. 18
18. 1.14	38. 36	58. 1111010	78. 125
19. 364	39. 26	59. 9000	79. 192
20. [80381, 88841]	40. [75994, 83992]	60. [651, 719]	80. [44, 47]

Sprint Round Solutions

1. When adding three positive whole numbers, the only ways the sum can be even is if all three numbers are even, or if two of the numbers are odd and one is even. There are no sums listed that have all three numbers even, and the only sum listed that has two numbers that are odd and one that is even is $\boxed{13 + 7 + 2}$.

2. To maximize the number of apples purchased, buy 4 sets of 3 apples for a total of $4 \times \$2 = \$8$. This is $4 \times 3 = 12$ apples, and the remaining dollar can be used to buy 1 more apple, for a total of $12 + 1 = \boxed{13}$.

3. The fortnight and single week total to 3 weeks, and since there are 7 days in one week, this is $3 \times 7 = 21$ days. The additional day brings the total number of days to $21 + 1 = \boxed{22}$.

4. Pete has $5 \times 10 + 3 \times 5 = 65$ cents. Ricky has 3 dimes and 5 nickels, so he has $3 \times 10 + 5 \times 5 = 55$ cents. Pete's total number of cents exceeds Ricky's total number of cents by $65 - 55 = \boxed{10}$.

5. The perimeter of the original square is $4 \times 4 = 16$ inches. The perimeter of the square that was removed, which is the perimeter of the hole in the original piece of paper, is $1 \times 4 = 4$ inches. The total perimeter of the piece of paper, in inches, is $16 + 4 = \boxed{20}$.

6. The product 12×14 can be thought of as $4 \times 3 \times 7 \times 2$, or $4 \times 2 \times 3 \times 7$. This is $8 \times 3 \times 7$, or 8×21, so the number Bethany multiplied by 8 was $\boxed{21}$.

7. Zach will vacuum his apartment on December 1st, 6th, 11th, 16th, 21st, 26th, and 31st. He will do a load of laundry on the 1st, 3rd, 5th, and so on, doing a load of laundry on every odd-numbered day of the month. The third odd-numbered day in the list of days where Zach vacuums is the $\boxed{21\text{st}}$.

8. Penny can paint 4 figurines in one hour, or 60 minutes. Then 1 figurine can be painted in $60 \div 4 = 15$ minutes, and the number of minutes to paint 7 figurines is $7 \times 15 = \boxed{105}$.

9. Because the sums of the digits of 57 is $5 + 7 = 12$, which is a multiple of 3, 57 is divisible by 3 and is therefore not prime. Similarly, 87 and 111 also have digits that sum to a multiple of 3 and are not prime. The number 91 is divisible by 7, and is therefore not prime. Additionally, because $(1 + 3) - (4) = 0$, which is a multiple of 11, the number 143 is divisible by 11. The number 97, however, is not divisible by any of the primes 2, 3, 5, or 7, which are all of the primes less than the square root of 97, so 97 is prime. The total number of primes in Priyana's list is $\boxed{1}$.

10. The triangle is a right triangle. One leg of the triangle has a length of $12 \div 2 = 6$ and the other leg has a length of $8 \div 2 = 4$. The area of a right triangle is half the product of the leg lengths, so the area of the shaded triangle is $\frac{1}{2} \times 6 \times 4 = \boxed{12}$.

11. The given expression can be rewritten as $(5) \times (11 + 4) \times (2 \times 11 + 3) \times (3 \times 11 + 2)$. When expanded, every term is a multiple of 11 except for $5 \times 4 \times 3 \times 2$. Thus the remainder of the entire product divided by 11 is the remainder of $2 \times 3 \times 4 \times 5 = 120$ divided by 11, which is $\boxed{10}$.

12. The number of years between these two times is $2000 - 1985 = 15$. So we want to find the greatest number of people who can serve in 15 years. Because two numbers equal to 4 and a third number less than 4 sums to less than 15, the fifteen-year period must cover at least 3 full four-year terms. Those 3 terms account for $3 \cdot 4 = 12$ years. The remaining $15 - 12 = 3$ years could be split between at most 2 Presidents. For example, the final year of one President could be year 1 of the 15 years, and the first two years of another President could be years 14 and 15 of the 15 years. Therefore the greatest number of people that could serve as President is $3 + 2 = \boxed{5}$.

13. The total width of the frame and picture is $6 + 2 + 2 = 10$ inches, and the total height of the frame and picture is $8 + 2 + 2 = 12$ inches. The area of the frame and picture is $12 \times 10 = 120$ square inches. The area of the picture is $6 \times 8 = 48$ square inches, so the area of the frame, in square inches, is $120 - 48 = \boxed{72}$.

14. If Samantha attempted 50 free throws and made exactly 70%, then she made exactly $0.7 \cdot 50 = 35$ free throws. To make exactly 75% of all free throws, 35 plus the additional number divided by 50 plus the additional number must be equal to $\frac{3}{4}$. Different answer choices could be tried. Alternatively, let m be the number of additional free throws, so $\frac{35+m}{50+m} = \frac{3}{4}$, or $140 + 4m = 150 + 3m$, and $m = \boxed{10}$.

15. When $\frac{17}{26}$ is compared to $\frac{2}{3}$, $3 \cdot 17 < 2 \cdot 26$, so $\frac{2}{3}$ is greater. Similarly, for $\frac{13}{20}$, $3 \cdot 13 < 2 \cdot 20$, so $\frac{2}{3}$ is greater. When $\frac{12}{17}$ is compared to $\frac{7}{10}$, $10 \cdot 12 > 7 \cdot 17$, so $\frac{7}{10}$ is less. Similarly, for $\frac{17}{24}$, $10 \cdot 17 > 7 \cdot 24$, so $\frac{17}{24}$ is greater. But for $\frac{9}{13}$, $2 \cdot 13 < 3 \cdot 9$, so $\frac{9}{13}$ is greater than $\frac{2}{3}$, and $7 \cdot 13 > 10 \cdot 9$, so $\frac{9}{13}$ is less than $\frac{7}{10}$, so the only fraction that meets both conditions is $\boxed{\dfrac{9}{13}}$.

16. By the Pythagorean Theorem, the hypotenuse of the right triangle has a length of $\sqrt{15^2 + 15^2} = \sqrt{450}$. Since $21^2 = 441$ and $22^2 = 484$, the perimeter of the triangle is between $15 + 15 + 21 = 51$ and $15 + 15 + 22 = 52$, so the greatest whole number that is less than the perimeter is $\boxed{51}$.

17. There are $3 + 4 + 5 + 6 = 18$ marbles in the bag. Because there are only three red marbles in the bag, it is possible to draw $18 - 3 = 15$ marbles from the bag and not select a red marble. But with only 2 marbles remaining, even if both are the same color, at least one marble of each color must have been removed. Therefore the number of marbles Selena must remove is $18 - 2 = \boxed{16}$.

18. If the average of the 4 numbers is 12, then the sum of the 4 numbers is $4 \cdot 12 = 48$. If the unique mode is 9, then at least 2 of the numbers must be 9, so the other two numbers must sum to $48 - 9 - 9 = 30$. If the range is 10, then either the remaining two numbers must differ by 10, with the lesser being less than or equal to 9, or the lesser is greater than 9 and the greater is $9 + 10 = 19$. The first case is impossible, as the only two numbers that differ by 10 with a sum of 30 are 10 and 20, which would mean the range of the four numbers would be $20 - 9 = 11$. In the second case, the greater number is 19, and the lesser is $30 - 19 = 11$. The range of the four numbers is $19 - 9 = 10$. Therefore the greatest of the four numbers is $\boxed{19}$.

19. There are 3 pairs of sides that are parallel. This can be subtracted from the total number of pairs of sides. The total number of pairs of sides that includes the top side is 5. The total number of pairs of sides that includes the side immediately to the right of the top side, but not the top side as that pair has already been counted, is 4. Similarly, the total number of pairs of sides that includes the side to the right of the bottom side is 3. And for the remaining two sides, the count is 2 and 1. Altogether, the total number of pairs of sides is $5 + 4 + 3 + 2 + 1 = 15$, so the total number of pairs of sides that are not parallel is $15 - 3 = \boxed{12}$.

20. The expression $x^2 - y^2$ can be factored as $(x + y)(x - y)$. Then $28\clubsuit26 = (28 + 26)(28 - 26)$, which is $54 \cdot 2 = 108$. Similarly, $24\clubsuit22 = (24 + 22)(24 - 22)$, which is $46 \cdot 2 = 92$. Finally, $108\clubsuit92 = (108 + 92)(108 - 92)$, which is $200 \cdot 16 = \boxed{3200}$.

21. A number is a perfect square if its prime factorization has exponents that are all even numbers. Considering each, $8^{2021} = \left(2^3\right)^{2021}$, which is 2^{6063}, so 8^{2021} is not a perfect square. But 3^{2022} is already a prime to an even power, so it is a perfect square. And 25^{2023} is $\left(5^2\right)^{2023} = 5^{4046}$, so 25^{2023} is also a perfect square. Because 2024 is an even power, the prime factorization of 12^{2024} must also have primes to even powers, so 12^{2024} is a perfect square. Finally, $15^{2025} = (5 \cdot 3)^{2025}$, which is $5^{2025} \cdot 3^{2025}$, so 15^{2025} is not a perfect square. Altogether, the number of perfect squares is $\boxed{3}$.

22. The numbers Mika wrote down were 111110_2, 111101_2, 111011_2, 110111_2, and 101111_2. There are 5 numbers, and a 1 appears in the 32-place 5 times, and a 1 appears in the 16, 8, 4, 2, and 1 places 4 times. The sum is $5 \cdot 32 + 4 \cdot (16 + 8 + 4 + 2 + 1) = 160 + 4 \cdot 31$, which is $\boxed{284}$.

23. If the triangle has an area of 1260, then the length of the altitude to the side of length 56 is $\frac{1260 \cdot 2}{56} = 45$. This altitude bisects the side length of 56, forming two congruent right triangles with legs of length 45 and $\frac{56}{2} = 28$. By the Pythagorean Theorem, the length of the hypotenuse of these triangles, which is also the unknown side length of the original isosceles triangle, is $\sqrt{28^2 + 45^2} = \sqrt{2809}$, which is 53. The perimeter of the isosceles triangle is $53 + 53 + 56 = \boxed{162}$.

24. In 1 minute, Max runs $\frac{1}{6}$ mile, Nate runs $\frac{1}{7}$ mile, and Phil runs $\frac{1}{8}$ mile. When all three are running, the total distance covered in 1 minute is $\frac{1}{6} + \frac{1}{7} + \frac{1}{8} = \frac{73}{168}$ mile. Thus the total number of minutes required to run 10 miles is $10 \div \frac{73}{168} = \frac{1680}{73}$, which to the nearest whole number is $\boxed{23}$.

25. Because there are 5 letters in *KAPPA*, but there are 2 instances of *P* and 2 instances of *A*, there are $\frac{5!}{2! \cdot 2!} = 30$ different arrangements. There are two cases where there is not an *A* between the two instances of *P*. In the first case, both instances of *P* are consecutive. Treating the two instances of *P* as a single letter, there are $\frac{4!}{2!} = 12$ different arrangements of *PP*, *A*, *A*, and *K*. In the second case, there is only the letter *K* between the instances of *P*. Treating *PKP* as a single letter, there are $\frac{3!}{2!} = 3$ different arrangements of *PKP*, *A*, and *A*. Therefore the number of arrangements where there is an *A* between the two instances of *P* is $30 - 12 - 3 = \boxed{15}$.

26. There are 365 days in the year 2021. Since 365 divided by 3 has a quotient of 121, Anna will volunteer on 121 of the days. Similarly, Brian will volunteer on 73 of the days, and Cameron will volunteer on 52 of the days. Since every 15 days both Anna and Brian both volunteer, there are 24 days when both volunteer. Similarly, both Anna and Cameron volunteer every 21 days, for 17 days when both volunteer, and both Brian and Cameron volunteer every 35 days, for 10 days when both volunteer. Finally, since $3 \cdot 5 \cdot 7 = 105$, there are 3 days when all three volunteer. Thus there are $24 - 3 = 21$ days when only Anna and Brian volunteer, $17 - 3 = 14$ days when only Anna and Cameron volunteer, and $10 - 3 = 7$ days when only Brian and Cameron volunteer. Therefore there are $121 - 21 - 14 - 3 = 83$ days when only Anna volunteers, $73 - 21 - 7 - 3 = 42$ days when only Brian volunteers, and $52 - 14 - 7 - 3 = 28$ days when only Cameron volunteers. Altogether, the number of days that at least one of the three volunteers is $83 + 42 + 28 + 21 + 14 + 7 + 3 = 198$, so the number of days when none volunteer is $365 - 198 = \boxed{167}$.

27. The area of the circle is $10^2 \cdot \pi$, which is very nearly $100 \cdot 3.14 = 314$. Because two radii and a side of the rectangle are sides of an equilateral triangle, the shorter side of the rectangle has length 10. Dropping a perpendicular from the center of the circle to the longer side of the rectangle bisects the longer side and forms a $30 - 60 - 90$ right triangle with a hypotenuse of length 10, so half the longer side is $\frac{\sqrt{3}}{2} \cdot 10 = 5\sqrt{3}$, and the longer side of the rectangle is $10\sqrt{3}$. The area of the rectangle is $10 \cdot 10\sqrt{3} = 100\sqrt{3}$. The square root of 3 is very nearly 1.73, so the area of the rectangle is very nearly 173, and the area of the region inside the circle but outside the rectangle is very nearly $314 - 173 = \boxed{141}$.

28. There are several cases to consider. The friends may ride as 6 individuals, 4 individuals and 1 pair, 2 individuals and 2 pairs, or 3 pairs. In the first case, there is only 1 way for the friends to ride, as all 6 must ride alone. In the second case, there are $\binom{6}{2} = 15$ ways, as once the pair of riders is set, the remaining 4 must ride alone. In the third case, there are $\binom{6}{2} = 15$ ways to select the first pair of riders, and $\binom{4}{2} = 6$ ways to select the second pair of riders from the remaining 4 friends, and the final 2 friends must ride alone. Since the order of the pairs does not matter, this yields $\frac{15 \cdot 6}{2!} = 45$ ways. The fourth case is identical to the third case, as once the first two pairs are selected, the final 2 friends must be paired together. Again, the order of the three pairs does not matter, therefore we have $\frac{15 \cdot 6}{3!} = 15$ ways. Summing over all cases, the total number of ways for the friends to ride is $1 + 15 + 45 + 15 = \boxed{76}$.

29. Let Sabrina's distance to home be *H* and her distance to school be *S*, so that the total distance from home to school is $H + S$. Additionally, let her walking speed be 1, so that her biking speed is 3. Then the time it will take Sabrina to walk to school is *S*, and the time it will take Sabrina to walk home and then ride her bike to school is $H + \frac{H+S}{3}$. Setting these two expressions equal, $S = H + \frac{H+S}{3}$, and $3S = 3H + H + S$. The value sought is $\frac{H}{S}$, and $2S = 4H$, so $\frac{H}{S} = \frac{2}{4}$, which is $\boxed{\frac{1}{2}}$.

30. Let $x = 21$ so that $x + 1 = 22$. Then the expression is $\dfrac{1}{\sqrt{1+\frac{1}{x^2}+\frac{1}{(x+1)^2}}-1}$. Considering only the portion under the radical, $1 + \frac{1}{x^2} + \frac{1}{(x+1)^2} = \dfrac{x^2(x+1)^2+(x+1)^2+x^2}{x^2(x+1)^2}$. The numerator is $x^2(x^2 + 2x + 1) + (x^2 + 2x + 1) + x^2 = x^4 + 2x^3 + 3x^2 + 2x + 1$. This is equivalent to $(x^2 + x + 1)^2$. Therefore the value of the radical is $\sqrt{\dfrac{(x^2+x+1)^2}{x^2(x+1)^2}} = \dfrac{x^2+x+1}{x(x+1)}$. Subtracting 1 from this expression, $\dfrac{x^2+x+1}{x(x+1)} - \dfrac{x^2+x}{x(x+1)} = \dfrac{1}{x(x+1)}$, and taking the reciprocal yields $x(x + 1)$. Thus the value of the expression is $21 \cdot 22 = 462$, and $4 + 6 + 2 = \boxed{12}$.

Target Round Solutions

1. If the sum of the units and tens digits was 8, then the digits must be 8 and 0, 7 and 1, 6 and 2, 5 and 3, or 4 and 4. Of these possible pairs, only 6 and 2 has a product of 12. Since the tens digit is greater than the units digit, the tens digit must be 6 and the units digit must be 2, and the number is $\boxed{62}$.

2. Each of the top, bottom, right, and left edges of the figure have three segments of length 6, for a combined length of $4 \times 3 \times 6 = 72$. Additionally, the interior of the figure has two vertical segments of length 6 that are not part of the left or right edges of the figure, for an additional length of $2 \times 6 = 12$. Altogether, the total perimeter is $72 + 12 = \boxed{84}$.

3. The total value of the $20 bills is $6 \times \$20 = \$120$, and the total value of the $10 bills is $5 \times \$10 = \$50$, for a total of $\$120 + \$50 = \$170$. Therefore, the $5 bills have a value of $\$200 - \$170 = \$30$, and the number of $5 bills is $\$30 \div \$5 = \boxed{6}$.

4. The sum of the ages of the fifth graders is $5 \cdot 10 = 50$, and the sum of the ages of the sixth graders is $7 \cdot 11 = 77$, so the sum of the ages of the fifth and sixth graders is 127. When Mrs. Moreau is included, there are 13 people with an average age of 13, so the sum of all ages is $13 \cdot 13 = 169$. Therefore Mrs. Moreau's age is $169 - 127 = \boxed{42}$.

5. Because the left column and bottom row include the number in lower right corner, the middle square on the bottom row must be $8 + 1 - 2 = 7$. Because the diagonal and the middle column include the number in the center, the middle square on the top row must be $8 + 2 - 7 = 3$. Similarly, the number in the middle of the right column must be $8 + 2 - 1 = 9$. Finally, the numbers in the upper right corner and lower left corner must also sum to $8 + 2 = 10$. But the rightmost column has $2 + 9 = 11$ and the bottom row has $2 + 7 = 9$, so the number in the lower left corner must be $11 - 9 = 2$ more than the number in the upper right corner. Therefore the number in the upper right corner must be $\boxed{4}$.

6. If the first chip is red, the remaining chips are two red, two blue, and one white. The number of different ways to arrange the letters *RRBBW* is $\frac{5!}{2! \cdot 2!} = 30$. Similarly, if the last chip is red, the number of ways to arrange the remaining chips is also 30. Summing, there appear to be $30 + 30 = 60$ ways to arrange the chips with the first red or last red. But this counts twice the arrangements where both the first and last chips are red. If both the first and last chip are red, the remaining chips are one red, two blue, and one white, and the number of different ways to arrange *RBBW* is $\frac{4!}{2!} = 12$. Therefore the number of ways to arrange the chips so that either the first or last chip is red is $60 - 12 = \boxed{48}$.

7. A multiple of 9 plus a multiple of 7 must sum to 110. The number 110 has a remainder of 2 when divided by 9, so the multiple of 7 must have a remainder of 2 when divided by 9. The only multiple of 7 that is less than 110 and has a remainder of 2 when divided by 9 is $7 \cdot 8 = 56$, so Tamara completed 8 word problems, and $\frac{110-56}{9} = 6$ geometry problems. Altogether, the number of problems she completed was $8 + 6 = \boxed{14}$.

8. Consider the triangle with vertices that are endpoints of the line segment and the circled dot. The altitude from the line segment to the circled dot is the shortest distance from the line segment to the circled dot, and the length of the line segment is, by the Pythagorean Theorem, $\sqrt{6^2 + 8^2} = 10$. The area of the triangle can be found by taking the area of the right triangle that contains the circled dot and has a hypotenuse that is the line segment, and removing the unwanted area. This right triangle has an area of $\frac{1}{2} \cdot 6 \cdot 8 = 24$. The unwanted area is a square with area 1, a right triangle with area $\frac{1}{2} \cdot 1 \cdot 5 = \frac{5}{2}$, and a right triangle with area $\frac{1}{2} \cdot 1 \cdot 7 = \frac{7}{2}$. Therefore the area of the triangle with vertices that are endpoints of the line segment and the circle dot is $24 - \left(1 + \frac{5}{2} + \frac{7}{2}\right) = 17$, and the altitude from the line segment to the circled dot is $\frac{2 \cdot 17}{10} = \boxed{\dfrac{17}{5}}$.

Team Round Solutions

1. The sum of the numbers less than 41 that are multiples of 5 is $5+10+15+20+25+30+35+40 = 180$. But 15 are 30 are multiples of 3 and must be removed from the sum, so the value of Sammy's sum is $180 - 15 - 30 = \boxed{135}$.

2. Working backwards, before Armando gave 6 marbles to Emily, he had $5 + 6 = 11$ marbles. Before he gave half to Daniel, he had $2 \times 11 = 22$. Before he gave 7 to Cindy, he had $22 + 7 = 29$. And before he gave half to Bianca, he had $29 \times 2 = \boxed{58}$.

3. If the number of stamps can be divided by 3 and 4, then the number of stamps can be divided by $3 \cdot 4 = 12$. Multiples of 12 greater than 30 are 36, 48, 60, 72, 84, 96, and so on. But 36 is divisible by 18, 48 is divisible by 16, 60 is divisible by 15, and 72 is also divisible by 18. But 84 is not divisible by any of 15, 16, or 18, so the fewest number of stamps that Colin could have is $\boxed{84}$.

4. Consider the squares that are not shaded, or white. If both of the squares that are white are in the middle column, there is 1 shading. If one of the squares in the middle column is white and a square sharing a side with that square is white, there is 1 shading. If one of the squares in the middle column is white and a square not sharing a side with that square is white, there is 1 shading. If both white squares are corner squares, then the second square that is shaded can be in the same row, the same column, or in neither the same row or the same column, for 3 shadings. Altogether, the number of possible shadings is $1 + 1 + 1 + 3 = \boxed{6}$.

5. The square root must be greater than 98.5, so the number must be greater than $98.5^2 = 9702.25$. Therefore the least possible whole number is 9703. The square root must be less than 99.5, so the number must be less than $99.5^2 = 9900.25$. Therefore the greatest possible whole number is 9900. The total count of numbers is $9900 - 9703 + 1 = \boxed{198}$.

6. Jeff's time for the race was $\frac{200}{87} \approx 2.2989$ hours. Since there are 60 minutes in one hour and 3600 seconds in one hour, Dale finished $\frac{10}{60} + \frac{13}{3600} \approx 0.1703$ hours after Jeff, so Jeff's time, in hours was approximately $2.2989 + 0.1703 = 2.4692$ hours. Therefore Dale's average speed in miles per hour was $\frac{200}{2.4692}$, which to the nearest whole number is $\boxed{81}$.

7. If there were no restrictions, there would be $12 \cdot 12 \cdot 12 = 1728$ secret codes. There is exactly 1 code that has three uses of the letter X. For codes that have exactly 2 uses of the letter X, there are 3 possible locations in the code for the letter that is not an X, and then $12 - 1 = 11$ possibilities for that letter, for $3 \cdot 11 = 33$ codes. The number of codes that have 0 or 1 use of the letter X is $1728 - 1 - 33 = \boxed{1694}$.

8. The number 1 is the only number with exactly 1 divisor. The only numbers with 2 divisors are primes, and there are 25 primes less than 100. The only numbers with 3 divisors are squares of primes, and 4, 9, 25, and 49 are the only such numbers, for a total of 4. The only numbers with 5 divisors are fourth powers of primes, and 16 and 81 are the only such numbers, for a total of 2. The numbers with 4 divisors fall into two categories. The first is cubes of primes, and there are 2 such numbers, 8 and 27. The second is numbers that are the product of two primes. If one of the primes is 2, the second prime could be any prime from 3 through 47, for a total of 14. If one of the primes is 3, the second prime could be any prime from 5 through 31, for a total of 9. If one of the primes is 5, the second prime could be any prime from 7 through 19, for a total of 5. Finally, if one of the primes is 7, the second prime could be either 11 or 13, for a total of 2. Altogether, the count of numbers with 4 divisors is $2 + 14 + 9 + 5 + 2 = 32$, and the count of numbers with five or fewer divisors is $1 + 25 + 4 + 2 + 32 = \boxed{64}$.

9. By the Pythagorean Theorem, the length of AC is $\sqrt{(9 + 27)^2 + (12 + 36)^2} = 60$, so the length of ZC is $60 - 45 = 15$. Additionally, triangle ABC is similar to a $3 - 4 - 5$ right triangle. From point Z, construct a perpendicular to BC, meeting BC at point M. Right triangle ZMC is also similar to a $3 - 4 - 5$ right triangle. Since ZC has length 15, the length of ZM is $\frac{3}{5} \cdot 15 = 9$. The area of triangle YZC is $\frac{1}{2} \cdot 36 \cdot 9 = 162$. Now from point Z, construct a perpendicular to AB, meeting AB at point N. Because MC has length $\frac{4}{5} \cdot 15 = 12$, the length of ZN is $48 - 12 = 36$. The area of triangle AXZ is $\frac{1}{2} \cdot 36 \cdot 9 = 162$. The area of triangle XBY is $\frac{1}{2} \cdot 12 \cdot 27 = 162$ as well. Finally, the area of ABC is $\frac{1}{2} \cdot 36 \cdot 48 = 864$, so the area of XYZ is $864 - 3 \cdot 162 = \boxed{378}$.

10. Let the first and second terms in the first list be a and b. Then the third term is $a + b$, the fourth is $a + 2b$, the fifth is $2a + 3b$, the sixth is $3a + 5b$, the seventh is $5a + 8b$, and the eighth is $8a + 13b$. Similarly, if the second list has first and second terms of c and d, then the eighth term is $8c + 13d$. Therefore $8a + 13b = 8c + 13d$. Rearranging and factoring, $8 \cdot (a - c) = 13 \cdot (d - b)$. Since a is not equal to c and the right side of the equation is a multiple of 13, $a - c$ must also be a multiple of 13. Because a and c are both positive whole numbers and the value of the eighth term must be minimized, let $a = 14$ and $c = 1$. Additionally, because b must be greater than or equal to a, the least possible value for b is 14, and the value of d is $\frac{8 \cdot 14 + 13 \cdot 14 - 8 \cdot 1}{13} = 22$. Both $8 \cdot 13 + 13 \cdot 14$ and $8 \cdot 1 + 13 \cdot 22$ produce the least possible value for the eighth term, which is $\boxed{294}$.

Number Sense
12224

Place ID Sticker
Inside This Box

Name _____

Grade _____

School _____

1. $222 + 21 = $ _____.

2. $631 - 469 = $ _____.

3. The units digit of 1312021 is _____.

4. $12 + 12 \times 4 = $ _____.

5. $32 + 45 + 55 + 38 = $ _____.

6. The remainder of $279 \div 5$ is _____.

7. $16 \times 30 = $ _____.

8. $429 + 285 = $ _____.

9. $156 \div 13 = $ _____.

10. (estimate) $492 + 1066 + 902 = $ _____.

11. $62 \times 11 = $ _____.

12. $561 - 138 - 218 = $ _____.

13. The remainder of $352 \div 9$ is _____.

14. $18 \times 5 \times 11 = $ _____.

15. $19^2 = $ _____.

16. $33 \times 27 = $ _____.

17. $36 \times 45 = $ _____.

18. *CCCXLVII* in Arabic numerals is _____.

19. $19.2 \div 1.2 = $ _____.

20. (estimate) $149 \times 601 = $ _____.

21. $25 \times 46 = $ _____.

22. The lesser of $\frac{6}{11}$ and $\frac{5}{9}$ is _____ (fraction).

23. $15 \times 49 \div 35 = $ _____.

24. $31^2 = $ _____.

25. The GCD of 35 and 55 is _____.

26. $544 \div 32 = $ _____.

27. $25 + 23 + 21 + 19 + 17 = $ _____.

28. $\frac{5}{6} - \frac{1}{12} - \frac{1}{4} = $ _____ (fraction).

29. If 1 yard is equal to 3 feet, then 5280 feet is equal to _____ yards.

30. (estimate) $89 \times 11 \times 91 = $ _____.

31. $99 \times 51 = $ _____.

32. $55^2 = $ _____.

33. $\frac{7}{10} = $ _____ %.

34. The perimeter of a square with area 196 is ___.

35. $39 \times 31 = $ _____.

36. The number of odd whole numbers between 92 and 184 is _____.

37. 25% of 76 is _____.

38. The LCM of 35 and 55 is _____.

39. $\sqrt{841} = $ _____.

40. (estimate) $\sqrt{262396} = $ _____.

41. The remainder of $3755 \div 11$ is _____.

42. $88 \times 28 =$ _____.

43. $36^2 - 25^2 =$ _____.

44. The twelfth term in the arithmetic sequence $13, 28, 43, \ldots$ is _____.

45. $8 \times 14 + 12 \times 4 =$ _____.

46. The diameter of a circle with area 49π is _____.

47. $75 \times 101 =$ _____.

48. 144_8 in base 10 is _____.

49. $2^5 \cdot 5^2 =$ _____.

50. (estimate) $27 \times 4444 =$ _____.

51. $103 \times 129 =$ _____.

52. The measure of an interior angle in a regular octagon is _____ $^\circ$.

53. $8\frac{1}{3}\%$ of 132 is _____.

54. The sum of the terms of the arithmetic sequence $7, 10, 13, \ldots 64$ is _____.

55. $12 \times 333 =$ _____.

56. The mean of the list $15, 21, 9, 34, 16$ is _____.

57. 10110_2 in base 8 is _____ $_8$.

58. The area of a right triangle with a leg of length 5 and a hypotenuse of length 13 is _____.

59. $96 \times 82 =$ _____.

60. (estimate) $7338768 \div 269 =$ _____.

61. The number of ways to choose 2 toys from a set of 6 different toys is _____.

62. $0.1\overline{3} =$ _____ (fraction).

63. $5\frac{1}{6} \times 7\frac{1}{6} =$ _____ (mixed number).

64. The number 93 in base 5 is _____ $_5$.

65. $\sqrt[3]{140608} =$ _____.

66. $99 \times 125 =$ _____.

67. If $w = 11$, then $w^2 + 8w + 16 =$ _____.

68. $16 \times 17 \times 42 =$ _____.

69. The area of a rhombus with diagonals of length 50 and 64 is _____.

70. (estimate) $31^4 =$ _____.

71. $\sqrt{20} \times \sqrt{90} \times \sqrt{2} =$ _____.

72. $185^2 =$ _____.

73. If $5^{1-x} = \frac{1}{5}$, then $5^{1+x} =$ _____.

74. The volume of a cube with a surface area of 864 is _____.

75. $13^3 =$ _____.

76. The number of positive whole number divisors of 98 is _____.

77. $729^{\frac{2}{3}} =$ _____.

78. $34 \times 15 \times 49 =$ _____.

79. The sum of the terms of the infinite geometric sequence $36, 24, 16, \ldots$ is _____.

80. (estimate) $108^4 \div 9^2 =$ _____.

Sprint Round
12224

Place ID Sticker
Inside This Box

Name _____

Grade _____

School _____

1. Ⓐ Ⓑ Ⓒ Ⓓ Ⓔ   11. Ⓐ Ⓑ Ⓒ Ⓓ Ⓔ   21. Ⓐ Ⓑ Ⓒ Ⓓ Ⓔ

2. Ⓐ Ⓑ Ⓒ Ⓓ Ⓔ   12. Ⓐ Ⓑ Ⓒ Ⓓ Ⓔ   22. Ⓐ Ⓑ Ⓒ Ⓓ Ⓔ

3. Ⓐ Ⓑ Ⓒ Ⓓ Ⓔ   13. Ⓐ Ⓑ Ⓒ Ⓓ Ⓔ   23. Ⓐ Ⓑ Ⓒ Ⓓ Ⓔ

4. Ⓐ Ⓑ Ⓒ Ⓓ Ⓔ   14. Ⓐ Ⓑ Ⓒ Ⓓ Ⓔ   24. Ⓐ Ⓑ Ⓒ Ⓓ Ⓔ

5. Ⓐ Ⓑ Ⓒ Ⓓ Ⓔ   15. Ⓐ Ⓑ Ⓒ Ⓓ Ⓔ   25. Ⓐ Ⓑ Ⓒ Ⓓ Ⓔ

6. Ⓐ Ⓑ Ⓒ Ⓓ Ⓔ   16. Ⓐ Ⓑ Ⓒ Ⓓ Ⓔ   26. Ⓐ Ⓑ Ⓒ Ⓓ Ⓔ

7. Ⓐ Ⓑ Ⓒ Ⓓ Ⓔ   17. Ⓐ Ⓑ Ⓒ Ⓓ Ⓔ   27. Ⓐ Ⓑ Ⓒ Ⓓ Ⓔ

8. Ⓐ Ⓑ Ⓒ Ⓓ Ⓔ   18. Ⓐ Ⓑ Ⓒ Ⓓ Ⓔ   28. Ⓐ Ⓑ Ⓒ Ⓓ Ⓔ

9. Ⓐ Ⓑ Ⓒ Ⓓ Ⓔ   19. Ⓐ Ⓑ Ⓒ Ⓓ Ⓔ   29. Ⓐ Ⓑ Ⓒ Ⓓ Ⓔ

10. Ⓐ Ⓑ Ⓒ Ⓓ Ⓔ   20. Ⓐ Ⓑ Ⓒ Ⓓ Ⓔ   30. Ⓐ Ⓑ Ⓒ Ⓓ Ⓔ

1. How many of the products 4×8, 5×5, 11×3, 2×15, and 7×4 are greater than 31?

   (A) 3   (B) 2   (C) 1   (D) 4   (E) 5

2. Hayden was given $20 by his mother to purchase snacks this week. On Monday, Hayden spent $4 on snacks. On Tuesday and Wednesday, Hayden spent $3 each day on snacks. On Thursday, Hayden spent $4 on snacks, and on Friday Hayden spent $5 on snacks. How many dollars of the $20 remained after Hayden bought snacks on Friday?

   (A) $3   (B) $4   (C) $1   (D) $2   (E) $0

3. What is the value of $11 + 15 + 19 + 21 + 25 + 29 + 31 + 35 + 39 + 41 + 45 + 49$?

   (A) 360   (B) 320   (C) 380   (D) 300   (E) 400

4. One rectangle shown below has a width of 8 and height of 6. Another rectangle has a width of 5 and a height of 9. What is the total area of both rectangles?

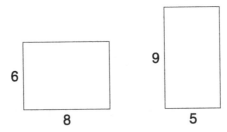

   (A) 93   (B) 98   (C) 88   (D) 95   (E) 87

5. Gary went to a showing of the latest *Ghostblasters* movie. The movie began at 7:18 PM and lasted for 124 minutes. At what time did the movie end?

   (A) 9:18 PM   (B) 9:26 PM   (C) 9:24 PM   (D) 9:28 PM   (E) 9:22 PM

6. Michelle is selling lemonade. She has five gallons of lemonade, and is selling the lemonade at a price of $2 per pint. If there are two pints in one quart, and four quarts in one gallon, then how many dollars will Michelle receive for selling all of her lemonade?

(A) $160   (B) $20   (C) $40   (D) $120   (E) $80

7. January 1st, 2022 was a Saturday. On what day of January 2022 does the last Wednesday of January 2022 occur?

(A) 26   (B) 27   (C) 25   (D) 29   (E) 28

8. A prime number is a whole number that is both greater than 1 and only evenly disible by 1 and itself. For example, since 5 is only divisible by 1 and 5, the number 5 is a prime number. Of the answer choices, which number is not prime?

(A) 83   (B) 73   (C) 91   (D) 97   (E) 79

9. The product of two positive whole numbers is 84. When one number is subtracted from the other, the difference is 8. What is the sum of the two numbers?

(A) 18   (B) 22   (C) 26   (D) 20   (E) 24

10. Cindy takes a square piece of paper measuring 12 inches on a side and makes four cuts, with each cut beginning and ending at the middle point of one of the sides of the paper. After she is done, she then has four triangles and a smaller square. What is the area of the smaller square, in square inches?

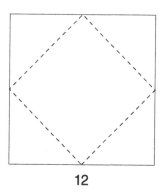

12

(A) 84   (B) 96   (C) 72   (D) 60   (E) 90

11. How many positive whole numbers evenly divide 165 but do not evenly divide 105?

    (A) 5   (B) 4   (C) 3   (D) 2   (E) 6

12. Colleen is collecting acorns. She collects 3 acorns on the first day, 7 acorns on the second day, 11 acorns on the third day, and so on, collecting four more acorns each day than she did on the previous day. On what day of her collecting will her total collection have more than 299 acorns?

    (A) 14   (B) 13   (C) 12   (D) 15   (E) 11

13. A piece of paper is in the shape of a right triangle with legs of length 40 centimeters and 30 centimeters. From the middle portion of this piece of paper, a piece of paper in the shape of a right triangle with legs of length 20 centimeters and 15 centimeters is cut out and removed. What is the area of the remaining piece of paper, in square centimeters?

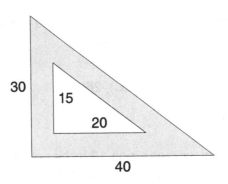

    (A) 550   (B) 480   (C) 400   (D) 450   (E) 420

14. The Ryde ride service charges users a fee of $5 for any ride, and this fee also pays for the first mile of travel. After the first mile, users are charged a fee of $1.25 per mile traveled. Andy is using Ryde to travel to a football stadium that is seventeen miles from his home. In addition to the fees for his Ryde ride, Andy plans to pay his Ryde driver a $4 tip. What is the total cost, in dollars, of Andy's ride to the football stadium using Ryde?

    (A) $25.25   (B) $29.00   (C) $31.50   (D) $28.00   (E) $30.25

15. The factorial of a positive whole number is written as a ! following the number, and it is calculated by multiplying all of the positive whole numbers from that number down to 1. For example, 4! is equal to $4 \times 3 \times 2 \times 1 = 24$. What is the value of $(9! + 8! + 7!) \div (7!)$?

(A) 100   (B) 81   (C) 90   (D) 80   (E) 99

16. Two rectangles have the same perimeter. One rectangle has a height of 10, and the other rectangle has a height of 7. The area of the larger rectangle exceeds the area of the smaller rectangle by 27. What is the perimeter of one of the rectangles?

10 ☐   7 ☐

(A) 52   (B) 50   (C) 54   (D) 56   (E) 58

17. In the 3×3 grid of squares below, each of the whole numbers from 1 through 9 is placed into one of the nine squares of the grid so that the sum of the numbers in any row or column of the grid is odd. Five of the squares already have numbers. In how many different ways can the remaining four numbers be placed into the remaining four squares?

2	6	3
1		
4		

(A) 8   (B) 12   (C) 6   (D) 9   (E) 24

18. What whole number is nearest in value to $17\sqrt{7}$?

(A) 48   (B) 45   (C) 44   (D) 47   (E) 46

19. Stan purchased a share of stock at the end of the day on Monday. On Tuesday, the value of the stock increased by 20%, and on Wednesday, the value of the stock increased by 25%. But on Thursday, the value of the stock only increased by 10%, and finally on Friday the stock lost 40% of its value. Stan incorrectly thought that since 20% + 25% + 10% − 40% = 15%, the stock increased by 15% since he bought it. But the stock actually lost value since he made his purchase. By what percent had the value of the stock decreased since Stan made his purchase?

   (A) 1%   (B) 5%   (C) 2%   (D) 10%   (E) 4%

20. If $a \clubsuit b = a^3 + 3a^2b + 3ab^2 + b^3$, then what is the value of $9 \clubsuit 5$?

   (A) 2704   (B) 2844   (C) 2854   (D) 2744   (E) 2684

21. How many different arrangements of the letters of the word *SNOWS* either begin with an *S* or end with an *S*?

   (A) 42   (B) 60   (C) 48   (D) 36   (E) 54

22. Henry and Isaac are riding their bikes on the same route. Henry rides his bike at a constant speed of 10 miles per hour, and Isaac rides his bike at a constant speed of 12 miles per hour. At noon, Henry rides his bike past a road sign. Exactly twelve minutes later, Isaac rides his bike past the same sign. At what time will Isaac catch up to Henry?

   (A) 1:30 PM   (B) 1:20PM   (C) 1:12 PM   (D) 1:06 PM   (E) 1:15 PM

23. What is the remainder when $35 \times 36 \times 37 \times 38 \times 39$ is divided by 25?

   (A) 20   (B) 0   (C) 15   (D) 10   (E) 5

24. A rectangular picture that has a width of 15 centimeters and a height of 10 centimeters is surrounded by a picture frame. Every point on the outer edge of the frame is 7 centimeters from the nearest point on the outer edge of the picture. To the nearest whole number, what is the area of the frame, in square centimeters?

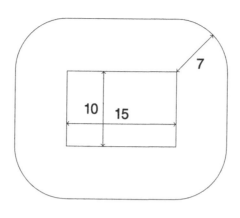

(A) 504   (B) 512   (C) 496   (D) 511   (E) 508

25. Stella has a bag that contains plenty of red, white, and blue beads to use to make bracelets. She removes beads from the bag one at a time, and when she has three beads of any one color, she sets that group of three beads aside for use on a bracelet. What is the fewest number of beads that Stella must remove from the bag in order to guarantee that she has at least six groups of beads for use on bracelets?

(A) 18   (B) 22   (C) 19   (D) 20   (E) 21

26. What is the smallest power of 5 that is greater than 2^{30}?

(A) 5^{14} (B) 5^{13} (C) 5^{16} (D) 5^{17} (E) 5^{15}

27. Micah and Noah are playing a game. A bag has 100 jellybeans. Micah and Noah take turns removing either 1, 2, 3, 4, 5, or 6 jellybeans from the bag. The player that removes the last jellybean loses. Micah gets to draw from the bag first, and realizes that he has a plan that guarantees that he wins the game by drawing a certain number of jellybeans on his first turn. How many jellybeans should Micah draw on his first turn to guarantee that he wins the game?

(A) 4   (B) 2   (C) 5   (D) 1   (E) 3

28. In the rectangle below, a diagonal intersects a segment that connects one vertex of the rectangle to the midpoint of a side. The diagonal and segment divide the rectangle into three triangles and a quadrilateral. The area of the quadrilateral is 45. The sum of the areas of the three triangles is a positive whole number. What is the sum of the digits of that positive whole number?

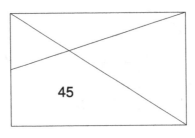

(A) 17   (B) 9   (C) 12   (D) 10   (E) 15

29. Kim chose a four-digit positive whole number. She noticed that the sum of the digits of the number was equal to the product of the digits of the number. How many different four-digit positive whole numbers could Kim have chosen?

(A) 12   (B) 16   (C) 6   (D) 8   (E) 24

30. The octal, or base 8 repeating value $0.1\overline{52}_8$ is equivalent to a fraction whose numerator and denominator are in base 10. What is the sum of the numerator and denominator of that fraction?

(A) 29   (B) 25   (C) 17   (D) 19   (E) 24

Target Round
12224

Place ID Sticker
Inside This Box

Name _____

Grade _____

School _____

Problems 1 & 2

1. Amber's history test had twenty multiple-choice questions. Each multiple-choice question was worth three points. Her history test also had eight short-answer questions. Each short-answer question was worth five points. Amber answered seventeen of the multiple-choice questions correctly, and seven of the short-answer questions correctly. Any questions answered incorrectly are worth zero points. How many points did Amber score on her history test?

1.

2. The rectangle below has a width of 15 and a height of 8. The rectangle is cut into four smaller rectangles by cuts along the dotted lines. What is the sum of the perimeters of the four smaller rectangles?

2.

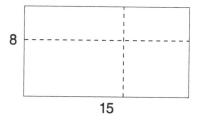

8

15

Place ID Sticker
Inside This Box

Name _____

Grade _____

School _____

Problems 3 & 4

3. The product of the tens and units digit of a three-digit whole number is 12. The product of the tens and hundreds digits of the same three-digit whole number is 4. What is the greatest possible value of the three-digit whole number?

3.

4. Three busy beavers can build six dams in two days. If all busy beavers always work at the same constant rate, then how many days will it take two busy beavers to build eight dams?

4.

Target Round
12224

Name _____

Grade _____

School _____

Problems 5 & 6

5. Chauncey chooses a two-digit whole number. If Chauncey divides his number by two, the result will be a two-digit whole number, and if Chauncey multiplies his number by two instead, the result will also be a two-digit whole number. How many different numbers could Chauncey have chosen?

5.

6. Mrs. Howard has six different prizes to award to students in her class this school week, which is every day from Monday through Friday. She wants to give at least one prize on each day of the school week. In how many different ways can Mrs. Howard select which prizes to award on each day of the school week?

6.

Target Round
12224

Place ID Sticker
Inside This Box

Name _____

Grade _____

School _____

Problems 7 & 8

7. Paul and his daughter Leah share the same birthday. When Leah turned one year old, Paul turned thirty-six years old, so Paul's age was a multiple of Leah's age. If Paul and Leah both live to be at least 100 years old, on how many other birthdays will Paul's age be a multiple of Leah's age?

7.

8. As shown below, diagonals are drawn in a trapezoid to create four triangles. The two triangles that have sides which are also bases of the trapezoid have areas of 25 and 49. What is the area of the trapezoid?

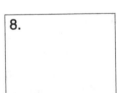

8.

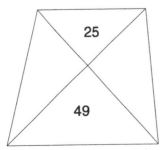

Team Round
12224

School or Team

Name _____

Name _____

Name _____

Name _____

Place ID Sticker
Inside This Box

Place ID Sticker
Inside This Box

Place ID Sticker
Inside This Box

Place ID Sticker
Inside This Box

1.

2.

3.

4.

5.

6.

7.

8.

9.

10.

1. Bhairav is buying candy with coins from his piggy bank. Bhairav has a number of coins worth 25 cents each. He buys six gobstoppers for 10 cents each, nine lemondrops for 5 cents each, and ten chocolate-covered peanuts for 12 cents each. How many 25 cent coins does Bhairav spend on candy?

2. What is the sum of the first 40 positive whole numbers that are odd but are not multiples of 5?

3. Emma is giving out butterfly stickers to her friends. Emma gave Stella half of her stickers. Then Emma gave Allison one dozen stickers. Finally, Emma gave Denise half of the stickers she had left. After Emma gave butterfly stickers to her friends, she had seven butterfly stickers left. How many butterfly stickers did Emma have before she gave any to her friends?

4. From a square piece of paper that has sides measuring 10 inches, two cuts are made to remove a square of side length 7 inches, as shown below. What is the area, in square inches, of the L-shaped piece of paper that remains?

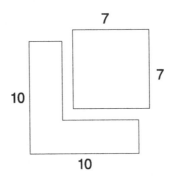

5. At the school fair, prize tokens are worth either 1 point, 2 points, or 4 points. Mr. Tolkein has ten prize tokens worth a total of 25 points. What is the greatest possible number of tokens worth 2 points that Mr. Tolkein could have?

6. Rafael chose a three-digit positive whole number. He then created a new number by reversing the digits of his original number, swapping the units and hundreds digit. For example, if Rafael chose the number 247, the new number would be 742. After Rafael created the new number, he multiplied the new number by the original number, and his product was 394695. What is the sum of Rafael's new number and old number?

7. In a list of positive whole numbers, each number after the first two numbers is the sum of the previous two numbers in the list. The sixth number in the list is 2022. What is the greatest possible value for the first number in the list?

8. A square is divided into four smaller squares, as shown below. Colin wants to color the four smaller squares. He has a red marker, a blue marker, and a green marker. But he does not want any two of the smaller squares that share a side to be colored the same color. How many different ways can Colin color the smaller squares?

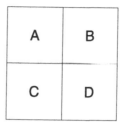

9. What is the sum of the tens digit and the units digit of 2022^{2022}?

10. The regular octagon below has a side of length 40. Eight conguent small circles are drawn with centers that are also vertices of the octagon. Each small circle is tangent to two other small circles. Finally, a large circle is drawn that is tangent to each of eight smaller circles, as shown below. To the nearest whole number, what is the area of the large circle?

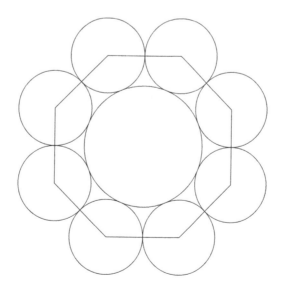

Sprint Round

1. B	11. B	21. A
2. C	12. C	22. C
3. A	13. D	23. C
4. A	14. B	24. A
5. E	15. B	25. B
6. E	16. A	26. B
7. A	17. C	27. D
8. C	18. B	28. B
9. D	19. A	29. A
10. C	20. D	30. A

Target Round

1. 86
2. 92
3. 226
4. 4
5. 15
6. 1800
7. 3
8. 144

Team Round

1. 9
2. 2000
3. 52
4. 51
5. 6
6. 1272
7. 669
8. 18
9. 12
10. 3270

Number Sense

1. 243	21. 1150	41. 4	61. 15
2. 162	22. $\frac{6}{11}$	42. 2464	62. $\frac{2}{15}$
3. 1	23. 21	43. 671	63. $37\frac{1}{36}$
4. 60	24. 961	44. 178	64. 333
5. 170	25. 5	45. 160	65. 52
6. 4	26. 17	46. 14	66. 12375
7. 480	27. 105	47. 7575	67. 225
8. 714	28. $\frac{1}{2}$	48. 100	68. 11424
9. 12	29. 1760	49. 800	69. 1600
10. [2337, 2583]	30. [84635, 93543]	50. [113989, 125987]	70. [877345, 969697]
11. 682	31. 5049	51. 13287	71. 60
12. 205	32. 3025	52. 135	72. 34225
13. 1	33. 70	53. 11	73. 125
14. 990	34. 56	54. 710	74. 1728
15. 361	35. 1209	55. 3996	75. 2197
16. 891	36. 46	56. 19	76. 6
17. 1620	37. 19	57. 26	77. 81
18. 347	38. 385	58. 30	78. 24990
19. 16	39. 29	59. 7872	79. 108
20. [85072, 94026]	40. [487, 537]	60. [25918, 28645]	80. [1595636, 1763596]

Sprint Round Solutions

1. The values of the products are $4 \times 8 = 32$, $5 \times 5 = 25$, $11 \times 3 = 33$, $2 \times 15 = 30$, and $7 \times 4 = 28$. Only 32 and 33 are greater than 31, for a total of $\boxed{2}$.

2. Hayden spent a total of $\$4 + \$3 + \$3 + \$4 + \$5 = \$19$ on snacks, so the number of dollars that remained was $\$20 - \$19 = \boxed{\$1}$.

3. There are 3 instances of $10 + 20 + 30 + 40 = 100$, for a total of $3 \times 100 = 300$. There are 4 instances of $1 + 5 + 9 = 15$, for a total of $4 \times 15 = 60$. Altogether, the sum is $300 + 60 = \boxed{360}$.

4. The area of the first rectangle is $8 \times 6 = 48$. The area of the second rectangle is $5 \times 9 = 45$. The total area of both rectangles is $48 + 45 = \boxed{93}$.

5. Since there are 60 minutes in 1 hour, a time 60 minutes after the start of the movie would be 8:18 PM, and a time $60 + 60 = 120$ minutes after the start of the movie would be 9:18 PM. An additional $124 - 120 = 4$ minutes would bring the time to $\boxed{9:22 \text{ PM}}$.

6. Michelle has 5 gallons, which is $5 \times 4 = 20$ quarts, or $20 \times 2 = 40$ pints. If Michelle sells 40 pints for $\$2$ per pint, she will receive a total of $40 \times \$2 = \boxed{\$80}$.

7. If day 1 of January was a Saturday, then day 2 was a Sunday, day 3 was a Monday, day 4 was a Tuesday, and day 5 was a Wednesday. If day 5 was a Wednesday, then so are days $5 + 7 = 12$, $12 + 7 = 19$, and $19 + 7 = 26$. The last Wednesday occurs on day $\boxed{26}$.

8. All of the answer choices are less than 100, so it is only necessary to check for divisibility by primes less than $\sqrt{100} = 10$. These primes are 2, 3, 5, and 7. None of 73, 79, 83, and 97 are divisible by 2, 3, 5, or 7, but $91 = 7 \times 13$, so the number that is not prime is $\boxed{91}$.

9. Considering numbers that differ by 8, $10 \times 18 = 180$ is too large, but $2 \times 10 = 20$ is too small. While $5 \times 13 = 65$ is closer, although still too small, $6 \times 14 = 84$, and the sum of 6 and 14 is $\boxed{20}$.

10. Two of the triangles created can be placed together to form a square of side length $12 \div 2 = 6$. The area of one of these squares is $6 \times 6 = 36$, so the area of 4 triangles, which is 2 squares, is $2 \times 36 = 72$. The area of the original square is $12 \times 12 = 144$, and the area of the four triangles is 72, so the area of the smaller square is $144 - 72 = \boxed{72}$.

11. The prime factorization of 105 is $3 \cdot 5 \cdot 7$. The prime factorization of 165 is $3 \cdot 5 \cdot 11$. The factors that divide 165 but do not divide 105 are those that are multiples of 11. That is $1 \cdot 11 = 11$, $3 \cdot 11 = 33$, $5 \cdot 11 = 55$, and $3 \cdot 5 \cdot 11 = 165$, for a total of $\boxed{4}$.

12. The number of acorns Colleen collected on the first 5 days is $3 + 7 + 11 + 15 + 19$. This is $5 \cdot 11 = 55$. Similarly, the number of acorns Colleen collected on the second 5 days, or days 6 through 10, is $23 + 27 + 31 + 35 + 39$, or $5 \cdot 31 = 155$. So in the first 10 days, she collected a total of $55 + 155 = 210$ acorns. On day 11, she collected 43 more, bringing her total to $210 + 43 = 253$, and on day 12 she collected 47 more, bringing her total to $253 + 47 = 300$. Her total collection exceeded 299 acorns on day $\boxed{12}$.

13. The area of a right triangle is half the product of the lengths of the legs, so the area of the original piece of paper is $\frac{1}{2} \cdot 40 \cdot 30 = 600$ square centimeters. The area of the piece of paper that was cut out and removed is $\frac{1}{2} \cdot 20 \cdot 15 = 150$ square centimeters. The area of the remaining piece of paper, in square centimeters, is $600 - 150 = \boxed{450}$.

14. The fee of \$5 covers pays for 1 of the 17 miles, so $17 - 1 = 16$ miles cost \$1.25 per mile, for an additional $16 \times \$1.25 = \$20$. Adding in the tip, the total cost of the Ryde ride is $\$5 + \$20 + \$4 = \boxed{\$29.00}$.

15. The number 9! can be written as $9 \cdot 8 \cdot 7!$, and the number 8! can be written as $8 \cdot 7!$. Then the expression becomes $(9 \cdot 8 \cdot 7! + 8 \cdot 7! + 7!) \div (7!)$, or $7! \cdot (9 \cdot 8 + 8 + 1) \div (7!)$. The 7! in the dividend and divisor cancel, leaving $9 \cdot 8 + 8 + 1 = \boxed{81}$.

16. If the perimeter for both rectangles is the same, then the width of the rectangle with height 7 exceeds the width of the rectangle of height 10 by $10 - 7 = 3$. Let the width of the rectangle with height 10 be W, and the rectangle with height 7 must have width $W + 3$. If the area of the rectangle with height 7 is greater, then $7(W + 3) - 10W = 27$, or $21 - 3W = 27$, which is impossible, since W must be positive. Therefore, the area of the rectangle with height 10 is greater, so $10W - 7(W+3) = 27$, or $3W - 21 = 27$. Then $W = 16$, and the perimeter of one of the rectangles is $2 \cdot (10 + 16) = \boxed{52}$.

17. The remaining four numbers are 5, 7, 8, and 9. If the two additional numbers in the middle column are both odd, then the sum of the numbers in the middle column will be even, which is not permitted. Similarly, if the two additional numbers in the bottom row are both odd, then the sum of the numbers in the bottom row will be even, which is not permitted. Thus the only remaining even number, 8, must be placed into the middle column and bottom row.

The remaining 3 odd numbers may be placed into the remaining three squares in any way. There are 3 possibilities for the square in the middle column of the middle row. Once that number is selected, there are 2 possibilities for the rightmost square in the middle row, and then there is only 1 possibility for the rightmost square square in the bottom row. Therefore the total number of ways to place the remaining four numbers is $3 \times 2 \times 1 = \boxed{6}$.

18. The number $17\sqrt{7}$ is equal to $\sqrt{17^2} \cdot \sqrt{7}$. This is $\sqrt{289} \cdot \sqrt{7}$, or $\sqrt{289 \cdot 7} = \sqrt{2023}$. Because $45^2 = 2025$ and $44^2 = 1936$, the number $\sqrt{2023}$ is nearest in value to $\boxed{45}$.

19. An increase of 20% multiplies the value of the stock by $1 + 0.20 = 1.2$. Similarly, an increase of 25% multiplies the value of the stock by $1 + 0.25$, and an increase of 10% multiplies the value of the stock by $1 + 0.1$. But a loss of 40% multiplies the value of the stock by $1 - 0.4$. In total, the value of the stock since Stan made his purchase was multiplied by $(1 + 0.25)(1 + 0.2)(1 + 0.1)(1 - 0.4)$. This is $1.25 \cdot 1.2 \cdot 1.1 \cdot 0.6$, or $1.5 \cdot 0.66$, which is 0.99. This is equivalent to multiplying the value by $1 - 0.01$, which is a decrease of $\boxed{1\%}$.

20. This could be evaluated directly, but $a^3 + 3a^2b + 3ab^2 + b^3$ is equal to $(a+b)^3$. Therefore, $9 \clubsuit 5 = (9+5)^3$, and $14^3 = 14 \times 196$, or $14 \cdot 200 - 14 \cdot 4 = \boxed{2744}$.

21. If S is the first letter, then there are $4! = 24$ ways to arrange *NOWS* in the remaining four positions. Similarly, if S is the last letter, then there are $4! = 24$ ways to arrange *SNOW* in the remaining four positions. Summing these results yields $24 + 24 = 48$ possible arrangement. But this double-counts arrangements that both begin an end with the letter S. If S is both the first and last letter, there are $3! = 6$ ways to arrange *NOW* in the remaining three positions. These 6 arrangements have been counted twice, so the total number of possible arrangements is $48 - 6 = \boxed{42}$.

22. When Isaac passes the sign, it is 12 minutes after noon, or 12:12 PM. At that time, Henry has ridden his bike for $\frac{12}{60} = \frac{1}{5}$ of an hour after he passed the sign, and is $\frac{1}{5} \cdot 10 = 2$ miles ahead of Isaac. Since Isaac rides his bike at 12 miles per hour and Henry rides his bike at 10 miles per hour, Isaac travels $12 - 10 = 2$ miles more than Henry in one hour, and he will catch up to Henry exactly one hour after he passes the road sign, which is $\boxed{1:12 \text{ PM}}$.

23. Because 35 is a multiple of 5, the product is a multiple of 5. So, if $35 \cdot 36 \cdot 37 \cdot 38 \cdot 39 = 25k + r$ for some quotient k and some remainder r, then, dividing both sides by 5, $7 \cdot 36 \cdot 37 \cdot 38 \cdot 39 = 5k + \frac{r}{5}$. The remainder of $7 \cdot 36 \cdot 37 \cdot 38 \cdot 39$ divided by 5 is determined by the units digit of the product, which is the units digit of $7 \cdot 6 \cdot 7 \cdot 8 \cdot 9$, or 8. Therefore, $\frac{r}{5}$ is 3, so r, the remainder when the product is divided by 25, is $3 \cdot 5 = \boxed{15}$.

24. Taken together, the four curved corners of the frame form a circle of radius 7. Using $\frac{22}{7}$ as an approximation for π, the area of this circle is $7^2 \cdot \frac{22}{7} = 154$. The remaining portions of the frame are two rectangles of width 15 and height 7, which together have an area of $2 \cdot 7 \cdot 15 = 210$, and two rectangles of height 10 and width 7, which together have an area of $2 \cdot 10 \cdot 7 = 140$. To the nearest whole number, the area of the frame, in square centimeters, is $154 + 210 + 140 = \boxed{504}$.

25. After creating a set of three beads, regardless of color, the greatest number of unmatched beads is 2 beads of each of the other 2 colors, for a total of 4 unmatched beads. Therefore, to guarantee 6 groups of beads, Stella would need to remove the $6 \cdot 3 = 18$ beads for those 6 groups plus the maximum of 4 unmatched that would remain after creating the sixth group, for a total of $6 \times 3 + 4 = \boxed{22}$.

26. The number 2^{30} can be expressed as $\left(2^7\right)^4 \cdot 2^2$, or $128^4 \cdot 4$. Because $5^{12} = \left(5^3\right)^4$, or 125^4, this number is greater than 5^{12}. Now consider 5^{13}, or $125^4 \cdot 5$, and the quotient when divided by 2^{30}. This quotient is $\left(\frac{125}{128}\right)^4 \cdot \frac{5}{4}$. If this is greater than 1, then $5^{13} > 2^{30}$. The quotient is greater than 1 if $\left(\frac{125}{128}\right)^4 > 0.8$. Since $\frac{125}{128} > 0.95$ and $0.95^4 > 0.8$, $\left(\frac{125}{128}\right)^4 > 0.8$, and the smallest power of 5 that is greater than 2^{30} is $\boxed{5^{13}}$.

27. To win the game, on his last turn Micah needs to leave exactly 1 jellybean in the bag. This can be guaranteed if, on the preceding turn for Noah, there are exactly 8 jellybeans in the bag. This is because no matter the number of jellybeans Noah draws from the bag, Micah can draw a number that, when combined with the number Noah drew, totals 7 jellybeans. If Noah draws 6, Micah draws 1. If Noah draws 5, Micah draws 2. And so on.

Exactly 8 jellybeans in the bag can be guaranteed if, one turn for Noah and Micah earlier, there are $8 + 7 = 15$ jellybeans in the bag. And as long as the number of jellybeans in the bag is 1 more than a multiple of 7 prior to Noah taking a turn, the number of jellybeans remaining in the bag can be reduced by Micah to a smaller number that is also 1 more than a multiple of 7. Thus, on his first turn Micah needs to reduce the number of jellybeans in the bag to a number that is 1 more than a multiple of 7. Since $7 \cdot 14 = 98$, Micah needs to reduce the number of jellybeans in the bag to $98 + 1 = 99$, so the number of jellybeans he should draw is $100 - 99 = \boxed{1}$.

28. Let the width of the rectangle be W and the height of the rectangle be H. Then the area of the rectangle is WH. The two triangles that share a vertical angle where the two segments intersect are similar. The base of one triangle is $\frac{H}{2}$ and the base of the other is H. By similarity, the altitudes, which sum to W, are $\frac{W}{3}$ and $\frac{2W}{3}$. Therefore the area of the smaller of the two triangles is $\frac{1}{2} \cdot \frac{H}{2} \cdot \frac{W}{3} = \frac{HW}{12}$. The third triangle, opposite the quadrilateral, and the larger triangle must have areas that sum to $\frac{HW}{2}$, so the area of all three triangles is $\frac{HW}{2} + \frac{HW}{12} = \frac{7HW}{12}$. Thus the area of the quadrilateral is $HW - \frac{7HW}{12} = \frac{5HW}{12}$. Since $\frac{5HW}{12} = 45$, $HW = 108$. The area of the three triangles is $\frac{7}{12} \cdot 108 = 63$, and $6 + 3 = \boxed{9}$.

29. Suppose the four-digit number is $ABCD$. Because no number with four of the same digit has a product of the digits that is equal to the sum of the digits, at least one digit must be less than the greatest digit. Additionally, no digit can be 0, since that would create a product of 0, and the sum would be greater. Since the order of the digits does not affect the value of the sum or product, let $A \geq B \geq C \geq D$, with $A > D$. Then $A + A + A + A > A + B + C + D$, so $A + A + A + A > A \cdot B \cdot C \cdot D$. That is, $4A > A \cdot B \cdot C \cdot D$, or $4 > B \cdot C \cdot D$.

If $B \cdot C \cdot D = 1$, then B, C, and D would all be 1, and $A + 1 + 1 + 1 = A \cdot 1 \cdot 1 \cdot 1$, which is impossible. If $B \cdot C \cdot D = 3$, then two of B, C, and D would be 1 and the other would be 3, so $A + 1 + 1 + 3 = A \cdot 1 \cdot 1 \cdot 3$, or $A + 5 = 3A$. Then $A = \frac{5}{2}$, which is also impossible. Finally, if $B \cdot C \cdot D = 2$, then two of B, C, and D would be 1 and the other would be 2, so $A + 1 + 1 + 2 = A \cdot 1 \cdot 1 \cdot 2$, or $A + 4 = 2A$. Then $A = 4$, which is possible. Therefore the only four-digit positive whole numbers that are possible are permutations of the digits 1, 1, 2, and 4. Since there are two instance of the digit 1, the number of distinct arrangements is $\frac{4!}{2!} = \boxed{12}$.

30. The digits to the right of the octal point in base 8 have a value of $\frac{1}{8}$, $\frac{1}{64}$, $\frac{1}{512}$, and so on, with each place being $\frac{1}{8}$ the value of the place immediately to the left. The non-repeating portion of the number has a value of $1 \cdot \frac{1}{8} = \frac{1}{8}$. The repeating portion that has places occupied by a 5 has the value $\frac{5}{64} + \frac{5}{64^2} + \frac{5}{64^3} + \cdots$. This is an infinite geometric series with a first term equal to $\frac{5}{64}$ and a ratio of $\frac{1}{64}$. The repeating portion that has places occupied by a 2 has the value $\frac{2}{512} + \frac{2}{512 \cdot 64} + \frac{2}{512 \cdot 64^2} + \cdots$. This is an infinite geometric series with a first term equal to $\frac{2}{512} = \frac{1}{256}$ and a ratio of $\frac{1}{64}$. The sum of both of these series is $\frac{\frac{1}{256} + \frac{5}{64}}{1 - \frac{1}{64}} = \frac{\frac{1}{256} + \frac{20}{256}}{\frac{252}{256}}$. This is $\frac{21}{252} = \frac{1}{12}$. Therefore the value is $\frac{1}{8} + \frac{1}{12} = \frac{5}{24}$, and $5 + 24 = \boxed{29}$.

Target Round Solutions

1. Amber's score on the multiple-choice portion of the test was $17 \times 3 = 51$, and her score on the short-answer portion of the test was $7 \times 5 = 35$, so her score on the entire test was $51 + 35 = \boxed{86}$.

2. The perimeter of the original rectangle is $15 + 15 + 8 + 8 = 46$. All of these edges exist on the four smaller rectangles. When the long cut parallel to the side of length 15 is made, edges are created with a total length of $15 + 15 = 30$. When the short cut parallel to the side of length 8 is made, edges are created with a total length of $8 + 8 = 16$. Therefore, the total perimeter of the four rectangles is $46 + 30 + 16 = \boxed{92}$.

3. If the product of the tens and hundreds digits is 4, then the tens and hundreds digits are either 4 and 1 in some order, or 2 and 2. If the hundreds digit is 4, then the tens digit is 1, and the units digit would be $12 \div 1 = 12$, which is impossible. If the hundreds digit is 1, then the tens digit is 4, and the units digit would be $12 \div 4 = 3$, so the number would be 143. If the hundreds digit is 2, then the tens digit is 2, and the units digit is $12 \div 2 = 6$, so the number would be 226. Of the two possibilities, the greatest is $\boxed{226}$.

4. If 3 busy beavers can build 6 dams in 2 days, then 3 busy beavers building 8 dams would take $2 \cdot \frac{8}{6} = \frac{8}{3}$ days. However, because only 2 busy beavers are working, not 3, the work will take $\frac{3}{2}$ as long, so the number of days required is $\frac{8}{3} \cdot \frac{3}{2} = \boxed{4}$.

5. Because the quotient when the number is divided by 2 is a whole number, the number must be even. Additionally, since the quotient is a two-digit whole number, the quotient must be at least 10, so the number must be at least 20. Additionally, because the product when the number is multiplied by 2 is a two-digit whole number, the product must be no more than 98, so the number must be no more than 49. The number of even numbers between 20 and 49, including 20, is $\frac{48-20}{2} + 1 = \boxed{15}$.

6. There are 5 days in total and 6 different prizes, and every day must have at least 1 prize, so there must be exactly 1 day that has 2 prizes, and all other days will have 1 prize. There are 5 ways to select the day that has 2 prizes. Additionally, there are $\binom{6}{2} = 15$ sets of two prizes that may be awarded on that day. Finally, there are $4 \cdot 3 \cdot 2 \cdot 1 = 24$ ways to assign the remaining four prizes to the four remaining days. Therefore, the total number of ways to select which prizes to award each day is $5 \cdot 15 \cdot 24 = \boxed{1800}$.

7. Paul will always be $36 - 1 = 35$ years older than Leah, and if Paul's age is a multiple of Leah's age, then the difference between their ages, 35, must also be a multiple of Leah's age. Leah's age must be a divisor of 35, so Paul's age will be a multiple of Leah's age when Leah is 5, 7, and 35, and the number of times this occurs is $\boxed{3}$.

8. Let the shorter base of the trapezoid be a and the longer base of the trapezoid be b. Additionally, let the altitude from the shorter base to the intersection of the diagonals be c and the altitude from the longer base to the intersection of the diagonals be d. Then $\frac{1}{2} \cdot ac = 25$, and $\frac{1}{2} \cdot bd = 49$, or $ac = 50$, and $bd = 98$. The area of the trapezoid is $\frac{1}{2} \cdot (a+b)(c+d)$, or $\frac{1}{2} \cdot (ac + ad + bc + bd)$. Since bd and ac are known, this is $\frac{1}{2}(148 + ad + bc)$. The triangles of area 49 and 25 are similar, so $\frac{a}{c} = \frac{b}{d}$, so $ad = bc$. Additionally, $adbc = 50 \cdot 98$, and since ad and bc are equal, each is $\sqrt{50 \cdot 98} = 70$. Thus the total area of the trapezoid is $\frac{1}{2}(148 + 70 + 70) = \boxed{144}$.

Team Round Solutions

1. The cost of the gobstoppers is $6 \times 10 = 60$ cents, the cost of the lemondrops is $9 \times 5 = 45$ cents, and the cost of the chocolate-covered peanutes is $10 \times 12 = 120$ cents each. The total cost of his candy purchases is $60 + 45 + 120 = 225$ cents. The number of 25 cent coins needed is $225 \div 25 = \boxed{9}$.

2. In each range of 10 units digits, the sum will include 4 the four numbers that have a units digit of 1, 3, 7, and 9. The value of $1 + 3 + 7 + 9$ is 20. The value of $11 + 13 + 17 + 19$ is 60. The value of $21 + 23 + 27 + 29$ is 100. This continues, and the final group of 4 is the 37th through 40th odd numbers, $91 + 93 + 97 + 99 = 380$. The total sum is $20 + 60 + 100 + 140 + 180 + 220 + 260 + 300 + 340 + 380$, which is $\boxed{2000}$.

3. Before Emma gave half her stickers to Denise, she had $7 \times 2 = 14$ stickers. Before she gave Allison one dozen stickers, she had $14 + 12 = 26$. Before she gave Stella half of her stickers, the number of stickers Emma had was $26 \times 2 = \boxed{52}$.

4. The area of the original piece of paper is $10 \times 10 = 100$ square inches. The area of the square that was removed is $7 \times 7 = 49$ square inches. Therefore, the area of the L-shaped piece of paper, in square inches, is $100 - 49 = \boxed{51}$.

5. First, note that since 25 is an odd number, Mr. Tolkein must have at least 1 token worth 1 point. Then we work backwards from 9 tokens worth 2 points. We find that 9 tokens worth 2 points does not work because $9 \cdot 2 + 1 = 19$. We also find that 8 tokens worth 2 points does not work because even with using a token worth 4 points, the total is only $8 \cdot 2 + 1 + 4 = 21$. Similarly, 7 tokens worth 2 points does not work as the max total can only be $7 \cdot 2 + 1 + 2 \cdot 4 = 23$. However, 6 tokens worth 2 points does work because Mr. Tolkein can also have 3 tokens worth 4 points and a token worth 1 point, where the total value sums to $6 \cdot 2 + 3 \cdot 4 + 1 = 25$. Therefore, the greatest possible number of tokens worth 2 points that Mr. Tolkien could have is $\boxed{6}$.

6. We can approach the problem with clues from divisibility and estimation. Because 394695 is a multiple of 5 (but not 25), either the hundreds or units digit of Rafael's number (but not both) must be a 5. Suppose 5 is the hundreds digit. Then because the units digit of the product is a 5, the units digit of his original number must be odd (since an even number would give the product a units digit of 0) and not equal to 5.

Next, we can note that a number with 5 as the hundreds digit is at least 500 but less than 600. Then we find that the other number should be at least 600 but less than 800. This narrows down the units digit to be 7. Finally, since 394695 is a multiple of 3, the original number must also be a multiple of 3. Because $5 + 7 = 12$, the tens digit must be a multiple of 3. Trying 507×705, 537×735, 567×765, and 597×795, the product of 537 and 735 is 394695, and $537 + 735 = \boxed{1272}$.

7. Let the first number in the list be a and the second number in the list be b. Then the third number is $a + b$, the fourth is $b + (a + b) = a + 2b$, the fifth is $(a + b) + (a + 2b) = 2a + 3b$, and the sixth is $(a + 2b) + (2a + 3b) = 3a + 5b$. Thus $3a + 5b = 2022$. To maximize a, $5b$ must be as small as possible. But $2022 - 5b$ must be a multiple of 3. Since 2022 is a multiple of 3, then $b = 3$ is the least positive value of b that makes $2022 - 5b$ a multiple of 3. So $2022 - 5 \cdot 3 = 2007$ is $3a$, and the greatest possible value of a is $\frac{2007}{3} = \boxed{669}$.

8. Because no two squares that share a side may be colored the same color, at least 2 of the 3 colors must be used. If 2 colors are used, one color must be used to color the squares labeled A and D, and the other color must be used to color the squares labeled B and C. There are 3 choices for the first color and 2 choices for the second, for a total of 6 possibilities when using 2 colors.

If 3 colors are used, one color must be used to color either squares A and D, or squares B and C. In either case, each of the remaining 2 colors must be used for one of the two remaining squares. If squares A and D are colored the same color, there are 3 choices for that color, then 2 choices for the color of square B, and 1 choice for the color of square C, for a total of $3 \cdot 2 \cdot 1 = 6$ possibilities. Similarly, if squares B and C are colored the same color, there are also 6 possibilities. Altogether, the total number of possible colorings is $6 + 6 + 6 = \boxed{18}$.

9. The only portion of the product that affects the tens digit and units digit of the result is the tens digit and units digit of each term of the product, so it is only necessary to find the tens and units digit of 22^{2022}. Each power of 22 after the first is a multiple of 4. There are only 20 multiples of 4 that are not multiples 5, as no power of 22 can be a multiple of 5, so the sequence of tens and units digits of powers of 22 beyond 22^2 can be at most 20 terms before a term repeats.

Powers 1 through 5 have tens and units digits of $22, 84, 48, 56, 32$. Then 22^{10} has the same tens and units digits as $32 \cdot 32 = 1024$, and 22^{20} has the same tens and units digits as $24 \cdot 24 = 576$. Power 21 has a tens and units digit of 72, and for power 22 the tens and units digits are 84, which are identical to the tens and units digits for 22^2. Therefore the tens and units digits repeat every 20 terms. Since $\frac{2022}{20}$ has a remainder of 2, the tens and units digits will be the same as those for 22^2 and 22^{22}, which are 84, and $8 + 4 = \boxed{12}$.

10. Label the octagon *ABCDEFGH*, and let r be the length of the radius of the smaller circles and R be the length of the radius of the bigger circle. Because two radii of the smaller circles are equal to a side length of the octagon, then r is equal to $\frac{40}{2} = 20$. Consider diagonal *AE* of the octagon. This passes through the center of the large circle and two points where the large circle is tangent to one of the smaller circles. The length of *AE* is equal to $r + 2R + r = 2R + 40$. *AE* is also the hypotenuse of right triangle *AEF*. The length of *AF* is equal to the sum of the side of the octagon, 40, plus the twice the length of a leg of an isosceles right triangle with hypotenuse *FG*. This leg length of the isosceles right triangle is $\frac{40}{\sqrt{2}} = 20\sqrt{2}$, so the length of *AF* is $40 + 2 \cdot 20\sqrt{2} = 40 + 40\sqrt{2}$. By the Pythagorean Theorem, *AE* has a length of $\sqrt{40^2 + (40 + 40\sqrt{2})^2} \approx 104.525$. Therefore R is approximately $\frac{104.525 - 2 \cdot 20}{2} \approx 32.2625$. The area of the large circle is then $32.2625^2 \cdot \pi$, which to the nearest whole number is $\boxed{3270}$.

Number Sense
12225

Place ID Sticker
Inside This Box

Name _____

Grade _____

School _____

1. $122 - 21 =$ _____.

2. $3 + 12 \times 3 =$ _____.

3. $478 + 227 =$ _____.

4. The thousands digit of 125663 is _____.

5. $531 - 295 =$ _____.

6. $51 \times 20 =$ _____.

7. The remainder of $104 \div 3$ is _____.

8. $84 \div 12 =$ _____.

9. The product of 17 and 6 is _____.

10. (estimate) $1067 + 582 + 1261 =$ _____.

11. $73 \times 11 =$ _____.

12. $14^2 =$ _____.

13. $451 - 233 - 96 =$ _____.

14. The remainder of $1246 \div 4$ is _____.

15. $13 \times 5 \times 12 =$ _____.

16. $62 \times 15 =$ _____.

17. *MMCLII* in Arabic numerals is _____.

18. $0.14 \times 60 =$ _____ (decimal).

19. $28 \times 12 =$ _____.

20. (estimate) $179 \times 399 =$ _____.

21. $25 \times 66 =$ _____.

22. The greater of $\frac{4}{13}$ and $\frac{3}{10}$ is _____ (fraction).

23. $23^2 =$ _____.

24. The GCD of 18 and 42 is _____.

25. $32 + 27 + 22 + 17 + 12 + 7 =$ _____.

26. If $\frac{1}{8}$ gallon is equal to 1 pint, then 48 pints is equal to _____ gallons.

27. $\frac{1}{2} - \frac{1}{6} - \frac{1}{21} =$ _____ (fraction).

28. $493 \div 29 =$ _____.

29. $14 \times 24 \div 21 =$ _____.

30. (estimate) $29 \times 50 \times 31 =$ _____.

31. The perimeter of a rectangle with area 20 and width 5 is _____.

32. $43 \times 99 =$ _____.

33. The number of even whole numbers between 31 and 81 is _____.

34. $\frac{3}{20} =$ _____ %.

35. The LCM of 18 and 42 is _____.

36. $45^2 =$ _____.

37. 20% of 95 is _____.

38. $58 \times 52 =$ _____.

39. 2.5 days is _____ hours.

40. (estimate) $273645 \div 136 =$ _____.

41. $14 \times 6 + 7 \times 18 =$ _____.

42. The area of a right triangle with legs of length 12 and 18 is _____.

43. $43 \times 63 =$ _____.

44. 88_9 in base 10 is _____.

45. The remainder of $2562 \div 11$ is _____.

46. $101 \times 29 =$ _____.

47. $44^2 - 36^2 =$ _____.

48. The fifteenth term in the arithmetic sequence $2, 9, 16, \ldots$ is _____.

49. $7^2 \cdot 2^2 =$ _____.

50. (estimate) $285714 \times 9 =$ _____.

51. $16\frac{2}{3}\%$ of 96 is _____.

52. $112 \times 105 =$ _____.

53. The mode of the list $5, 7, 9, 11, 7, 5, 3, 1, 7$ is ___.

54. $31 \times 222 =$ _____.

55. 323_4 in base 2 is _____ $_2$.

56. $96 \times 89 =$ _____.

57. The perimeter of a right triangle with legs of length 9 and 12 is _____.

58. $49^2 =$ _____.

59. The measure of an interior angle in a regular decagon is _____°.

60. (estimate) $8333 \times 36 =$ _____.

61. $11\frac{4}{9} \times 11\frac{5}{9} =$ _____ (mixed number).

62. The number 77 in base 6 is _____ $_6$.

63. $0.\overline{117} =$ _____ (fraction).

64. $375 \times 11 =$ _____.

65. If $u = 23$, then $u^2 - 6u + 9 =$ _____.

66. The area of a trapezoid with bases of length 6 and 11 and a height of 4 is _____.

67. $\sqrt{23409} =$ _____.

68. The number of different arrangements of the letters $PEEP$ is _____.

69. $19 \times 55 \times 9 =$ _____.

70. (estimate) $5.5^4 =$ _____.

71. The sum of the prime divisors of 182 is _____.

72. $1019 \times 1018 =$ _____.

73. The sum of the terms of the infinite geometric sequence $5, 4, \frac{16}{5}, \ldots$ is _____.

74. $305^2 =$ _____.

75. The diameter of a sphere with surface area 100π is _____.

76. $25^3 =$ _____.

77. The number of positive whole number divisors of 50 is _____.

78. $45 \times 22 \times 55 =$ _____.

79. If $5^{1-y} = 10$, then $5^{2y} =$ _____ (fraction).

80. (estimate) $\sqrt{20.22 \times 2022 \times 2} =$ _____.

Sprint Round
12225

Place ID Sticker
Inside This Box

Name _____

Grade _____

School _____

1. Ⓐ Ⓑ Ⓒ Ⓓ Ⓔ   11. Ⓐ Ⓑ Ⓒ Ⓓ Ⓔ   21. Ⓐ Ⓑ Ⓒ Ⓓ Ⓔ

2. Ⓐ Ⓑ Ⓒ Ⓓ Ⓔ   12. Ⓐ Ⓑ Ⓒ Ⓓ Ⓔ   22. Ⓐ Ⓑ Ⓒ Ⓓ Ⓔ

3. Ⓐ Ⓑ Ⓒ Ⓓ Ⓔ   13. Ⓐ Ⓑ Ⓒ Ⓓ Ⓔ   23. Ⓐ Ⓑ Ⓒ Ⓓ Ⓔ

4. Ⓐ Ⓑ Ⓒ Ⓓ Ⓔ   14. Ⓐ Ⓑ Ⓒ Ⓓ Ⓔ   24. Ⓐ Ⓑ Ⓒ Ⓓ Ⓔ

5. Ⓐ Ⓑ Ⓒ Ⓓ Ⓔ   15. Ⓐ Ⓑ Ⓒ Ⓓ Ⓔ   25. Ⓐ Ⓑ Ⓒ Ⓓ Ⓔ

6. Ⓐ Ⓑ Ⓒ Ⓓ Ⓔ   16. Ⓐ Ⓑ Ⓒ Ⓓ Ⓔ   26. Ⓐ Ⓑ Ⓒ Ⓓ Ⓔ

7. Ⓐ Ⓑ Ⓒ Ⓓ Ⓔ   17. Ⓐ Ⓑ Ⓒ Ⓓ Ⓔ   27. Ⓐ Ⓑ Ⓒ Ⓓ Ⓔ

8. Ⓐ Ⓑ Ⓒ Ⓓ Ⓔ   18. Ⓐ Ⓑ Ⓒ Ⓓ Ⓔ   28. Ⓐ Ⓑ Ⓒ Ⓓ Ⓔ

9. Ⓐ Ⓑ Ⓒ Ⓓ Ⓔ   19. Ⓐ Ⓑ Ⓒ Ⓓ Ⓔ   29. Ⓐ Ⓑ Ⓒ Ⓓ Ⓔ

10. Ⓐ Ⓑ Ⓒ Ⓓ Ⓔ   20. Ⓐ Ⓑ Ⓒ Ⓓ Ⓔ   30. Ⓐ Ⓑ Ⓒ Ⓓ Ⓔ

1. Evan walked one mile on Monday, two miles on Tuesday, three miles on Wednesday, four miles on Thursday, and five miles on Friday. On Saturday, Evan walked as many miles as he did the previous five days. How many total miles did Evan walk on all six days?

(A) 20   (B) 30   (C) 28   (D) 15   (E) 24

2. Which of the following values is not a multiple of 4?

(A) 2×14 (B) 10×6 (C) 8×7 (D) 6×9 (E) 12×3

3. A square, a pentagon, a hexagon, a heptagon, and an octagon are shown below. How many sides do the shapes have altogether?

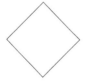

(A) 31   (B) 27   (C) 28   (D) 29   (E) 30

4. At the school store, five pencils can be purchased for $2. Mr. Lewis has thirty students in his class, and for the upcoming test he wants to buy two pencils for each student. How many dollars does Mr. Lewis spend buying pencils for his class?

(A) $20   (B) $24   (C) $30   (D) $28   (E) $18

5. How many positive whole numbers less than 29 are even or evenly divisible by three?

(A) 18   (B) 21   (C) 23   (D) 17   (E) 19

6. The product of the tens digit and the units digit of a two-digit positive whole number is 24, and the sum of the tens digit and units digit of the same number is 11. What is the sum of the two possible values of the number?

(A) 154   (B) 143   (C) 132   (D) 121   (E) 110

7. The drive from Beaumont, Texas to El Paso, Texas along the Interstate 10 freeway is 845 miles. If Hector drives at a speed of 65 miles per hour, then how long, in hours, will it take Hector to drive from Beaumont to El Paso on the Interstate 10 freeway?

(A) 12   (B) 13   (C) 15   (D) 17   (E) 14

8. Charlie, Donnie, Eddie, and Frankie decided to play games of chess. If each person played every other person exactly once, then how many total games of chess were played?

(A) 3   (B) 8   (C) 12   (D) 9   (E) 6

9. Three squares are arranged to form a rectangle, as shown below. If the perimeter of the rectangle is 30, then what is the area of the largest square?

(A) 25   (B) 81   (C) 18   (D) 36   (E) 54

10. What is the remainder when $21 \times 23 \times 27 \times 29$ is divided by 5?

(A) 1   (B) 4   (C) 0   (D) 3   (E) 2

11. January 1st of the year 2022 was a Saturday. How many days of the year 2022 are either Saturdays or Sundays?

(A) 106   (B) 105   (C) 104   (D) 102   (E) 103

12. Three right triangles have the same area. The first right triangle has legs of length 20 and 24. The second right triangle has a leg of length 30, and the third right triangle has a leg of length 12. What is the sum of the lengths of all of the legs of all three triangles?

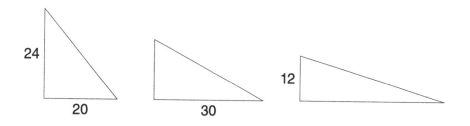

(A) 150   (B) 148   (C) 146   (D) 144   (E) 142

13. Emery studied every day from Sunday through Thursday for a history test on Friday. Each day after Sunday, she studied for four more minutes than she did the previous day. Over the five days, she studied for a total of two hours. How many minutes did Emery study for her test on Thursday?

(A) 34   (B) 32   (C) 30   (D) 26   (E) 28

14. Henry has 868 cards in his baseball card collection, and Isaiah has 1316 cards in his baseball card collection. Henry sorted his collection into groups of cards, with the same number of cards in each of his groups. Isaiah also sorted his collection into groups of cards, with the same number of cards in each of his groups. When finished, Isaiah and Henry had the same number of groups of cards. What is the greatest possible value for the number of groups of cards that Isaiah or Henry had?

(A) 28   (B) 4   (C) 14   (D) 56   (E) 7

15. What is the greatest whole number that is less than $\frac{1}{2} + \frac{2}{3} + \frac{3}{4} + \frac{4}{5} + \frac{5}{6} + \frac{6}{7} + \frac{7}{8} + \frac{8}{9} + \frac{9}{10}$?

(A) 6   (B) 5   (C) 9   (D) 7   (E) 8

16. A gallon is equal to 231 cubic inches. There are 12 inches in one foot. To the nearest whole number, how many gallons are in two cubic feet of water?

(A) 15   (B) 16   (C) 12   (D) 13   (E) 14

17. A right triangle has legs of length 13 and 19. What whole number is nearest the value of the perimeter of the triangle?

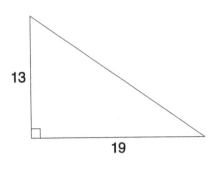

(A) 53   (B) 56   (C) 54   (D) 57   (E) 55

18. Rohil and Sohil each chose a positive whole number. Rohil noticed that $\frac{2}{3}$ of his number was equal to $\frac{3}{5}$ of Sohil's number. What was the value of Rohil's number divided by Sohil's number?

(A) $\frac{9}{10}$ (B) 1   (C) $\frac{3}{5}$ (D) $\frac{10}{9}$ (E) $\frac{2}{5}$

19. If $a \heartsuit b = ab + a - b$, then what is the value of $376 \heartsuit 239$?

(A) 90001   (B) 80001   (C) 96001   (D) 84001   (E) 92001

20. Motorcycles are vehicles that have two wheels and cars are vehicles that have four wheels. In a five-minute period at a busy intersection, Talia tallied 97 vehicles, all of which were either cars or motorcycles, with a total of 352 wheels. How many more cars than motorcycles did Talia tally?

(A) 60   (B) 59   (C) 63   (D) 61   (E) 62

21. In the figure below, dots are in a square grid so that each dot has a horizontal and vertical distance of 1 unit from neighboring dots, and the area of the entire grid is $5 \times 5 = 25$. What is the area of the shaded region in the figure below?

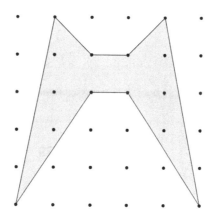

(A) 9   (B) $\frac{21}{2}$ (C) $\frac{19}{2}$ (D) 10   (E) 8

22. May had a jar that contained a number of marbles. In the jar, 30% of the marbles are blue, and the rest are red. After May removed 12 blue marbles from the jar, exactly 25% of the marbles in the jar were blue. How many red marbles were in the jar?

(A) 132   (B) 126   (C) 120   (D) 144   (E) 112

23. How many perfect squares are greater than $3^6 - 1$, but less than $3^{16} + 1$?

(A) 6535   (B) 80   (C) 3267   (D) 721   (E) 6536

24. Two circles share the same center. The large circle has a radius of 29. A chord of the larger circle has length 42 and is tangent to the smaller circle. To the nearest whole number, what is the area of the region between the two circles?

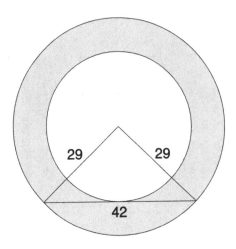

(A) 1345   (B) 1265   (C) 1385   (D) 1305   (E) 1425

25. Two different odd positive whole numbers are squared. The smaller square is then subtracted from the larger square. What is the greatest positive whole number that must divide this result?

(A) 1   (B) 2   (C) 8   (D) 3   (E) 4

26. Kevin and Liam earn extra money by washing cars. Kevin can wash a car in twenty minutes, while Liam can wash a car in sixteen minutes. One Saturday, Kevin and Liam have agreed to wash one dozen cars. Initially, Kevin works alone for half an hour, but is then joined by Liam. Before they finish washing the cars, Kevin has to leave, so Liam finishes the cars by himself. The total time from when Kevin started washing the first car until Liam finished washing the last car was two hours and fourteen minutes. How many minutes did Liam wash cars by himself?

(A) 24   (B) 28   (C) 20   (D) 40   (E) 32

27. Ajene chose three different numbers from the list $-7, -6, -2, -1, 0, 3, 4, 8, 9$ and then calculated the product of the three numbers. What is the probability that Ajene's product was positive?

(A) $\frac{3}{7}$ (B) $\frac{2}{5}$ (C) $\frac{1}{2}$ (D) $\frac{2}{7}$ (E) $\frac{1}{3}$

28. What is the remainder when the sum of the first 2022 perfect squares is divided by 15?

(A) 10   (B) 5   (C) 1   (D) 0   (E) 14

29. Points A, B, C, and D lie on a circle with center O. Chord BD and diameter AC intersect at point P. The length of segment OP is 3, the length of segment OC is 15, the length of segment BC is 18, and the length of segment PB is 16. What is the length of segment DC?

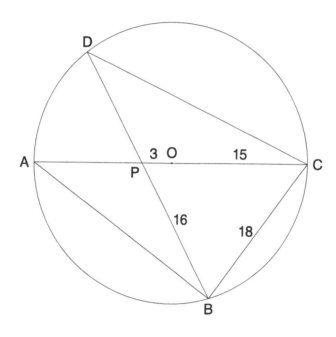

(A) 30   (B) 28   (C) 29   (D) 26   (E) 27

30. Jason and Pradeep each chose a rational number. The sum of Jason's number and the reciprocal of Pradeep's number was $\frac{19}{10}$. The sum of Pradeep's number and the reciprocal of Jason's number was $\frac{19}{6}$. The greatest possible value of the product of Jason's number and Pradeep's number is a common fraction. What is the value of the numerator of that fraction minus the denominator of that fraction?

(A) 9   (B) 16   (C) 11   (D) 12   (E) 6

Place ID Sticker
Inside This Box

Name _____

Grade _____

School _____

Problems 1 & 2

1. Michelle, Nicole, Olivia, and Patricia each have several pieces of candy. Michelle has three more pieces than Nicole. Nicole has two fewer pieces than Olivia. Olivia has half as many pieces as Patricia. Patricia has eight pieces of candy. How many pieces of candy do Michelle, Nicole, Olivia, and Patricia have altogether?

1.

2. Carlos has a math book, a history book, and a science book. Carlos is arranging the three books on a shelf, but since he loves math and uses the math book often, he does not want the math book to be between the other two books. How many different ways can Carlos arrange his three books on the shelf?

2.

Place ID Sticker
Inside This Box

Name _____

Grade _____

School _____

Problems 3 & 4

3. Angela chose a positive whole number. She told her friend Benjamin, "My number is greater than four and less than twenty. Also, my number is odd, is not prime, and is not a perfect square." With this information, Benjamin knew Angela's number. What was Angela's number?

3.

4. A large rectangle is formed by arranging a number of identical smaller rectangles, as shown below. The area of the large rectangle is 168. What is the perimeter of the large rectangle?

4.

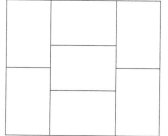

Place ID Sticker
Inside This Box

Name _____

Grade _____

School _____

Problems 5 & 6

5. Dimes are coins worth 10 cents and nickels are coins worth 5 cents. Nigel has 9 coins, all of which are dimes or nickels. The total value of Nigel's coins is 75 cents. Oscar has as many nickels as Nigel has dimes, and as many dimes as Nigel has nickels. What is the total value, in cents, of Oscar's nickels and dimes?

5.

6. How many positive whole numbers less than 1000 have exactly nine positive whole number divisors?

6.

Place ID Sticker
Inside This Box

Name _____

Grade _____

School _____

Problems 7 & 8

7. In the addition problem below, each letter represents a different digit. What is the sum of the values of the digits represented by *A*, *B*, and *C*?

```
    A  A
+   B  B
─────────
 C  B  C
```

7. [   ]

8. The area of the large triangle shown below is 420. Two segments are drawn in the triangle, each from a vertex of the triangle to a point on the opposite side. One segment partitions the opposite side into two segments in the ratio of 1 : 1, and the other segment partitions the opposite side into two segments in the ratio of 1 : 3, as shown. Together, the two segments partition the large triangle into four regions. Three of these regions are triangles, and one is a quadrilateral. What is the area of the quadrilateral?

8. [   ]

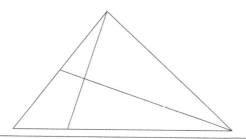

Team Round
12225

School or Team

Name _____

Name _____

Name _____

Name _____

Place ID Sticker
Inside This Box

Place ID Sticker
Inside This Box

Place ID Sticker
Inside This Box

Place ID Sticker
Inside This Box

1.

2.

3.

4.

5.

6.

7.

8.

9.

10.

1. At 9 : 44 PM, a hacker started a computer program to crack a password. At 7 : 07 AM the next morning, the computer program finished and the hacker had the password. How many minutes did it take the program to crack the password?

2. The figure below is formed by two rectangles that overlap, with the sides of the rectangles intersecting at right angles. Using only lines shown as sides of rectangles, how many different rectangles are in the figure below?

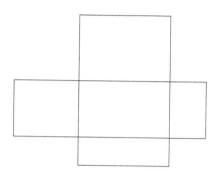

3. Mr. Olive summed all of the two-digit positive whole numbers. Mr. Stevens summed all of the two-digit even positive whole numbers. What is the value of Mr. Olive's result minus Mr. Stevens' result?

4. Vai cleans her room once every seven days, and does her laundry once every four days. On January 1st, 2022, Vai cleaned her room and did her laundry. On how many days in January 2022 did Vai either clean her room or do her laundry, but did not do both?

5. This past fall, the ratio of fifth graders to fourth graders on the Armstrong Elementary Math Team was 7 : 5. After the start of the new year, four more fifth graders joined the team, and the ratio of fifth graders to fourth graders is now 5 : 3. How many total fourth graders and fifth graders are now on the Armstrong Elementary Math Team?

6. An isosceles triangle is drawn on a piece of paper. Aria accurately measures one of the angles in the triangle as 50°. Brayden accurately measures another one of the angles in the triangle. What is the sum, in degrees, of all of the different possible values of Brayden's measurement?

7. Fahrenheit and Celsius are two different scales for measuring temperature. A temperature of 32° Fahrenheit is equivalent to a temperature of 0° Celsius. Additionally, an increase of 1° on the Fahrenheit scale is equivalent to an increase of $\frac{5}{9}$° on the Celsius scale. At what temperature, in degrees Fahrenheit, is the measurement of the temperature in degrees Fahrenheit numerically 100 greater than the temperature in degrees Celsius? For example, at 32° Fahrenheit, or 0° Celsius, the temperature in degrees Fahrenheit is numerically $32 - 0 = 32$ greater than the temperature in degrees Celsius.

8. What is the sum of the tens digit and units digit of 12^{2022}?

9. The square below has three shaded regions. One region is a kite, and the other two regions are isosceles right triangles. Each isosceles triangle shares a vertex with the kite, as shown. The area of the kite is $\frac{1}{3}$ the area of the square. What fraction of the square is not shaded? Express your answer as a common fraction.

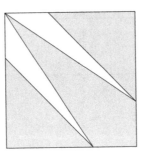

10. An 8×8 checkerboard is shown below. A number of rectangles exist on this board, with boundaries of each rectangle that are boundaries of the small squares or boundaries of the board. A single small square is one such rectangle, and the entire board is another such rectangle. One of these rectangles is randomly chosen. What is the probability that the rectangle chosen contains more small grey squares than small white squares? Express your answer as a common fraction.

Sprint Round

1. B	11. B	21. A
2. D	12. E	22. B
3. E	13. B	23. A
4. B	14. A	24. C
5. E	15. D	25. C
6. D	16. A	26. A
7. B	17. E	27. E
8. E	18. A	28. A
9. D	19. A	29. E
10. B	20. D	30. C

Target Round

1. 19
2. 4
3. 15
4. 52
5. 60
6. 8
7. 12
8. 75

Team Round

1. 563
2. 11
3. 2475
4. 9
5. 40
6. 195($°$)
7. 185($°$)
8. 8
9. $\frac{2}{9}$
10. $\frac{25}{162}$

Number Sense

1. 101	21. 1650	41. 210	61. $132\frac{20}{81}$
2. 39	22. $\frac{4}{13}$	42. 108	62. 205
3. 705	23. 529	43. 2709	63. $\frac{13}{111}$
4. 5	24. 6	44. 80	64. 4125
5. 236	25. 117	45. 10	65. 400
6. 1020	26. 6	46. 2929	66. 34
7. 2	27. $\frac{2}{7}$	47. 640	67. 153
8. 7	28. 17	48. 100	68. 6
9. 102	29. 16	49. 196	69. 9405
10. [2765, 3055]	30. [42703, 47197]	50. [2442855, 2699997]	70. [870, 960]
11. 803	31. 18	51. 16	71. 22
12. 196	32. 4257	52. 11760	72. 1037342
13. 122	33. 25	53. 7	73. 25
14. 2	34. 15	54. 6882	74. 93025
15. 780	35. 126	55. 111011	75. 10
16. 930	36. 2025	56. 8544	76. 15625
17. 2152	37. 19	57. 36	77. 6
18. 8.4	38. 3016	58. 2401	78. 54450
19. 336	39. 60	59. 144	79. $\frac{1}{4}$
20. [67850, 74992]	40. [1912, 2112]	60. [284989, 314987]	80. [272, 300]

Sprint Round Solutions

1. From Monday through Friday, Evan walked $1 + 2 + 3 + 4 + 5 = 15$ miles. On Saturday, Evan walked an additional 15 miles, so the total number of miles Evan walked was $15 + 15 = \boxed{30}$.

2. Any product that is the product of two even numbers must be a multiple of 4, so 2×14 and 10×6 are multiples of 4. Since both 12 and 8 are multiples of 4, both 12×3 and 8×7 are multiples of 4. But the product of an even number that is not a multiple of 4 and an odd number is not a multiple of 4, so the value that is not a multiple of 4 is $\boxed{6 \times 9}$.

3. A square has 4 sides, a pentagon has 5 sides, a hexagon has 6 sides, a heptagon has 7 sides, and an octagon has 8 sides. Altogether, the total number of sides is $4 + 5 + 6 + 7 + 8 = \boxed{30}$.

4. There are 30 students in the class, and each student needs 2 pencils, so $30 \times 2 = 60$ pencils must be purchased. This is $60 \div 5 = 12$ sets of five pencils, and since each set of five costs $2, the total cost is $12 \times \$2 = \boxed{\$24}$.

5. The even whole numbers less than 29 are $2, 4, 6, 8, 10, 12, 14, 16, 18, 20, 22, 24, 26,$ and 28, for a count of 14. This count includes numbers that are both even and divisible by 3. The numbers that are evenly divisible by 3 and not even are $3, 9, 15, 21,$ and 27, for a count of 5. Altogether, the count of numbers that are even or divisible by 3 is $14 + 5 = \boxed{19}$.

6. If the product of the digits is 24, then the digits must be either 4 and 6 or 3 and 8. Because the sum of the digits is 11, the digits must be 8 and 3. The two possible values of the number are 38 and 83, and their sum is $\boxed{121}$.

7. Time is equal to distance divided by rate, or speed. Therefore the time, in hours, required to drive 845 miles at a speed of 65 miles per hour is $845 \div 65 = \boxed{13}$.

8. Charlie plays games against Donnie, Eddie, and Frankie, for 3 games. Donnie, having already played Charlie, plays games against Eddie and Frankie, for 2 games. Eddie, having already played Charlie and Donnie, plays a game against Frankie, for 1 game. Frankie does not need to play any additional games, as he has already played everyone. The total number of games played is $3 + 2 + 1 = \boxed{6}$.

9. The height of the rectangle is equal to the side length of the largest square. Since each of the smaller squares has a side length half that of the larger square, the width of the rectangle is equal to the side length of the largest square plus $\frac{1}{2}$ the side length of the largest square. Therefore the perimeter of the rectangle is $1+1+1+1+\frac{1}{2}+\frac{1}{2}=5$ side lengths of the largest square. The side length of the largest square is $30 \div 5 = 6$, so the area is $6 \times 6 = \boxed{36}$.

10. The remainder when a number is divided by 5 is determined by the units digit of the number. The units digit of the product $21 \times 23 \times 27 \times 29$ is the units digit of $1 \times 3 \times 7 \times 9$, which is the units digit of 3×3, or 9. The remainder when a number with a units digit of 9 is divided by 5 is $\boxed{4}$.

11. There are 365 days in the year 2022. Because $365 \div 7$ has a quotient of 52 and a remainder of 1, the length of the year is 52 weeks and 1 day. Thus all days of the week will occur 52 times, except for the day of the week that is the first day of the year, as it will occur an additional time on the last day of the year. So the total number of Saturdays and Sundays in 2022 is $52+52+1=\boxed{105}$.

12. The product of the leg lengths of a right triangle is equal to twice the area of the triangle. Since the areas of the triangles are all equal, the product of the leg lengths of each triangle must also be all equal. The product of the leg lengths of the first triangle is $20 \cdot 24 = 480$. The unknown leg of the second triangle has length $\frac{480}{30} = 16$, and the unknown leg of the third triangle has length $\frac{480}{12} = 40$. The sum of the lengths of all of the legs of all three triangles is $20+24+16+30+12+40=\boxed{142}$.

13. Two hours is $2 \cdot 60 = 120$ minutes, and Emery studied for 5 days. The number of minutes studied each day is an arithmetic sequence. Therefore the average number of minutes studied, $120 \div 5 = 24$, is the number of minutes Emery studied on Tuesday, which is the middle of the 5 days. The number of minutes Emery studied on Thursday is $24+4+4=\boxed{32}$.

14. The number of groups must be a number that divides both 868 and 1316. The greatest possible value of this number is the *GCD* of 868 and 1316. Applying Euclid's method, $1316 \div 868$ has a remainder of 448, $868 \div 448$ has a remainder of 420, $448 \div 420$ has a remainder of 28, and $420 \div 28$ has a remainder of 0. Therefore the *GCD* of 868 and 1316, which is also the greatest possible value for the number of groups of cards that Isaiah or Henry had, is $\boxed{28}$.

15. Comparing to decimals, $0.5 = \frac{1}{2}$, $0.66 < \frac{2}{3}$, $0.75 = \frac{3}{4}$, $0.8 = \frac{4}{5}$, $0.83 < \frac{5}{6}$, $0.85 < \frac{6}{7}$, $0.87 < \frac{7}{8}$, $0.88 < \frac{8}{9}$, and $0.9 = \frac{9}{10}$. The sum of these decimals is $0.5+0.66+0.75+0.8+0.83+0.85+0.87+0.88+0.9 = 7.04$. This is slightly less than the sum of the fractions, so the greatest whole number that is less than the sum of the fractions is $\boxed{7}$.

16. The number of cubic inches in one cubic foot is $12 \cdot 12 \cdot 12 = 1728$, and the number of cubic inches in 2 cubic feet is $1728 \cdot 2 = 3456$. The number of gallons in 2 cubic feet is $\frac{3456}{231} = \frac{1152}{77}$. This is $14\frac{74}{77}$, which is very nearly $\boxed{15}$.

17. By the Pythagorean Theorem, the length of the hypotenuse is $\sqrt{13^2 + 19^2} = \sqrt{530}$. The value of 23^2 is 529, so $\sqrt{530}$ is very near 23, and the perimeter of the triangle is very near $13 + 19 + 23 = \boxed{55}$.

18. Suppose that $\frac{2}{3}$ of Rohil's number, and $\frac{3}{5}$ of Sohil's number was equal to 6. Then Rohil's number would be $\frac{3}{2} \cdot 6 = 9$, and Sohil's number would be $\frac{5}{3} \cdot 6 = 10$. The value of Rohil's number divided by Sohil's number would be $\boxed{\frac{9}{10}}$.

19. This is $376 \cdot 239 + 376 - 239$, or $376 \cdot 240 - 239$, which is $375 \cdot 240 + 1$. This can also be expressed as $1000 \cdot \frac{3}{8} \cdot 240 + 1$, or $1000 \cdot 90 + 1 = \boxed{90001}$.

20. If each of the 97 vehicles tallied was a car, then the total number of wheels would be $97 \cdot 4 = 388$. But this is an excess of $388 - 352 = 36$ wheels. When a car is replaced by a motorcycle in the count, the number of wheels counted decreases by $4 - 2 = 2$, so the number of motorcycles must be $\frac{36}{2} = 18$. The number of cars is $97 - 18 = 79$, and the number of cars exceeds the number of motorcycles by $79 - 18 = \boxed{61}$.

21. The area of the entire grid is 25. The area of the shaded region can be found by subtracting the unshaded portions of the grid. On each of the left and right sides is a right triangle with legs of length 1 and 5. These two triangles have a total area of $1 \cdot 5 = 5$. On the top is a trapezoid with bases of length 1 and 3 and a height of length 1. This trapezoid has an area of $\frac{1}{2} \cdot (1 + 3) \cdot 1 = 2$. On the bottom is a trapezoid with bases of length 1 and 5 and a height of length 3. This trapezoid has an area of $\frac{1}{2} \cdot (1 + 5) \cdot 3 = 9$. Therefore the shaded region has an area of $25 - 5 - 2 - 9 = \boxed{9}$.

22. Let the total number of marbles in the jar be M. Then the number of red marbles in the jar is 70% of the total number of marbles in the jar, or $0.7 \cdot M$. After removing 12 blue marbles from the jar, the number of red marbles is unchanged, but is 75% of the total number of marbles in the jar, or $0.75 \cdot (M - 12)$. Setting these two expressions equal, $0.7M = 0.75 \cdot (M - 12)$, or $9 = 0.05M$, so $M = 180$. The number of red marbles in the jar is $0.7 \cdot 180 = \boxed{126}$.

23. The number $3^6 - 1$ is equal to $\left(3^3\right)^2 - 1$, or $27^2 - 1$, so the least square greater than $3^6 - 1$ is 27^2. Similarly, the number $3^{16} + 1$ is equal to $\left(3^8\right)^2 + 1$. The number 3^8 is the square of 3^4, or $81^2 = 6561$, so the greatest square less than $3^{16} + 1$ is 6561^2. The number of perfect squares from 27^2 through 6561^2 is $6561 - 27 + 1 = \boxed{6535}$.

24. The chord and the two radii shown form an isosceles triangle. Dropping an altitude to the side of length 42 partitions this triangle into two congruent right triangles, each with one leg of length $\frac{42}{2} = 21$, and the length of the altitude is the second leg as well as the radius of the smaller circle. By the Pythagorean Theorem, the length of the altitude is $\sqrt{29^2 - 21^2} = 20$. The area of the larger circle is $29^2 \cdot \pi = 841\pi$, and the area of the smaller circle is $20^2 \cdot \pi = 400\pi$, so the area between the two circles is $841\pi - 400\pi = 441\pi$. Approximating π as $\frac{22}{7}$ yields an area of $\frac{22}{7} \cdot 441 = 1386$, and while this is a very slight overestimate, the only nearby answer choice is $\boxed{1385}$.

25. Let the greater odd number be $2a - 1$ and the lesser odd number be $2b - 1$ for positive whole numbers a and b. Then the difference of the squares of these numbers is $(2a - 1)^2 - (2b - 1)^2 = (2a - 1 + 2b - 1)((2a - 1) - (2b - 1))$. This is $(2a + 2b - 2)(2a - 2b)$, or $4 \cdot (a + b - 1)(a - b)$. If a and b are both odd or even, then $a - b$ is even. If only one of a and b are even, then $a + b - 1$ is even. Therefore the product $(a + b - 1)(a - b)$ must be even, and contains an additional factor of 2. No other numbers must divide this product, so the greatest number that must divide the difference of the squares is $4 \cdot 2 = \boxed{8}$.

26. Since Kevin can wash a car in 20 minutes, when he washes cars by himself for half an hour, or 30 minutes, he washes $\frac{30}{20} = \frac{3}{2}$ cars. This leaves $12 - \frac{3}{2} = \frac{21}{2}$ cars remaining to be washed. The total time remaining to wash these cars is $2 \cdot 60 + 14 - 30 = 104$ minutes. Working alone for 1 minute, Liam can wash $\frac{1}{16}$ of a car. Working together for 1 minute, Kevin and Liam can wash $\frac{1}{16} + \frac{1}{20} = \frac{9}{80}$ of a car. Let M be the number of minutes that Liam and Kevin work together. Then $\frac{9}{80}M + \frac{1}{16} \cdot (104 - M) = \frac{21}{2}$, or $9M + 5 \cdot (104 - M) = 840$, so $4M = 840 - 520$ and $M = 80$. The number of minutes Liam washed cars by himself is $104 - 80 = \boxed{24}$.

27. There are 9 numbers in the list, and the total number of groups of 3 numbers that Ajene could select is $\binom{9}{3} = 84$. Because there are 4 positive numbers in the list, there are $\binom{4}{3} = 4$ ways to choose 3 positive numbers. The only other way to have a product that is positive is to choose 2 negative numbers and 1 positive number. There are $\binom{4}{2} = 6$ ways to choose 2 negative numbers, and $\binom{4}{1} = 4$ ways to choose a positive number, so there are $6 \cdot 4 = 24$ ways to choose 2 negative numbers and 1 positive number. Altogether, the total number of ways to have a product that is positive is $4 + 24 = 28$, for a probability of $\frac{28}{84} = \boxed{\dfrac{1}{3}}$.

28. The sum of the first n perfect squares is $\frac{n \cdot (n+1)(2n+1)}{6}$, so the sum of the first 2022 perfect squares is $\frac{2022 \cdot 2023 \cdot 4045}{6}$, or $337 \cdot 2023 \cdot 4045$. This expression is equal to $15q + r$, for some r greater than or equal to 0 and less than 15. But the expression is also a multiple of 5, so r must be a multiple of 5. Letting $r = 5s$, $337 \cdot 2023 \cdot 4045 = 15q + 5s$, or $337 \cdot 2023 \cdot 809 = 3q + s$. The remainder when $337 \cdot 2023 \cdot 809$ is divided by 3 is equivalent to the product of the remainders of 337, 2023, and 809 each divided by 3, which is $1 \cdot 1 \cdot 2 = 2$. Therefore s is 2, and r is $5 \cdot 2 = \boxed{10}$.

29. Because OC is a radius, the length of AC is $2 \cdot 15 = 30$. Because AC is a diameter, triangle ABC must be a right triangle, so by the Pythagorean Theorem, the length of AB is $\sqrt{30^2 - 18^2} = 24$. Angles CAB and CDB both subtend arc CB and are therefore congruent, and angles DBA and DCA both subtend are DA and are therefore congruent. Thus triangle DPC is similar to triangle APB. Then $\frac{CP}{BP} = \frac{CD}{BA}$, or $\frac{18}{16} = \frac{CD}{24}$, and the length of CD is $\boxed{27}$.

30. Let Jason's number be x and Pradeep's number be y. Then $x + \frac{1}{y} = \frac{19}{10}$, and $y + \frac{1}{x} = \frac{19}{6}$. Multiplying these equations yields $xy + 1 + 1 + \frac{1}{xy} = \frac{361}{60}$. Letting $xy = k$, this is $k + 2 + \frac{1}{k} = \frac{361}{60}$, or $60k^2 - 241k + 60 = 0$. This quadratic factors as $(15k - 4)(4k - 15) = 0$, so k is either $\frac{4}{15}$ or $\frac{15}{4}$. The maximum possible value is $\frac{15}{4}$, and $15 - 4 = \boxed{11}$.

Target Round Solutions

1. If Patricia has 8 pieces of candy, then Olivia, having half as many, has $8 \div 2 = 4$ pieces of candy. If Olivia has 4 pieces of candy, then Nicole, having 2 fewer, has $4 - 2 = 2$ pieces of candy. Finally, if Nicole has 2 pieces of candy, then Michelle, having 3 more, has $2 + 3 = 5$ pieces of candy. Alttogether, the number of pieces of candy is $8 + 4 + 2 + 5 = \boxed{19}$.

2. The math book must be either the leftmost or right most book in the arrangement. If the math book is the leftmost book, then there are 2 ways to arrange the other 2 books. Similarly, if the math book is the rightmost book, then there are also 2 ways to arrange the other 2 books. The total number of ways to arrange the books is $2 + 2 = \boxed{4}$.

3. The odd numbers greater than 4 and less than 20 are $5, 7, 9, 11, 13, 15, 17, 19$. Of these, $5, 7, 11, 13, 17, 19$ are prime, leaving only 9 and 15. But 9 is a perfect square, so Angela's number must be $\boxed{15}$.

4. There are 7 smaller rectangles, each of which has an area of $\frac{168}{7} = 24$. From the height of the large rectangle, 2 times the longer side of the small rectangle must be equal to 3 times the shorter side of the small rectangle, or the longer side of the rectangle must be $\frac{3}{2}$ as long as the shorter side. Considering factor pairs of 24, the longer side must be 6 and the shorter side length must be 4. Thus the height of the large rectangle is $6 + 6 = 12$, the width is $4 + 6 + 4 = 14$, and the perimeter is $12 + 12 + 14 + 14 = \boxed{52}$.

5. If Nigel had 9 nickels then his coins would be worth $9 \times 5 = 45$ cents. But Nigel has $75 - 45 = 30$ cents more. Replacing a nickel with a dime adds $10 - 5 = 5$ cents. Therefore Nigel has $30 \div 5 = 6$ dimes, and $9 - 6 = 3$ nickels. Oscar has 6 nickels and 3 dimes, for a total value, in cents, of $6 \times 5 + 3 \times 10 = \boxed{60}$.

6. For a number to have 9 positive whole number divisors, the prime factorization of the number must be either p^8, where p is a prime, or $p^2 \cdot q^2$, where p and q are both prime. In the first case, the only possible value of p for which p^8 is less than 1000 is 2. In the second case, the number must be a perfect square. If $p^2 \cdot q^2 < 1000$, then $p \cdot q < \sqrt{1000}$. Since $\sqrt{1000}$ is between 31 and 32, the product of p and q must be less than 32. Let p be the smaller of the two primes. If p is 2, then q can be $3, 5, 7, 11$, or 13, for 5 possibilities. If p is 3, then q can be 5 or 7, for 2 possibilities. If p is 5 or larger, there is no greater prime q for which $p \cdot q < 32$. Altogether, the number of whole numbers less than 1000 with exactly 9 positive whole number divisors is $1 + 5 + 2 = \boxed{8}$.

7. Because the two-digit numbers AA and BB have repeated digits, each must be a multiple of 11. Therefore the number CBC, being the sum of two multiples of 11, must also be a multiple of 11. And the sum of two two-digit numbers must be less than 200, so C must be 1. The only multiple of 11 between 100 and 200 that has a units digit of 1 is 121, so B is 2. Then AA is $121 - 22 = 99$, and A is 9. The sum of A, B, and C is $9 + 2 + 1 = \boxed{12}$.

8. Draw an additional segment from the unused vertex to the point of intersection partitioning the quadrilateral into two triangles. Let the areas of the five triangles be a, b, c, d, and e, as shown below. The segment that partitions the opposite side into two segments in the ratio of 1 : 1 creates two regions, each of which is half the entire triangle, so $a + b = 210$ and $c + d + e = 210$. The segment that partitions the opposite side into two segments in the ratio of 1 : 3 creates two regions, one of which is $\frac{1}{1+3} = \frac{1}{4}$ of the entire triangle, and the other is $\frac{3}{4}$, so $a + c + d = 105$ and $b + e = 315$. Additionally, since each triangle has a base of equal length and the two share a common altitude, $a = c$. And since one triangle has a base 3 times the other and the two share a common altitude, $e = 3d$. Substituting $a = c$ into $a + c + d = 105$ yields $2a + d = 105$. Substituting $e = 3d$ and $a = c$ into $c + d + e = 210$ yields $a + 4d = 210$. Solving this system for a and d, $a = 30$ and $d = 45$. Since the area of the quadrilateral is $c + d$, which is equivalent to $a + d$, the area of the quadrilateral is $30 + 45 = \boxed{75}$.

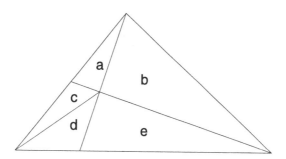

Team Round Solutions

1. After running for $60 - 44 = 16$ minutes, it was $10:00$ PM. After running for an additional $2 \times 60 = 120$ minutes, it was $12:00$ AM, the start of the next day. After running for an additional $7 \times 60 = 420$ minutes, it was $7:00$ AM the next day, and the program ran for an additional 7 minutes after that. The total number of minutes the program ran was $16 + 120 + 420 + 7 = \boxed{563}$.

2. There are 5 total regions in the figure. There are 5 rectangles that use 1 region, there are 4 rectangles that use 2 regions, and there are 2 rectangles that use 3 regions. Altogether the total number of rectangles is $5 + 4 + 2 = \boxed{11}$.

3. Mr. Olive's sum is $10 + 11 + 12 + \cdots + 99$, and Mr. Steven's sum is $10 + 12 + 14 + \cdots + 98$. When Mr. Stevens' result is subtracted from Mr. Olive's result, the remaining terms are $11 + 13 + 15 + \cdots + 99$. This is an arithmetic sequence with $\frac{99-11}{2} + 1 = 45$ terms having an average value of $\frac{99+11}{2} = 55$, for a sum of $45 \cdot 55 = \boxed{2475}$.

4. Vai will do her laundry on days $1, 5, 9, 13, 17, 21, 25, 29$. Vai will clean her room on days $1, 8, 15, 22, 29$. The days that appear in exactly one of the two lists are $5, 8, 9, 13, 15, 17, 21, 22, 25$, for a count of $\boxed{9}$.

5. The number of fourth graders is unchanged, and since the fourth grade portion of both ratios is 5 and 3, the number of fourth graders must be a multiple of $5 \cdot 3 = 15$. If the number of fourth graders is 15, then the number of fifth graders is initially $\frac{15}{5} \cdot 7 = 21$. When 4 fifth graders join the team, the number of fifth graders is $21 + 4 = 25$, and the ratio of fifth graders to fourth graders is $25:15$, or $5:3$. So the number of fourth graders must be 15, the number of fifth graders is now 25, and the total number of fourth and fifth graders on the team is $15 + 25 = \boxed{40}$.

6. The measures of the interior angles of a triangle must sum to $180°$. An isosceles triangle has two angles that are equal. There are two cases to consider. In the first case, Aria measured the unequal angle, so Brayden's measurement is $\frac{180° - 50°}{2} = 65°$. In the second case, Aria measured one of the equal angles, so the triangle has two angles that measure $50°$ and one angle that measures $180° - 50° - 50° = 80°$. In this case, Brayden could have measured either the $80°$ angle or the other $50°$ angle. The sum of all of the possible values of Brayden's measurement is $65° + 50° + 80° = \boxed{195°}$.

7. For the numerical difference of $32 - 0 = 32$ at the given temperature to increase to 100, the difference must increase by $100 - 32 = 68$. Because an increase of $1°$ Celsius is an increase of $\frac{9}{5}°$ Fahrenheit, each increase of $1°$ Celsius increases the numerical difference of Fahrenheit over Celsius by $\frac{9}{5} - 1 = \frac{4}{5}$. To gain the additional increase of 68 in the numerical difference requires an increase of $68 \div \frac{4}{5} = 85$ degrees Celsius. Therefore the desired temperature in Celsius is $0° + 85° = 85°$, and since the temperature in degrees Fahrenheit is numerically 100 greater, the temperature in degrees Fahrenheit is $\boxed{185°}$.

8. Every power of 12 is a multiple of 4, and no powers of 12 are multiples of 20. Thus there are only $\frac{100}{4} - 5 = 20$ possibilities for the tens digit and units digit. That is, the tens digit and units digit must repeat at least once in any list of 20 consecutive powers of 12. Now consider the tens and units digits of powers of 12. The first five powers of 12 have tens and units digits of $12, 44, 28, 36, 32$. The next five have tens and units digits of $84, 08, 96, 52, 24$. The next five, powers 11 through 15, have tens and units digits of $88, 56, 72, 64, 68$. The next five, powers 16 through 20, have tens and units digits of $16, 92, 04, 48, 76$. Finally, 12^{21} has a tens and units digits of 12, which is the same as 12^1. Therefore the pattern repeats every 20 powers of 12. Since $2022 \div 20$ has a remainder of 2, the tens and units digit will be the same as 12^2, which is 44. The sum of the tens and units digits is $4 + 4 = \boxed{8}$.

9. Because the kite is $\frac{1}{3}$ of the square, the portion of the square that is not the kite is $1 - \frac{1}{3} = \frac{2}{3}$ of the square. This portion of the square is comprised of two congruent right triangles, each of which has one leg that is a side of the square. The area of one of these triangles is $\frac{1}{2} \cdot \frac{2}{3} = \frac{1}{3}$ of the square. Because one leg is a side of the square, the length of the other leg must have a length that is $\frac{2 \cdot \frac{1}{3}}{1} = \frac{2}{3}$ of the side of the square. This leg is also the leg of the shaded isosceles right triangle. Therefore the base of one of the white triangles has a length that is $1 - \frac{2}{3} = \frac{1}{3}$ of the side of the square and an altitude that is $\frac{2}{3}$ of the side length of the square, for an area that is $\frac{1}{2} \cdot \frac{1}{3} \cdot \frac{2}{3} = \frac{1}{9}$ of the square. The two white triangles together, as a fraction of the square, are $2 \cdot \frac{1}{9} = \boxed{\frac{2}{9}}$.

10. There are 9 possible vertical boundaries for the rectangle, and therefore $\binom{9}{2} = 36$ different pairs of vertical boundaries for the rectangle. Similarly, there are 36 possible horizontal boundaries of the rectangle, so there are $36 \cdot 36 = 1296$ total possible rectangles. For a rectangle to have an unequal number of small gray squares, both dimensions of the rectangle must be odd. To have an odd dimension, one of the boundaries must be chosen from the 5 boundaries that are edges of the board or an even number of squares from the edge of the board, and the other boundary must be chosen from the 4 boundaries that are an odd number of squares from the edge of the board. For both vertical and horizontal boundaries, there are $5 \cdot 4 = 20$ such pairs, and therefore $20 \cdot 20 = 400$ such rectangles. By symmetry, exactly half of these rectangles, or 200 will have more small gray squares than small white squares, for a probability of $\frac{200}{1296} = \boxed{\frac{25}{162}}$.

Number Sense
12226

Place ID Sticker
Inside This Box

Name _____

Grade _____

School _____

1. $212 - 21 =$ _____.

2. The thousands digit of 519615 is _____.

3. $314 - 96 =$ _____.

4. $8 + 11 \times 8 =$ _____.

5. $98 \div 7 =$ _____.

6. The remainder of $129 \div 4$ is _____.

7. $787 + 316 =$ _____.

8. The product of 19 and 9 is _____.

9. $54 + 32 + 47 + 56 =$ _____.

10. (estimate) $1105 + 2431 + 1326 =$ _____.

11. $515 - 159 - 158 =$ _____.

12. $83 \times 11 =$ _____.

13. The remainder of $243 \div 9$ is _____.

14. $18^2 =$ _____.

15. $28 \times 35 =$ _____.

16. $22 \times 5 \times 7 =$ _____.

17. *CMLXXIV* in Arabic numerals is _____.

18. $14.4 \div 0.12 =$ _____.

19. $28 \times 32 =$ _____.

20. (estimate) $301 \times 419 =$ _____.

21. $14 \times 15 \div 35 =$ _____.

22. The GCD of 24 and 54 is _____.

23. $31 + 29 + 27 + 25 + 23 + 21 =$ _____.

24. The greater of $\frac{3}{4}$ and $\frac{13}{17}$ is _____ (fraction).

25. $1 - \frac{1}{3} - \frac{1}{4} =$ _____ (fraction).

26. $26^2 =$ _____.

27. If 1 teaspoon is equal to $\frac{1}{3}$ tablespoon, then 6 tablespoons equals _____ teaspoons.

28. $55 \times 25 =$ _____.

29. $765 \div 45 =$ _____.

30. (estimate) $49 \times 21 \times 51 =$ _____.

31. $75^2 =$ _____.

32. The perimeter of a rectangle with area 21 and width 7 is _____.

33. $\frac{4}{25} =$ _____ %.

34. The LCM of 24 and 54 is _____.

35. $61 \times 99 =$ _____.

36. 75% of 60 is _____.

37. $84 \times 86 =$ _____.

38. 1860 minutes is _____ hours.

39. The number of odd whole numbers between 88 and 156 is _____.

40. (estimate) $\sqrt{285482} =$ _____.

41. The side length of a regular octagon with perimeter 184 is _____.

42. $36 \times 76 =$ _____.

43. $14 \times 16 + 22 \times 8 =$ _____.

44. The twentieth term in the arithmetic sequence $4, 13, 22, \ldots$ is _____.

45. $42^2 - 12^2 =$ _____.

46. The remainder of $3447 \div 11$ is _____.

47. $29 \times 101 =$ _____.

48. $8^3 \cdot 2 =$ _____.

49. 120_{12} in base 10 is _____.

50. (estimate) $846721 \div 209 =$ _____.

51. $125 \times 63 =$ _____.

52. 110011_2 in base 8 is _____ ${}_8$.

53. The area of a right triangle with a leg of length 5 and a hypotenuse of length 13 is _____.

54. $121 \times 103 =$ _____.

55. The measure of an interior angle in a regular nonagon is _____ °.

56. $6\frac{2}{3}\%$ of 105 is _____.

57. The median of the list $18, 29, 21, 54, 15, 30$ is _____.

58. $97 \times 82 =$ _____.

59. The sum of the terms of the arithmetic sequence $24, 28, 32, \ldots 64$ is _____.

60. (estimate) $6667 \times 51 =$ _____.

61. $0.5\overline{6} =$ _____ (fraction).

62. $6\frac{1}{5} \times 14\frac{1}{5} =$ _____ (mixed number).

63. The number 100 in base 6 is _____ ${}_6$.

64. $333 \times 27 =$ _____.

65. If $w = 41$ then $w^2 + 8w + 16 =$ _____.

66. Two standard dice are rolled. The probability the sum of the numbers shown on the dice is 2 or 12 is _____ (fraction).

67. $38 \times 9 \times 34 =$ _____.

68. The area of a square with a diagonal of length 24 is _____.

69. $66^2 =$ _____.

70. (estimate) The radius of a circle with an area of 1386 is _____.

71. The number of positive whole number divisors of 48 is _____.

72. $979 \times 989 =$ _____.

73. If $6^{-z} = \frac{1}{18}$, then $6^{z-1} =$ _____.

74. $243^{0.6} =$ _____.

75. The surface area of a $8 \times 1 \times 4$ right rectangular prism is _____.

76. $44 \times 75 \times 27 =$ _____.

77. The sum of the terms of the infinite geometric sequence $12, 9, \frac{27}{4}, \ldots$ is _____.

78. $\frac{2}{5}$ of 22 is $\frac{11}{10}$ of _____.

79. $\sqrt{44} \times \sqrt{99} =$ _____.

80. (estimate) $10^2 \cdot 1.2^6 =$ _____.

Sprint Round
12226

Name _____

Grade _____

School _____

1. Ⓐ Ⓑ Ⓒ Ⓓ Ⓔ   11. Ⓐ Ⓑ Ⓒ Ⓓ Ⓔ   21. Ⓐ Ⓑ Ⓒ Ⓓ Ⓔ

2. Ⓐ Ⓑ Ⓒ Ⓓ Ⓔ   12. Ⓐ Ⓑ Ⓒ Ⓓ Ⓔ   22. Ⓐ Ⓑ Ⓒ Ⓓ Ⓔ

3. Ⓐ Ⓑ Ⓒ Ⓓ Ⓔ   13. Ⓐ Ⓑ Ⓒ Ⓓ Ⓔ   23. Ⓐ Ⓑ Ⓒ Ⓓ Ⓔ

4. Ⓐ Ⓑ Ⓒ Ⓓ Ⓔ   14. Ⓐ Ⓑ Ⓒ Ⓓ Ⓔ   24. Ⓐ Ⓑ Ⓒ Ⓓ Ⓔ

5. Ⓐ Ⓑ Ⓒ Ⓓ Ⓔ   15. Ⓐ Ⓑ Ⓒ Ⓓ Ⓔ   25. Ⓐ Ⓑ Ⓒ Ⓓ Ⓔ

6. Ⓐ Ⓑ Ⓒ Ⓓ Ⓔ   16. Ⓐ Ⓑ Ⓒ Ⓓ Ⓔ   26. Ⓐ Ⓑ Ⓒ Ⓓ Ⓔ

7. Ⓐ Ⓑ Ⓒ Ⓓ Ⓔ   17. Ⓐ Ⓑ Ⓒ Ⓓ Ⓔ   27. Ⓐ Ⓑ Ⓒ Ⓓ Ⓔ

8. Ⓐ Ⓑ Ⓒ Ⓓ Ⓔ   18. Ⓐ Ⓑ Ⓒ Ⓓ Ⓔ   28. Ⓐ Ⓑ Ⓒ Ⓓ Ⓔ

9. Ⓐ Ⓑ Ⓒ Ⓓ Ⓔ   19. Ⓐ Ⓑ Ⓒ Ⓓ Ⓔ   29. Ⓐ Ⓑ Ⓒ Ⓓ Ⓔ

10. Ⓐ Ⓑ Ⓒ Ⓓ Ⓔ   20. Ⓐ Ⓑ Ⓒ Ⓓ Ⓔ   30. Ⓐ Ⓑ Ⓒ Ⓓ Ⓔ

1. Which of the following products has the smallest value?

    (A) 16×3 (B) 9×5 (C) 7×7 (D) 4×11 (E) 2×23

2. At the supermarket, the price of three apples is $1, and the price of four bananas is also $1. Armando purchases two dozen apples and one dozen bananas. What is the total cost, in dollars, of Armando's apples and bananas?

    (A) $10   (B) $8   (C) $11   (D) $9   (E) $12

3. Billy can ride two miles on his bicycle in eleven minutes. If Billy always rides his bicycle at the same speed, then how many minutes will it take Billy to ride his bicycle twelve miles?

    (A) 60   (B) 66   (C) 72   (D) 56   (E) 55

4. What is the thousands digit of 1234×9999?

    (A) 0   (B) 1   (C) 7   (D) 9   (E) 8

5. A triangle has side lengths of 17, 10, and 21. A square has the same perimeter as the triangle. What is the area of the square?

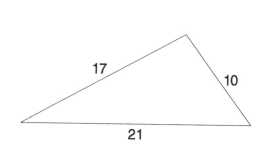

    (A) 196   (B) 169   (C) 144   (D) 100   (E) 121

6. The first day of February of the year 2022 is a Tuesday. The month of February has 28 days, and the month of March has 31 days. In the year 2022, what day of the week is the last day of March?

    (A) Monday   (B) Thursday   (C) Wednesday   (D) Friday   (E) Tuesday

7. What is the value of $4 + 8 + 12 + 16 + 20 + 24 + 28 + 32$ minus $2 + 6 + 10 + 14 + 18 + 22 + 24$?

    (A) 46   (B) 36   (C) 24   (D) 40   (E) 16

8. Nickels are coins worth 5 cents, dimes are coins worth 10 cents, and quarters are coins worth 25 cents. Penny has thirteen nickels, eight dimes, and three quarters. Penny uses these coins to purchase eight pencils for 180 cents. After making this purchase, what is the fewest number of coins that Penny could have remaining?

    (A) 8   (B) 5   (C) 3   (D) 2   (E) 4

9. James, Kevin, and Laura are lining up to swing at a piñata at a friend's birthday party. James does not want to swing at the piñata before Kevin swings at the piñata. How many different ways can James, Kevin, and Laura line up to swing at the piñata?

    (A) 6   (B) 1   (C) 4   (D) 2   (E) 3

10. The square below has an area of 81, and is divided into five identical smaller squares and one larger square. What is the sum of the perimeters of the five smaller squares and one larger square?

    (A) 80   (B) 96   (C) 92   (D) 90   (E) 84

11. How many positive whole numbers that evenly divide 108 are both less than 108 and even?

   (A) 8   (B) 7   (C) 4   (D) 5   (E) 6

12. Tickets for Saturday's school play were sold throughout the week. The number of tickets sold each day is displayed in the bar graph below. The average number of tickets sold each day is between which two numbers?

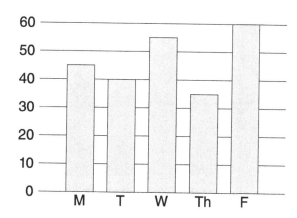

   (A) 50 and 56   (B) 32 and 38   (C) 44 and 50   (D) 26 and 32   (E) 38 and 44

13. Jasmine chose a positive whole number and divided the number by 20. Jasmine's result was greater than $1\frac{1}{3}$ but less than $1\frac{3}{7}$. What is the sum of all possible values of Jasmine's number?

   (A) 28   (B) 84   (C) 53   (D) 55   (E) 27

14. Two identical right triangles, each with legs of length 8 centimeters, are cut from a square sheet of paper measuring 10 centimeters on a side, as shown below. After the triangles are removed, the remaining piece of paper is a hexagon. What is the area of the hexagon, in square centimenters?

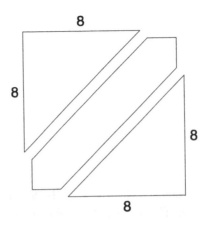

(A) 34   (B) 40   (C) 42   (D) 36   (E) 38

15. Chase chose a positive whole number that was greater than 2000 but less than 3000. The number Chase chose was a perfect square. How many different numbers could Chase have chosen?

(A) 13   (B) 10   (C) 12   (D) 9   (E) 11

16. Rita needed to read 75 pages in her book over the weekend. On Friday evening, Rita read 20% of the pages. On Saturday, Rita read 30% of the remaining pages. She read all of the remaining pages on Sunday. How many pages did Rita read on Sunday?

(A) 45   (B) 50   (C) 42   (D) 44   (E) 48

17. A rectangle has a height of 7 and a width of 16. To the nearest whole number, what is the sum of the lengths of the diagonals of the rectangle?

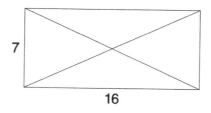

(A) 40   (B) 38   (C) 37   (D) 35   (E) 32

18. Quincy, Robert, and Samir had a total of $10,000 to invest in the stock market, but not everyone had the same amount of money. One year later, both Quincy and Robert had doubled their money, but Samir had lost $500. The total amount of money all three had after one year was $16,700. How much of the initial $10,000 belonged to Samir?

(A) $2,900   (B) $2,600   (C) $2,500   (D) $2,700   (E) $2,800

19. If $x \diamond y = 6xy + 4x + 3y$, then what is the value of $43 \diamond 27$?

(A) 7225   (B) 7217   (C) 7221   (D) 7223   (E) 7219

20. Tony is riding his electric skateboard at a speed of 10 miles per hour on a long, straight road. One mile ahead of Tony on the road, Scott is running at a speed of 7 miles per hour. If both Tony and Scott keep travelling at the same speed, in how many minutes will Tony be one mile ahead of Scott on the road?

(A) 45   (B) 42   (C) 40   (D) 48   (E) 30

21. Which of the following numbers is prime?

(A) 4409   (B) 4405   (C) 4411   (D) 4407   (E) 4403

22. The National Football League has eight divisions, with four teams in each division. A league game has two teams in the league playing against each other. Each year in the regular season, each team in the league plays seventeen games. Each year after the regular season, fourteen teams enter a playoff. Every playoff game has a losing team, and when a team loses a playoff game, it is eliminated from the playoff. Playoff games continue until all but one team has been eliminated. Including the regular season and the playoff, how many games are played in the National Football League each year?

(A) 547   (B) 272   (C) 286   (D) 548   (E) 285

23. What is the least power of 10 that is greater than the product of 16^{16} and 25^{25}?

(A) 10^{55} (B) 10^{53} (C) 10^{54} (D) 10^{51} (E) 10^{52}

24. In the concave quadrilateral shown below, one angle measures $79°$, and another angle measures $222°$. What is the sum of the degree measures of the other two angles of the quadrilateral?

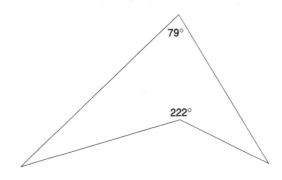

(A) $63°$ (B) $60°$ (C) $61°$ (D) $62°$ (E) $59°$

25. Kim created a list of positive whole numbers. She chose different positive whole numbers for the first two numbers in her list. Each number after the first two numbers in her list was the sum of the previous two numbers in the list. For example, if the first two numbers in Kim's list were 1 and 2, the third number in her list would be $1 + 2 = 3$, the fourth number in her list would be $2 + 3 = 5$, and the fifth number in her list would be $3 + 5 = 8$. When Kim created her list, however, the sixth number in her list was 2022. What is the greatest possible value of the first number in Kim's list?

(A) 661   (B) 674   (C) 656   (D) 648   (E) 669

26. What is the units digit of the sum of the first 2022 perfect squares?

(A) 1   (B) 5   (C) 0   (D) 4   (E) 6

27. The triangle shown below is divided into two trapezoids and a triangle, and segments AB, BC, and CD all have equal length. What is the ratio of the area of the unshaded trapezoid to the total area of the shaded triangle and shaded trapezoid?

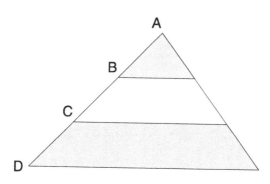

(A) $\frac{1}{4}$ (B) $\frac{1}{2}$ (C) $\frac{1}{3}$ (D) $\frac{2}{7}$ (E) $\frac{4}{9}$

28. Milena, Nala, and Oscar are playing a game of Rock, Paper, Scissors. In this game, each player chooses one of Rock, Paper, or Scissors. A player choosing Scissors beats a player choosing Paper, a player choosing Paper beats a player choosing Rock, and and a player choosing Rock beats a player choosing Scissors. If two players choose the same item, then neither player wins. If each of Milena, Nala, and Oscar each randomly choose Rock, Paper, or Scissors at the same time, then what is the probability that one player beats the other two?

(A) $\frac{1}{9}$ (B) $\frac{1}{3}$ (C) $\frac{2}{9}$ (D) $\frac{8}{27}$ (E) $\frac{7}{27}$

29. Carlos wants to color the six squares that make up the rectangle below so that each square is completely one color. Carlos plans to use exactly four different colors to color the squares, but he also wants exactly four of the squares to share a side with a square that has the same color. How many different ways can Carlos color the six squares?

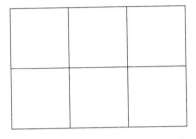

(A) 216   (B) 240   (C) 264   (D) 288   (E) 192

30. For three numbers x, y, and z, $4x + 17 = z^2$, $6y - 14 = x^2$, and $10z - 41 = y^2$. What is the value of xyz?

(A) 18   (B) 30   (C) 36   (D) 40   (E) 24

Place ID Sticker
Inside This Box

Name _____

Grade _____

School _____

Problems 1 & 2

1. Cathy exercises by walking around the track at her local high school. Every four laps walked around the track is one mile of walking. This week, Cathy walked six laps around the track on Monday. Each day after Monday she walked one more lap around the track than she did the previous day. From Monday through Friday of this week, how many miles did Cathy walk around the track?

1.

2. Sixteen identical squares are arranged to form a rectangle as shown. The perimeter of the rectangle is 136. The same sixteen squares are then arranged, without overlapping, to form a rectangle with the least possible perimeter. What is the perimeter of that rectangle?

2.

Place ID Sticker
Inside This Box

Name _____

Grade _____

School _____

Problems 3 & 4

3. Each of the digits 2, 3, 5, and 7 is used exactly once to replace each □ symbol in the expression □□□ ÷ □. After making the replacements, the expression is a three-digit number divided by a single-digit number. For example, 753 ÷ 2 is one possibility. If the result of the three-digit number divided by the single-digit number is a whole number, then what is the greatest possible value of that result?

3.

4. On the Ratioville Elementary School math team, the ratio of the number of fourth graders to the number of fifth graders last fall was 3 : 4. This spring, nine more fourth graders joined the team, and two more fifth graders joined the team. After these team members joined, the ratio of the number of fourth graders to the number of fifth graders was 7 : 6. This spring, how many total fourth and fifth graders were members of the Ratioville Elementary School math team this spring?

4.

Name _____

Grade _____

School _____

Problems 5 & 6

5. How many different positive whole numbers that are greater than 1 and less than 672 evenly divide 672?

5.

6. In triangle *ABC*, shown below, the measure of angle *CBA* is 135°, the measure of angle *CAB* is 30°, and the length of segment *AC* is 100. To the nearest whole number, what is the area of triangle *ABC*?

6.

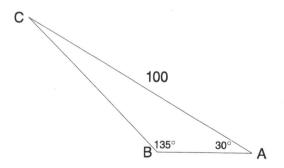

Place ID Sticker
Inside This Box

Name _____

Grade _____

School _____

Problems 7 & 8

7. Divesh chose a three-digit positive whole number. The value of the units digit divided by the tens digit was a whole number greater than one. The value of the tens digit divided by the hundreds digit was also a whole number greater than one. How many different numbers could Divesh have chosen?

7.

8. Four standard dice are rolled. What is the probability that at least three different numbers are shown on the four dice? Express your answer as a common fraction.

8.

Team Round
12226

School or Team

Name _____

Name _____

Name _____

Name _____

Place ID Sticker
Inside This Box

Place ID Sticker
Inside This Box

Place ID Sticker
Inside This Box

Place ID Sticker
Inside This Box

1.	2.	3.	4.	5.
6.	7.	8.	9.	10.

1. What is the sum of the two-digit positive whole numbers that are divisible by 7 and odd?

2. For Catie's thirteenth birthday party, she went to see a movie with six of her friends. Some of her friends were only twelve years old, and some of her friends were thirteen years old. The price of a child ticket, which is available for those aged twelve and younger, was $5. The price of an adult ticket, which is required for those aged thirteen and older, was $8. The total cost of the seven tickets for Catie and her friends was $50. How many of the tickets were adult tickets?

3. A fortnight is a length of time equal to two weeks. If the years 2012, 2016 and 2020 were all leap years, then how many fortnights occurred from the beginning of the year 2011 through the end of the year 2021?

4. Four rectangular strips of paper, each measuring 2 inches by 10 inches, are placed on a table as shown. Two of the strips are placed perfectly vertical, and two of the strips are perfectly horizontal. What is the total number of square inches in the part of the table covered by the strips of paper?

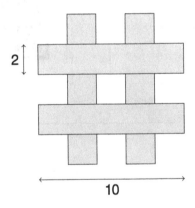

5. Diana, Erica, Francesca, and Greta each chose a different positive whole number from the first ten positive whole numbers. The sums of each possible pair of their numbers were 10, 11, 13, 15, 17, and 18. What was the product of their four numbers?

6. The figure below is a regular decagon, or figure with ten equal sides and ten equal angles. One diagonal is drawn in the decagon. This diagonal is parallel, or in the same direction, as at least one side of the decagon. How many different diagonals of the decagon are parallel to at least one side of the decagon?

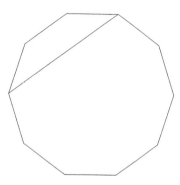

7. Fiona and Ginny each ran in a local race. Fiona finished the race in 66 minutes, and Ginny finished the race in 54 minutes. Fiona's average speed for the race was 1 mile per hour slower than Ginny's average speed. How many miles was the length of the race? Express your answer as a decimal to the nearest hundredth.

8. What is the remainder when 2022^{2022} is divided by 25?

9. A token is placed on one of the three squares in the diagram below. Every minute, the token is moved either one square clockwise or counterclockwise, with each direction being equally likely. What is the probability that after three moves or after four moves, the token is at the square where it was initially placed? Express your answer as a common fraction.

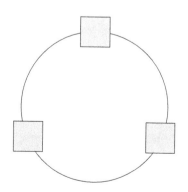

10. Amy and Ben each chose a two-digit positive whole number. Amy then told Charlie, "When you square my number and add Ben's number, and then subtract the sum of my number and the square of Ben's number, the result is 202." Charlie thought for a few minutes, and then announced that he knew Amy's number. What was Amy's number?

Sprint Round

1. D	11. B	21. A
2. C	12. C	22. E
3. B	13. D	23. A
4. E	14. D	24. E
5. C	15. B	25. E
6. B	16. C	26. B
7. A	17. D	27. B
8. C	18. E	28. B
9. E	19. E	29. C
10. E	20. C	30. B

Target Round

1. 10
2. 64
3. 76
4. 39
5. 22
6. 915
7. 7
8. $\frac{5}{6}$

Team Round

1. 336
2. 5
3. 287
4. 64
5. 1680
6. 15
7. 4.95
8. 9
9. $\frac{5}{8}$
10. 52

Number Sense

1. 191	21. 6	41. 23	61. $\frac{17}{30}$
2. 9	22. 6	42. 2736	62. $88\frac{1}{25}$
3. 218	23. 156	43. 400	63. 244
4. 96	24. $\frac{13}{17}$	44. 175	64. 8991
5. 14	25. $\frac{5}{12}$	45. 1620	65. 2025
6. 1	26. 676	46. 4	66. $\frac{1}{18}$
7. 1103	27. 18	47. 2929	67. 11628
8. 171	28. 1375	48. 1024	68. 288
9. 189	29. 17	49. 168	69. 4356
10. [4619, 5105]	30. [49856, 55102]	50. [3849, 4253]	70. [20, 22]
11. 198	31. 5625	51. 7875	71. 10
12. 913	32. 20	52. 63	72. 968231
13. 0	33. 16	53. 30	73. 3
14. 324	34. 216	54. 12463	74. 27
15. 980	35. 6039	55. 140	75. 88
16. 770	36. 45	56. 7	76. 89100
17. 974	37. 7224	57. 25	77. 48
18. 120	38. 31	58. 7954	78. 8
19. 896	39. 34	59. 484	79. 66
20. [119814, 132424]	40. [508, 561]	60. [323017, 357017]	80. [284, 313]

Solutions
12226

Sprint Round Solutions

1. The values of the products are $7 \times 7 = 49$, $16 \times 3 = 48$, $2 \times 23 = 46$, $9 \times 5 = 45$, and $4 \times 11 = 44$. The smallest product is $\boxed{4 \times 11}$.

2. Armando is purchasing $2 \times 12 = 24$ apples. This is $24 \div 3 = 8$ groups of 3. Because 3 apples cost \$1, the apples will cost \$8. Armando is also purchasing $1 \times 12 = 12$ bananas. This is $12 \div 4 = 3$ groups of 4. Because 4 bananas cost \$1, the bananas will cost \$3. The total cost of Armando's apples and bananas is $\$8 + \$3 = \boxed{\$11}$.

3. A distance of 12 miles is $12 \div 2 = 6$ distances of 2 miles. Since 2 miles requires 11 minutes, the number of minutes required to travel 12 miles is $6 \times 11 = \boxed{66}$.

4. This is $1234 \times 10000 - 1234 \times 1$, or $12340000 - 1234$, which is 12338766. The thousands digit is $\boxed{8}$.

5. The perimeter of the triangle is $17 + 10 + 21 = 48$. Since the perimeter of the square is 48, the side length of the square is $48 \div 4 = 12$, and the area of the square is $12 \times 12 = \boxed{144}$.

6. There are $28 + 31 = 59$ days in February and March. Since day 1 is a Tuesday, days 8, 15, 22, 29, 36, 43, 50, and 57 of these 59 days will also be Tuesdays. If day 57 is a Tuesday, then day 59, the last day of March, is a $\boxed{\text{Thursday}}$.

7. The first 7 terms of the first sum each exceed the first 7 terms of the second sum by 2 each, so among the first 7 terms, the first sum exceeds the second sum by $7 \times 2 = 14$. The first sum also includes an eighth term of 32, while the second sum has no eighth term, so the first sum exceeds the second by $14 + 32 = \boxed{46}$.

8. The total value of Penny's coins is $13 \times 5 + 8 \times 10 + 3 \times 25 = 220$ cents. After purchasing the pencils, Penny has $220 - 180 = 40$ cents remaining. There is no way to make 40 cents with only 1 coin, and there is no way to make 40 cents with only 2 coins. However, 40 cents can be made with 1 quarter, 1 dime, and 1 nickel, so the fewest number of coins Penny could have remaining is $\boxed{3}$.

9. Kevin must be in line before James. If Kevin is first in line, the possible ways to line up are Kevin, James, and Laura, or Kevin, Laura, and James, for 2 possibilities. If Kevin is second in line, the only possible way to line up is Laura, Kevin, and James, for 1 possibility. There are no possible ways to line up if Kevin is third in line. Therefore the total number of ways for the three to line up is $2 + 1 = \boxed{3}$.

10. The side length of the original square is $\sqrt{81} = 9$. The side length of one of the smaller squares is therefore $9 \div 3 = 3$, and the side length of the larger square is $9 - 3 = 6$. The perimeter of one of the smaller squares is $4 \times 3 = 12$, so the total perimeter of the five smaller squares is $12 \times 5 = 60$. The perimeter of the larger square is $4 \times 6 = 24$. The total perimeter of all of the squares is $60 + 24 = \boxed{84}$.

11. The factor pairs of 108 are 1×108, 2×54, 3×36, 4×27, 6×18, and 9×12. Those that are less than 108 and also even are 2, 54, 36, 4, 6, 18, and 12, for a total of $\boxed{7}$.

12. Monday's total is greater than 40 and less than 50. Tuesday's total is 40. Wednesday's total is greater than 50 and less than 60. Thursday's total is greater than 30 and less than 40. Friday's total is 60. The average must be greater than $(40 + 40 + 50 + 30 + 60) \div 5 = 44$. The average must also be less than $(50 + 40 + 60 + 40 + 60) \div 5 = 50$. Therefore the average must be between $\boxed{44 \text{ and } 50}$.

13. Jasmine's number must be greater than $1\frac{1}{3} \cdot 20$. This is $\frac{4}{3} \cdot 20 = \frac{80}{3}$, or $26\frac{2}{3}$. Jasmine's number must be less than $1\frac{3}{7} \cdot 20$. This is $\frac{10}{7} \cdot 20 = \frac{200}{7}$, or $28\frac{4}{7}$. The only possible values for Jasmine's number are 27 and 28, and $27 + 28 = \boxed{55}$.

14. The area of the original square is $10 \cdot 10 = 100$ square centimeters. The area of each triangle is $\frac{1}{2} \cdot 8 \cdot 8 = 32$ square centimeters, so the total area of both triangles is $32 + 32 = 64$ square centimeters. The area of the hexagon, in square centimeters, is $100 - 64 = \boxed{36}$.

15. Because $40^2 = 1600$ and $60^2 = 3600$, the number Chase chose must have been the square of a number between 40 and 60. Narrowing further, $45^2 = 2025$, so 44^2 must be less than 2000, and the least number Chase could have chosen was 2025. Additionally, $55^2 = 3025$, so 54^2 must be less than 3000, and the greatest number Chase could have chosen was 54^2. Therefore the possibilities are all perfect squares from 45^2 through 54^2, and the total count of the numbers Chase could have chosen is $54 - 45 + 1 = \boxed{10}$.

16. After Rita read 20% of the 75 pages on Friday, she had $75 \cdot (1 - 0.2) = 60$ pages remaining. After Rita read 30% of the 60 remaining pages on Saturday, the number of pages remaining was $60 \cdot (1 - 0.3) = \boxed{42}$.

17. In this rectangle, each diagonal is the hypotenuse of a right triangle with legs of length 7 and 16. By the Pythagorean Theorem, the length of each diagonal is $\sqrt{7^2 + 16^2} = \sqrt{305}$. The sum of the lengths of both diagonals is $2\sqrt{305}$, or $\sqrt{4}\sqrt{305} = \sqrt{1220}$. Because $35^2 = 1225$, the value of $\sqrt{1220}$, to the nearest whole number, is $\boxed{35}$.

18. If Quincy and Robert both doubled their money, but Samir's amount remained unchanged, at the end of one year the three would have $\$16,700 + \$500 = \$17,200$. If all three had doubled their money, at the end of one year the three would have $\$10,000 \cdot 2 = \$20,000$. The difference between $\$20,000$ and $\$17,200$ is the difference between Samir having the same amount of money and doubling his money. Thus, the amount Samir must have had initially is $\$20,000 - \$17,200 = \boxed{\$2,800}$.

19. The binomial product $(2x+1)(3y+2)$ expands to $6xy+4x+3y+2$, so $6xy+4x+3y = (2x+1)(3y+2)-2$. Then $43\diamond 27$ is $(2\cdot 43+1)(3\cdot 27+2)-2$, or $87\cdot 83-2$. This evaluates to $7221-2 = \boxed{7219}$.

20. To progress from 1 mile behind Scott to 1 mile ahead of Scott, Tony needs to move $1+1=2$ miles relative to Scott. Tony is moving at a speed of $10-7=3$ miles per hour relative to Scott, so to move 2 miles relative to Scott will require $\frac{2}{3}$ hours. In minutes, this is $\frac{2}{3}\cdot 60 = \boxed{40}$.

21. The number 4405 is a multiple of 5 and not prime. The number 4407 has digits that sum to a multiple of 3 and is therefore a multiple of 3 and not prime. The number 4411 is divisible by 11 and is not prime. And the number 4403 is equal to $7\cdot 629$. Thus the prime number must be $\boxed{4409}$.

22. There are 8 divisions with 4 teams in each division, for a total of 32 teams. Each team plays 17 games, but there are 2 teams playing each game, so the regular season has $\frac{1}{2}\cdot 32\cdot 17 = 272$ games. Finally, to eliminate all but 1 of the 14 playoff teams requires $14-1=13$ playoff games. The total number of games played is $272+13 = \boxed{285}$.

23. The number 16^{16} can be written as $\left(2^4\right)^{16} = 2^{64}$. Similarly, the number 25^{25} can be written as $\left(5^2\right)^{25} = 5^{50}$. The product of 2^{64} and 5^{50} is $2^{14}\cdot 2^{50}\cdot 5^{50} = 2^{14}\cdot 10^{50}$. Because $2^{10} = 1024$ and $2^4 = 16$, the least power of 10 that is greater than 2^{14} is 10^5. Therefore the least power of 10 that is greater than the given product is $10^5\cdot 10^{50} = \boxed{10^{55}}$.

24. Construct a segment connecting the two vertices with unknown angles. This creates a triangle exterior to the quadrilateral. One angle of this triangle measures $360°-222° = 138°$, so the other two angles of this triangle must sum to $180°-138° = 42°$. Now consider the triangle that is the original quadrilateral along with this exterior triangle. One angle of this triangle is $79°$, so the other two angles must sum to $180°-79° = 101°$. These two angles are comprised of the two angles that sum to $42°$ from the exterior triangle along with the two unknown angles of the quadrilateral. Therefore the two unknown angles of the quadrilateral must sum to $101°-42° = \boxed{59°}$.

25. Let the first number in Kim's list be a and the second number in Kim's list be b. Then the third number in the list is $a+b$, the fourth is $a+2b$, the fifth is $2a+3b$, and the sixth is $3a+5b$. If $3a+5b = 2022$, then the greatest possible value of a occurs when b is as small as possible. Additionally, since $3a$ is a multiple of 3 and 2022 is also a multiple of 3, $5b$ must be a multiple of 3. The smallest possible positive value of b for which this is true is $b = 3$. When b is 3, the value of a is $\frac{2022-5\cdot 3}{3} = \boxed{669}$.

26. The units digit of the square of a number that has a units digit of 1 or 9 is 1. The units digit of the square of a number that has a units digit of 2 or 8 is 4. The units digit of the square of a number that has a units digit of 3 or 7 is 9. The units digit of the square of a number that has a units digit of 4 or 6 is 6. The units digit of the square of a number that has a units digit of 5 is 5, and the units digit of the square of a number that has a units digit of 0 is 0. Therefore the sum of the units digits of the squares of 10 positive whole numbers greater than one multiple of 10 and less than or equal to the next multiple of 10 is $1+4+9+6+5+6+9+4+1+0$, which has a units digit of 5. Thus the sum of the first 2020 perfect squares has the same units digit of $202\cdot 5$, which is 0. The units digit of 2021^2 is 1, and the units digit of 2022^2 is 4, so the units digit of the sum of the first 2022 perfect squares is $1+4 = \boxed{5}$.

27. The small shaded triangle is similar to the entire triangle, with sides $\frac{1}{3}$ of the larger triangle, so the area of the smaller triangle is $\left(\frac{1}{3}\right)^2 = \frac{1}{9}$ of the entire triangle. The unshaded trapezoid and the small shaded triangle together form a triangle that is similar to the entire triangle, with sides $\frac{2}{3}$ of the entire triangle, so the area of the smaller triangle is $\left(\frac{2}{3}\right)^2 = \frac{4}{9}$ of the larger triangle. The area of the unshaded trapezoid is $\frac{4}{9} - \frac{1}{9} = \frac{1}{3}$ of the entire triangle, so the total shaded area is $1 - \frac{1}{3} = \frac{2}{3}$ of the entire triangle. The ratio of the unshaded area to the shaded area is $\frac{\frac{1}{3}}{\frac{2}{3}} = \boxed{\frac{1}{2}}$.

28. There are $3 \cdot 3 \cdot 3 = 27$ total possible outcomes. There are 3 ways to select the winning player, and 3 ways to select the winning player's item. Once these selections are made, the other two players must both choose the item that loses to the winning player's item. Therefore there are $3 \cdot 3 = 9$ outcomes where one player beats the other two, for a probability of $\frac{9}{27} = \boxed{\frac{1}{3}}$.

29. For exactly 4 of the squares to share a side with a square that has the same color while still using 4 different colors to color all 6 squares, there must be 2 pairs of squares that share a side and have the same color, with a different color for each pair. The remaining 2 squares must be colored with the remaining 2 colors. These two pairs can be arranged in multiple ways. If both pairs are horizontal, in a 1 row by 2 column position, the pair in the top row can have 2 positions and the pair in the bottom row can have 2 positions, for $2 \cdot 2 = 4$ possible locations for the two pairs. If both pairs are vertical, in a 2 row by 1 column position, the pairs can occupy the two leftmost columns, the two rightmost columns, or the leftmost and rightmost column, for 3 possible locations for the two pairs. If one pair is horizontal and the other is vertical, there are 2 possible locations for the vertical pair, either in the leftmost or rightmost column, and 2 possible locations for the horizontal pair, either in the top or bottom row, for $2 \cdot 2 = 4$ possible locations for the two pairs. Altogether, there are $4 + 3 + 4 = 11$ possible locations for the two pairs. Once the two pairs are placed, there are $4! = 24$ ways to choose a color for the 2 pairs and 2 single squares. Therefore the total number of ways to color the 6 squares is $11 \cdot 24 = \boxed{264}$.

30. Summing the three equations, $4x + 6y + 10z - 38 = x^2 + y^2 + z^2$. This is equivalent to $x^2 - 4x + y^2 - 6y + z^2 - 10z + 38 = 0$. Completing the square, $x^2 - 4x + 4 + y^2 - 6y + 9 + z^2 - 10z + 25 = 0$, or $(x - 2)^2 + (y - 3)^2 + (z - 5)^2 = 0$. This is only true when $x - 2$, $y - 3$, and $z - 5$ are all equal to 0, so $x = 2$, $y = 3$, and $z = 5$. The product xyz is $2 \cdot 3 \cdot 5 = \boxed{30}$.

Target Round Solutions

1. Cathy walked 6 laps on Monday, 7 on Tuesday, 8 on Wednesday, 9, on Thursday, and 10 on Friday. This is a total of $6 + 7 + 8 + 9 + 10 = 40$ laps. Since 4 laps is equal to 1 mile, this distance, in miles, is $40 \div 4 = \boxed{10}$.

2. There are $16 + 16 + 1 + 1 = 34$ sides of the squares that form the perimeter of the rectangle shown, so the side length of one of the squares is $136 \div 34 = 4$. To minimize the perimeter, the squares must be arranged into a rectangle that is a square comprised of 4 rows with 4 squares in each row. The side length of this square is $4 \times 4 = 16$, so the perimeter of this square is $16 \times 4 = \boxed{64}$.

3. Because the result must be a whole number, the single-digit number cannot be a 2 because there is no way to form an even number using the digits 3, 5, and 7. The single-digit number can also not be a 3, since any number with the digits 2, 5, and 7 has digits that sum to 14 and is therefore not divisible by 3. The single-digit number cannot be a 5 because there is no way to form a multiple of 5 using the digits 2, 3, and 7. Therefore the single-digit number must be 7. To maximize the value of the result, the three-digit number must be as large as possible. The greatest possible three-digit number using the digits 2, 3, and 5 is 532, and $532 \div 7 = \boxed{76}$.

4. In the fall, the number of fourth graders is $3k$ for some positive whole number k, and the number of fifth graders is $4k$, for the same whole number k. In the spring, the number of fourth graders is $3k+9$, and the number of fifth graders is $4k+2$. Additionally, $\frac{3k+9}{4k+2} = \frac{7}{6}$. Cross-multiplying yields $18k + 54 = 28k + 14$, and $k = 4$. The total number of fourth and fifth graders in the spring is $3k + 9 + 4k + 2 = 7k + 11$, and $7 \cdot 4 + 11 = \boxed{39}$.

5. The prime factorization of 672 is $2^5 \cdot 3^1 \cdot 7^1$. The number of divisors is therefore $(5+1)(1+1)(1+1) = 24$. However, 2 of these divisors are 1 and 672, and should not be counted, so the number of divisors greater than 1 and less than 672 is $24 - 2 = \boxed{22}$.

6. Drop an altitude from C to meet the line containing segment AB at point D. Then triangle ACD is a $30 - 60 - 90$ triangle with a hypotentuse of length 100, so leg CD has length $\frac{100}{2} = 50$ and leg AD has length $\frac{100}{2} \cdot \sqrt{3} = 50\sqrt{3}$. The area of ACD is $\frac{1}{2} \cdot 50 \cdot 50\sqrt{3} = 1250\sqrt{3}$. Triangle CBD is a $45 - 45 - 90$ triangle with legs of length 50, and has an area of $\frac{1}{2} \cdot 50 \cdot 50 = 1250$. The area of ABC is the area of ACD minus the area of CBD, or $1250\sqrt{3} - 1250 = 1250(\sqrt{3} - 1)$. To the nearest whole number, this is $\boxed{915}$.

7. If the hundreds digit is 1, then the tens digit could be any digit greater than 1. If the tens digit is a 2, the units digit could be 4, 6, or 8. If the tens digit is a 3, then the units digit could be a 6 or 9. If the tens digit is a 4, then the units digit could only be an 8. The tens digit cannot be anything greater, as there would be no possibilities for the units digit. This yields the numbers 124, 126, 128, 136, 139, and 148. If the hundreds digit is a 2, the tens digit could be a 4, 6, or 8. If the tens digit is a 4, then the units digit could only be an 8, and as before, the tens digit cannot be anything greater. This yields the number 248. The hundreds digit cannot be 3 or greater, as $3 \times 2 \times 2 = 12$, which is too large for the units digit. Thus the total count of possible numbers is $\boxed{7}$.

8. There are a total of $6^4 = 1296$ outcomes when rolling four dice. The outcomes where at least three different numbers shown can be considered in two cases. In the first case, all four dice show a different number. There are $6 \cdot 5 \cdot 4 \cdot 3 = 360$ such outcomes. In the second case, two dice show the same number, and the other two dice show a different number. There are 6 possibilities for the number that is repeated, and $\binom{5}{2} = 10$ possibilities for the two numbers that appear once. There are $\frac{4!}{2!} = 12$ ways to permute this set of 3 numbers among the four dice, so there are $6 \cdot 10 \cdot 12 = 720$ outcomes where exactly two dice show the same number. Altogether, the total number of outcomes where at least three

different numbers are shown is $720 + 360 = 1080$, for a probability of $\frac{1080}{1296} = \boxed{\dfrac{5}{6}}$.

Team Round Solutions

1. The odd multiples of 7 between 10 and 100 are 21, 35, 49, 63, 77, and 91, and $21 + 35 + 49 + 63 + 77 + 91 = \boxed{336}$.

2. If every ticket purchased was an adult ticket, the total cost would be $7 \times \$8 = \$56$. But for each ticket that is a child ticket instead of an adult ticket, the total cost is lowered by $\$8 - \$5 = \$3$. Since $\$56 - \$50 = \$6$, the number of child tickets is $\$6 \div \$3 = 2$, so the number of adult tickets is $7 - 2 = \boxed{5}$.

3. There were $2021 - 2011 + 1 = 11$ years that passed from the beginning of 2011 until the end of 2021. A period of 11 years is $11 \times 365 = 4015$ days. But since 2012, 2016, and 2020 were leap years, the total number of days that passed is $4015 + 3 = 4018$. A fortnight is 2 weeks, or 14 days, so the number of fortnights that occurred was $4018 \div 14 = \boxed{287}$.

4. When not overlapping, the total area of the 4 strips of paper, in square inches, is $4 \times 2 \times 10 = 80$. The area of the table covered by 2 strips of paper is 4 squares, each measuring 2 inches by 2 inches. This area, $4 \times 2 \times 2 = 16$, is counted twice. So the total area, in square inches, covered by the four strips is $80 - 16 = \boxed{64}$.

5. Because each selected a different number from the first 10 numbers, the only way two can sum to 18 is if one is 10 and another is 8. The only way two can sum to 17 is for another number to be 7, since $10 + 7 = 17$. Observe that $9 + 8 = 17$ is not possible, since that would also yield a sum of $10 + 9 = 19$ in the list of sums. If three of the numbers are 7, 8, and 10, the only way two can sum to 10, 11, and 13 is if the fourth number is 3. The product of 3, 7, 8, and 10 is $\boxed{1680}$.

6. As with the diagonal shown, any diagonal with endpoints separated by exactly 3 sides of the decagon will be parallel to 2 sides of the decagon. There are 10 such diagonals. Additionally, any diagonal that passes through the center of the decagon, or that is separated by exactly 5 sides of the decagon, will be parallel to 2 sides of the decagon as well. There are 5 such diagonals. Altogether, the total number of diagonals that are parallel to at least one side of the decagon is $10 + 5 = \boxed{15}$.

7. Let D be the length of the race, and let F be Fiona's speed in miles per hour. Then Ginny's speed is $F + 1$. Additionally, Fiona's time, in hours, is $\frac{66}{60} = 1.1$, and Ginny's time, in hours is $\frac{54}{60} = 0.9$. Then since distance divided by rate is time, $\frac{D}{F} = 1.1$, and $\frac{D}{F+1} = 0.9$. From the first equation, $D = 1.1 \cdot F$. Substituting into the second equation, $\frac{1.1F}{F+1} = 0.9$, or $1.1F = 0.9F + 0.9$, so $F = 4.5$. Since $F = 4.5$, D, the length of the race, in miles, is $4.5 \cdot 1.1 = \boxed{4.95}$.

8. The number 2022 can be written as $81 \cdot 25 - 3$. The expansion of $(81 \cdot 25 - 3)^{2022}$ has terms that are all multiples of 25 except for $(-3)^{2022}$. Thus only the remainder of $(-3)^{2022}$ divided by 25 needs to be determined. The value of $(-3)^{10}$ is 59049, which is 1 less than a multiple of 25, so $(-3)^{2022}$ can be written as $\left((-3)^{10}\right)^{202} \cdot (-3)^2$, or $(59050 - 1)^{202} \cdot 9$. The expansion of $(59050 - 1)^{202}$ has terms that are all multiples of 25 except for $(-1)^{202}$, and $(-1)^{202} = 1$. Therefore the remainder of 2022^{2022} is equal to $1 \cdot 9 = \boxed{9}$.

9. If the token returns to the initial square on the third move, then it cannot also return to the initial square on the fourth move, so the two outcomes are mutually exclusive. Suppose the square the token is initially placed is labeled A, and the other two squares are labeled B and C. To return to A in three moves, the token must either complete the sequence BCA or CBA. This is 2 possible sequences out of a total of $2 \cdot 2 \cdot 2 = 8$ possible three-move sequences, for a probability of $\frac{2}{8} = \frac{1}{4}$. To return to A in four moves, the token must not be at A on the third move, which occurs with probability $1 - \frac{1}{4} = \frac{3}{4}$. The token is therefore at B or C, where there is a $\frac{1}{2}$ probability the token moves to A. Therefore the probability the token returns to A in four moves is $\frac{3}{4} \cdot \frac{1}{2} = \frac{3}{8}$. The total probability the token returns to the square where it was initially placed in either three or four moves is $\frac{1}{4} + \frac{3}{8} = \boxed{\frac{5}{8}}$.

10. Let Amy's number be a and Ben's number be b. From what Amy told Charlie, $(a^2 + b) - (b^2 + a) = 202$. This can be rewritten as $(a^2 - b^2) - (a - b) = 202$, or $(a+b)(a-b) - (a-b) = 202$. This can be further factored as $(a + b - 1)(a - b) = 202$. Since a and b are whole numbers, both $a + b - 1$ and $a - b$ must be divisors of 202. The only factor pairs of 202 are 202 and 1, and 101 and 2. If $a + b - 1 = 202$ and $a - b = 1$, then $a = 102$ and $b = 101$. But a and b must be two-digit whole numbers, so $a + b - 1 = 101$ and $a - b = 2$. This system yields a solution of $a = 52$ and $b = 50$, so Amy's number was $\boxed{52}$.

Place ID Sticker
Inside This Box

Name _____

Grade _____

School _____

1. $221 - 22 =$ _____.

2. $569 + 242 =$ _____.

3. $9 + 11 \times 9 =$ _____.

4. The units digit of 72801 is _____.

5. $602 - 396 =$ _____.

6. The remainder of $117 \div 5$ is _____.

7. $24 + 53 + 56 + 26 =$ _____.

8. $7 \times 17 =$ _____.

9. The quotient of 92 divided by 4 is _____.

10. (estimate) $1506 + 2761 + 3263 =$ _____.

11. $94 \times 11 =$ _____.

12. $16^2 =$ _____.

13. The remainder of $327 \div 8$ is _____.

14. $531 - 229 - 212 =$ _____.

15. $56 \times 15 =$ _____.

16. $58 + 87 + 145 =$ _____.

17. $19 \times 5 \times 18 =$ _____.

18. *MCCCLI* in Arabic numerals is _____.

19. $1.92 \div 0.024 =$ _____.

20. (estimate) $199 \times 329 =$ _____.

21. The GCD of 28 and 52 is _____.

22. $57 \times 25 =$ _____.

23. The lesser of $\frac{7}{12}$ and $\frac{3}{5}$ is _____ (fraction).

24. $15 \times 77 \div 35 =$ _____.

25. $41 + 34 + 27 + 20 + 13 + 6 =$ _____.

26. $\frac{3}{35} + \frac{1}{7} + \frac{1}{5} =$ _____ (fraction).

27. $918 \div 34 =$ _____.

28. If 1 mile is equal to 1760 yards, then 176 yards is equal to _____ mile (fraction).

29. $31^2 =$ _____.

30. (estimate) $99 \times 9 \times 99 =$ _____.

31. $46 \times 44 =$ _____.

32. The area of a rectangle with width 9 and perimeter 42 is _____.

33. $\sqrt{784} =$ _____.

34. 2 days is _____ minutes.

35. $\frac{31}{50} =$ _____ %.

36. The LCM of 28 and 52 is _____.

37. $95^2 =$ _____.

38. The number of even whole numbers between 41 and 191 is _____.

39. $99 \times 41 =$ _____.

40. (estimate) $444 \times 629 =$ _____.

41. $39^2 - 14^2 =$ _____.

42. The fifteenth term in the arithmetic sequence $9, 20, 31, \ldots$ is _____.

43. $87 \times 27 =$ _____.

44. $18 \times 7 + 26 \times 9 =$ _____.

45. The remainder of $2986 \div 11$ is _____.

46. $101 \times 51 =$ _____.

47. 144_9 in base 10 is _____.

48. The perimeter of an isosceles triangle with sides of length 2 and 7 is _____.

49. $4^5 =$ _____.

50. (estimate) $428571 \times 9 =$ _____.

51. $105 \times 117 =$ _____.

52. The perimeter of a right triangle with a leg of length 9 and a hypotenuse of length 41 is ____.

53. 65_8 in base 2 is _____ $_2$.

54. $64 \times 111 =$ _____.

55. $36\frac{4}{11}\%$ of 143 is _____.

56. $\sqrt{6889} =$ _____.

57. The mean of the list $18, 15, 32, 11, 29$ is ____.

58. $97 \times 77 =$ _____.

59. The measure of an interior angle in a regular dodecagon is _____ $^\circ$.

60. (estimate) $938772 \div 229 =$ _____.

61. $15 \times 375 =$ _____.

62. $11\frac{2}{3} \times 1\frac{2}{3} =$ _____ (mixed number).

63. The number of different two-letter arrangements of the letters *HOWDY* is _____.

64. $0.5\overline{6} =$ _____ (fraction).

65. $12^3 =$ _____.

66. If $v = 16$, then $v^2 + 28v + 196 =$ _____.

67. $16 \times 42 \times 13 =$ _____.

68. The number 74 in base 5 is _____ $_5$.

69. $28\frac{4}{7}\% =$ _____ (fraction).

70. (estimate) $7.07^6 =$ _____.

71. $1029 \times 1031 =$ _____.

72. The sum of the terms of the infinite geometric sequence $3, -\frac{3}{2}, \frac{3}{4}, \ldots$ is _____.

73. $44 \times 15 \times 64 =$ _____.

74. The number of subsets of the set $\{Q, U, A, L, I, F, Y\}$ is _____.

75. $729^{\frac{5}{6}} =$ _____.

76. The number of positive whole number divisors of 154 is _____.

77. $\sqrt{32} \times \sqrt{162} =$ _____.

78. If $4^{x-1} = 9$, then $2^{x+1} =$ _____.

79. The volume of a cube with surface area 726 is _____.

80. (estimate) $(2.022 \times 20 \times 2.2)^2 =$ _____.

Sprint Round
12227

 Place ID Sticker
Inside This Box

Name _____

Grade _____

School _____

1. Ⓐ Ⓑ Ⓒ Ⓓ Ⓔ
2. Ⓐ Ⓑ Ⓒ Ⓓ Ⓔ
3. Ⓐ Ⓑ Ⓒ Ⓓ Ⓔ
4. Ⓐ Ⓑ Ⓒ Ⓓ Ⓔ
5. Ⓐ Ⓑ Ⓒ Ⓓ Ⓔ
6. Ⓐ Ⓑ Ⓒ Ⓓ Ⓔ
7. Ⓐ Ⓑ Ⓒ Ⓓ Ⓔ
8. Ⓐ Ⓑ Ⓒ Ⓓ Ⓔ
9. Ⓐ Ⓑ Ⓒ Ⓓ Ⓔ
10. Ⓐ Ⓑ Ⓒ Ⓓ Ⓔ

11. Ⓐ Ⓑ Ⓒ Ⓓ Ⓔ
12. Ⓐ Ⓑ Ⓒ Ⓓ Ⓔ
13. Ⓐ Ⓑ Ⓒ Ⓓ Ⓔ
14. Ⓐ Ⓑ Ⓒ Ⓓ Ⓔ
15. Ⓐ Ⓑ Ⓒ Ⓓ Ⓔ
16. Ⓐ Ⓑ Ⓒ Ⓓ Ⓔ
17. Ⓐ Ⓑ Ⓒ Ⓓ Ⓔ
18. Ⓐ Ⓑ Ⓒ Ⓓ Ⓔ
19. Ⓐ Ⓑ Ⓒ Ⓓ Ⓔ
20. Ⓐ Ⓑ Ⓒ Ⓓ Ⓔ

21. Ⓐ Ⓑ Ⓒ Ⓓ Ⓔ
22. Ⓐ Ⓑ Ⓒ Ⓓ Ⓔ
23. Ⓐ Ⓑ Ⓒ Ⓓ Ⓔ
24. Ⓐ Ⓑ Ⓒ Ⓓ Ⓔ
25. Ⓐ Ⓑ Ⓒ Ⓓ Ⓔ
26. Ⓐ Ⓑ Ⓒ Ⓓ Ⓔ
27. Ⓐ Ⓑ Ⓒ Ⓓ Ⓔ
28. Ⓐ Ⓑ Ⓒ Ⓓ Ⓔ
29. Ⓐ Ⓑ Ⓒ Ⓓ Ⓔ
30. Ⓐ Ⓑ Ⓒ Ⓓ Ⓔ

1. Annalise purchased three packages of gum at the store. Each package of gum cost $2. Annalise paid the cashier for the gum with a $10 bill. How many dollars did Annalise receive in return from the cashier?

(A) $8   (B) $6   (C) $5   (D) $4   (E) $2

2. Which of the following sums is odd?

(A) $12 + 17 + 18$ (B) $14 + 19 + 15$ (C) $14 + 10 + 18$ (D) $11 + 15 + 16$ (E) $13 + 16 + 19$

3. Kaitlyn is purchasing fruit for a large picnic. At the store, Kaitlyn bought two bags of oranges, and each bag held one dozen oranges. She bought four bunches of bananas. Three of the bunches had seven bananas and one bunch had six bananas. She also purchased two sacks of apples, and each sack held ten apples. Altogether, how many oranges, bananas, and apples did Kaitlyn purchase for her picnic?

(A) 81   (B) 62   (C) 70   (D) 71   (E) 61

4. A square and a rectangle have the same area. The side length of the square is 6, and the width of the rectangle is 4. What is the perimeter of the rectangle?

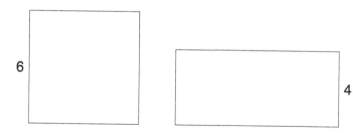

(A) 28   (B) 22   (C) 24   (D) 20   (E) 26

5. Linus chose a positive whole number. He tripled the number, and then subtracted five from that result. Then he doubled that result. The result of Linus' operations was 44. What number did Linus choose?

(A) 12   (B) 11   (C) 9   (D) 13   (E) 10

6. Evan calculated $222 \times 17 + 333 \times 17 + 444 \times 17$ and then summed the digits of the result. What was Evan's sum?

   (A) 33   (B) 27   (C) 29   (D) 36   (E) 31

7. April 1st of the year 2022 was a Friday. The month of April has 30 days. How many days in the month of April in the year 2022 were either Saturdays or Sundays?

   (A) 8   (B) 7   (C) 10   (D) 6   (E) 9

8. How many positive whole numbers less than 200 are evenly divisible by 9 but not evenly divisible by 6?

   (A) 14   (B) 10   (C) 11   (D) 22   (E) 12

9. Chip chose a number on the number line. The distance between Chip's number and 30 was twice the distance between Chip's number and 21. What is the sum of all possible numbers that Chip chose?

   (A) 36   (B) 39   (C) 24   (D) 27   (E) 12

10. The sum of three numbers is $\frac{1}{2}$. Two of the numbers are $\frac{1}{5}$ and $\frac{1}{4}$. What is the value of the second greatest of the three numbers minus the least of the three numbers?

   (A) $\frac{1}{4}$ (B) $\frac{1}{5}$ (C) $\frac{3}{20}$ (D) $\frac{1}{10}$ (E) $\frac{1}{20}$

11. George is arranging his four Transformers toys in a row on a shelf. He wants to place his Optimus Prime toy next to his Bumblebee toy, but he does not want to place his Megatron toy next to his Bumblebee toy. He does not care where his Starscream toy is placed. How many different ways can George arrange his Transformers toys?

   (A) 6   (B) 2   (C) 8   (D) 9   (E) 4

12. The corners of a smaller shaded rectangle lie on the sides of a larger rectangle, as shown below. One side of the larger rectangle is divided into lengths of 4 and 6 by one corner of the shaded rectangle, and another side of the larger rectangle is divided into lengths of 8 and 3 by another corner of the shaded rectangle. What is the area of the shaded rectangle?

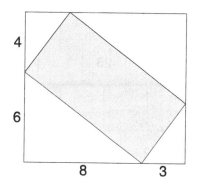

(A) 60   (B) 56   (C) 54   (D) 48   (E) 50

13. At Highville Park Middle School, the ratio of fifth grade students to sixth grade students on the Math Team was 5 : 6. After Spring Break, 4 more fifth grade students and 1 more sixth grade student joined the team, and the new ratio of fifth grade students to sixth grade students on the Math Team was 1 : 1. After the additional students joined, how many total fifth and sixth grade students were on the Math Team?

(A) 32   (B) 34   (C) 36   (D) 40   (E) 38

14. Andrew, Brandon, and Clint are friends competing against one another in swimming, running, and cycling races. Andrew finished in first place in the swimming race, and Brandon finished in second place in the running race. None of the three friends finished in the same place in more than one race. Using the letter A to represent Andrew, the letter B to represent Brandon, and the letter C to represent Clint, in what order, from first through third, did the three friends finish in the cycling race?

(A) C, B, A   (B) B, C, A   (C) C, A, B   (D) B, A, C   (E) A, B, C

15. In the number pyramid below, the number in a square is the sum of the numbers in the two squares in the row below and next to the square. For example, 8 is the sum of 5 and the number in the square marked *X*. What number belongs in the top square of the number pyramid?

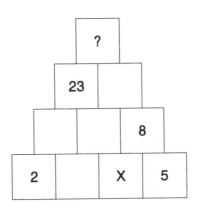

(A) 43   (B) 48   (C) 39   (D) 46   (E) 45

16. Emily is a star libero on her volleyball team. In volleyball, a match has three games. In two matches of a recent tournament, Emily averaged 11 digs per game in the first match, and in the three games of the second match, Emily had 9 digs, 14 digs, and 16 digs. How many digs per game did Emily average for the two matches?

(A) 13   (B) 12   (C) 11.5   (D) 12.5   (E) 13.5

17. In the large triangle below, one side has length 13. A segment drawn from one vertex to another side is perpendicular to that side, and partitions that side into segments of length 5 and 9. What is the perimeter of the large triangle?

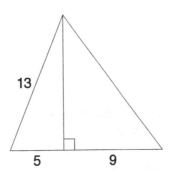

(A) 48   (B) 41   (C) 44   (D) 43   (E) 42

18. How many prime numbers are greater than 150 and less than 200?

(A) 12   (B) 11   (C) 10   (D) 13   (E) 9

19. Yesterday, Devan walked one mile of his trip from home to school and then, because he was running late, he ran the last quarter mile to school. Devan runs twice as fast as he walks, and the running portion of his trip lasted $2\frac{1}{2}$ minutes. How many total minutes was Devan's trip to school yesterday?

(A) 18   (B) 20   (C) $22\frac{1}{2}$ (D) $17\frac{1}{2}$ (E) 25

20. An artist is constructing a rectangular mosaic. The artist is using 1 inch by 1 inch square tiles, with a border of 0.25 inches around each tile, including around the outside of the outer edge of tiles. One corner of the mosaic is shown below. If the rectangular mosaic is 27 tiles wide and 17 tiles high, then what is the total area covered by the mosaic, in square inches?

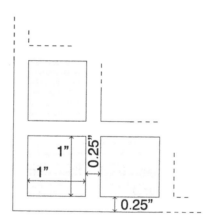

(A) $722\frac{1}{2}$ (B) 459   (C) $725\frac{5}{8}$ (D) $717\frac{3}{16}$ (E) 731

21. If $a \diamond b = 4ab + 2a + 2b + 1$, then what is the value of $126 \diamond 128$?

(A) 65001   (B) 65010   (C) 65025   (D) 65000   (E) 65021

22. A pyramid has a square base of edge length 16, and all four edges from the base to the apex, or peak, of the pyramid have length 17. What is the total surface area of the pyramid?

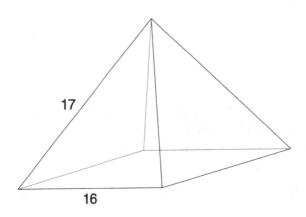

(A) 784   (B) 736   (C) 756   (D) 748   (E) 800

23. How many different arrangements of the letters *KENOBI* do not have the *K* next to the *N*, the *K* next to the *B*, or the *N* next to the *B*?

(A) 72   (B) 144   (C) 36   (D) 108   (E) 120

24. Huey chose a positive whole number in base 10. He then converted the number to base 9 and wrote it on a piece of paper. Louie saw the number on the piece of paper, and he read the digits of the number correctly, but he mistakenly read base 9 as base 7. He then converted what he thought was a base 7 number to base 10. Louie's result was 512. What number did Huey choose in base 10?

(A) 1331   (B) 512   (C) 1728   (D) 729   (E) 1000

25. How many perfect squares evenly divide 10!?

(A) 36   (B) 30   (C) 48   (D) 24   (E) 40

26. Dan is running clockwise around a track at a constant speed. His son Dave is walking slowly around the same track at a constant speed, but in a counterclockwise direction. Dan completes one lap around the track every 90 seconds, and he passes Dave every 65 seconds. How many seconds does it take Dave to complete one lap around the track?

(A) 240   (B) 234   (C) 221   (D) 231   (E) 216

27. A circle of radius 6 is inscribed in a regular hexagon. The same circle is also circumscribed about a regular hexagon. What is the area of the region within exactly one of the hexagons?

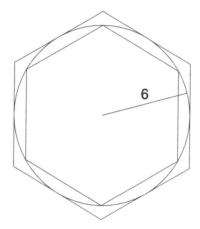

(A) $42 - 6\sqrt{3}$ (B) $24\sqrt{3}$ (C) $54 - 12\sqrt{3}$ (D) $12 + 12\sqrt{3}$ (E) $18\sqrt{3}$

28. Cassidy wrote down a list of seven positive whole numbers that formed an arithmetic sequence. The first number in Cassidy's list was 3, and the average of the last four numbers in Cassidy's list was three times the average of the first three numbers of Cassidy's list. What was the sum of the fourth and fifth numbers of Cassidy's list?

(A) 34   (B) 42   (C) 31   (D) 29   (E) 39

29. What is the value of $\sqrt{1.5 + 0.5\sqrt{5}} - 0.5\sqrt{5} + 0.5$?

(A) $\frac{5}{2}$ (B) $\sqrt{5} - 1$ (C) 1   (D) $\frac{2}{5}$ (E) $\frac{\sqrt{5}}{2}$

30. The figure below shows 100 dots arranged into ten rows and ten columns. In each row, the dots are one unit apart horizontally, and in each column, the dots are one unit apart vertically. How many different straight lines pass through the circled dot in the lower left corner of the figure and at least one other dot in the figure?

(A) 57   (B) 51   (C) 99   (D) 65   (E) 64

Place ID Sticker
Inside This Box

Name _____

Grade _____

School _____

Problems 1 & 2

1. Maddy purchased a box of Mint Thins cookies from her friend Claudia, who was selling them as a fundraiser. Inside the box of Mint Thins, the cookies were arranged in two columns. In each column, there were two packets of cookies. In each packet of cookies, there were nine cookies. If Maddy ate three cookies per day, then how many days did it take her to eat all of the cookies in her box of Mint Thins?

1.

2. Thomas chose a three-digit positive whole number. The number Thomas chose was divisible by both 7 and 11, but it had a remainder of 2 when divided by 13. What number did Thomas choose?

2.

Target Round
12227

Name _____

Grade _____

School _____

Problems 3 & 4

---

3. Captain Marbles the kitten weighed 4 pounds at the beginning of January. In the month of January, Captain Marbles gained 1 pound of weight. For each of the three months after January, Captain Marbles gained $\frac{1}{2}$ pound more of weight than he did the previous month. What was the weight of Captain Marbles, in pounds, at the end of April?

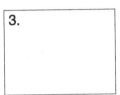

3.

4. A clock displaying a time of 2 o'clock is shown below. At how many times in the five hour period between 2 o'clock and 7 o'clock do the hour hand and minute hand of the clock form a right angle?

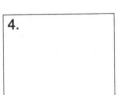

4.

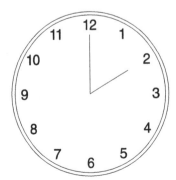

Place ID Sticker
Inside This Box

Name _____

Grade _____

School _____

Problems 5 & 6

5. A palindrome is a number that is unchanged when the order of its digits is reversed. For example, the numbers 1551 and 515 are both palindromes. Mala chose a three-digit positive whole number that was a palindrome, and Nikki chose a four-digit positive whole number that was palindrome. The difference between Nikki's number and Mala's number was 544. What was Mala's number?

5.

6. A convex polygon has exactly four interior angles that are obtuse. What is the greatest possible number of sides for the polygon?

6.

Place ID Sticker
Inside This Box

Name _____

Grade _____

School _____

Problems 7 & 8

7. What is the only four-digit perfect square with a thousands digit that is greater than or equal to the hundreds digit, a hundreds digit that is greater than or equal to the tens digit, a tens digit that is greater than or equal to the units digit, and a units digit that is greater than zero?

7.

8. When performing addition, a carry is required when the sum of the digits in the same place in each number is greater than 9. For example, when adding 15 and 16, since 5 and 6 are in the units place and $5 + 6 = 11$, a carry to the tens place is required when adding 15 and 16. How many different pairs of consecutive three-digit positive integers require no carry when adding their values? For example, 123 and 124 are one such pair, since $4 + 4 = 8$, $2 + 2 = 4$, and $1 + 1 = 2$, and $123 + 124 = 247$.

8.

School or Team

Name _____

Name _____

Name _____

Name _____

Place ID Sticker
Inside This Box

Place ID Sticker
Inside This Box

Place ID Sticker
Inside This Box

Place ID Sticker
Inside This Box

1.	2.	3.	4.	5.
6.	7.	8.	9.	10.

1. Mikey took a road trip with his family for Spring Break. Mikey and his family drove from their home in Houston to visit Mikey's aunt in Dallas, a distance of 246 miles. From Dallas, Mikey and his family drove to Little Rock to visit Mikey's grandmother, a distance of 324 miles. From Little Rock, Mikey and his family drove home to Houston. But Mikey and his family took a more direct route home, and the distance traveled was 131 miles shorter than the total distance they traveled from Houston to Dallas and then Dallas to Little Rock. How many total miles did Mikey and his family travel on their Spring Break road trip?

2. Wright wrote all of the whole numbers from 1 through 50. How many of the numbers Wright wrote contained either the digit 2 or the digit 3?

3. In the addition problem below, each letter represents a different digit. What is the greatest possible sum of the values of the digits represented by A, B, and C?

$$\begin{array}{r} A\ B \\ +\ A\ B \\ \hline C\ A \end{array}$$

4. The figure below shows a triangle partitioned into a number of smaller triangles. How many different triangles can be drawn by tracing some or all of the figure?

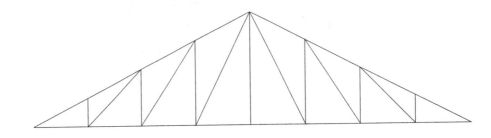

5. In the country of Primeland, coins have values of either 23 cents or 29 cents. What is the greatest whole number of cents less than 200 cents that a citizen of Primeland could make using an unlimited supply of these coins?

6. Elizabeth and her mother have the same birthday. The age of Elizabeth's mother is four times the age of Elizabeth. Four years ago, the age of Elizabeth's mother was seven times the age of Elizabeth. In how many years will the age of Elizabeth's mother be twice the age of Elizabeth?

7. Rhonda rolled two standard dice. She looked at the result and told Samuel that the sum of the numbers shown on the dice was at least 8. With this information, Samuel calculated the probability that at least one of the dice showed a 4. What probability did Samuel calculate? Express your answer as a common fraction.

8. Jalen and Jason each picked a positive whole number less than 50. The greatest common divisor of Jalen's number and Jason's number was 6. How many different pairs of numbers could Jalen and Jason have picked? For example, Jalen picking 12 and Jason picking 18 is one such pair, and Jalen picking 18 and Jason picking 12 is another such pair.

9. As shown below, a triangle with sides of length 45, 28, and 53 shares one of its vertices with the vertex of a square, and the other two vertices of the triangle lie on sides of the square. To the nearest whole number, what is the area of the square?

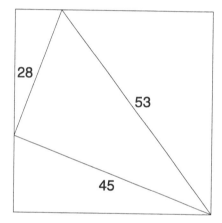

10. In Pascal's triangle, the value of a number is the sum of the number above it just to the left and the number above it just to the right. The first few rows of Pascal's triangle are shown below. The top row is row 0. On what row number of Pascal's Triangle do three consecutive numbers appear that are in the ratio 2 : 3 : 4?

Row 0						1					
Row 1					1		1				
Row 2				1		2		1			
Row 3			1		3		3		1		
Row 4		1		4		6		4		1	
Row 5	1		5		10		10		5		1

Sprint Round

1. D	11. C	21. E
2. A	12. E	22. B
3. D	13. E	23. B
4. E	14. D	24. E
5. C	15. A	25. B
6. B	16. B	26. B
7. E	17. E	27. E
8. C	18. B	28. A
9. A	19. C	29. C
10. C	20. E	30. A

Target Round

1. 12
2. 847
3. 11
4. 9
5. 787
6. 7
7. 7744
8. 124

Team Round

1. 1009
2. 26
3. 20
4. 30
5. 197
6. 16
7. $\frac{1}{3}$
8. 43
9. 1772
10. 34

Number Sense

1. 199	21. 4	41. 1325	61. 5625
2. 811	22. 1425	42. 163	62. $19\frac{4}{9}$
3. 108	23. $\frac{7}{12}$	43. 2349	63. 20
4. 1	24. 33	44. 360	64. $\frac{17}{30}$
5. 206	25. 141	45. 5	65. 1728
6. 2	26. $\frac{3}{7}$	46. 5151	66. 900
7. 159	27. 27	47. 121	67. 8736
8. 119	28. $\frac{1}{10}$	48. 16	68. 244
9. 23	29. 961	49. 1024	69. $\frac{2}{7}$
10. [7154, 7906]	30. [83799, 92619]	50. [3664283, 4049995]	70. [118643, 131131]
11. 1034	31. 2024	51. 12285	71. 1060899
12. 256	32. 108	52. 90	72. 2
13. 7	33. 28	53. 110101	73. 42240
14. 90	34. 2880	54. 7104	74. 128
15. 840	35. 62	55. 52	75. 243
16. 290	36. 364	56. 83	76. 8
17. 1710	37. 9025	57. 21	77. 72
18. 1351	38. 75	58. 7469	78. 12
19. 80	39. 4059	59. 150	79. 1331
20. [62198, 68744]	40. [265313, 293239]	60. [3895, 4304]	80. [7520, 8311]

Sprint Round Solutions

1. The total cost of 3 packages of gum is $3 \times \$2 = \$6$. When paying with a \$10 bill, the number of dollars received in return is $\$10 - \$6 = \boxed{\$4}$.

2. Each of the sums includes three whole numbers. If the sum of three whole numbers is odd, then either all three numbers must be odd, or two numbers must be even and the third must be odd. There is no answer choice where all three numbers are odd, and the only answer choice where two numbers are even and the third is odd is $\boxed{12 + 17 + 18}$.

3. The total number of oranges was $2 \times 12 = 24$, the total number of bananas was $3 \times 7 + 6 = 27$, and the total number of apples was $2 \times 10 = 20$. Altogether, the total number of oranges, bananas, and apples Kaitlyn purchased was $24 + 27 + 20 = \boxed{71}$.

4. The area of the square is $6 \times 6 = 36$. Since the rectangle has the same area, the length of the rectangle is $36 \div 4 = 9$. The perimeter of the rectangle is $9 + 9 + 4 + 4 = \boxed{26}$.

5. Before the doubling, the result was $44 \div 2 = 22$. Before subtracting 5, the result was $22 + 5 = 27$. And before the tripling, Linus' original number was $27 \div 3 = \boxed{9}$.

6. Evan's expression is equivalent to $(222 + 333 + 444) \times 17$, or 999×17. This is $17 \times 1000 - 17 \times 1$, or $17000 - 17 = 16983$, and $1 + 6 + 9 + 8 + 3 = \boxed{27}$.

7. The days of the month that were Saturdays were 2, 9, 16, 23, and 30, for a total of 5 Saturdays. The days of the month that were Sundays were 3, 10, 17, and 24, for a total of 4 Sundays. Altogether, the total number of days that were either Saturdays or Sundays was $4 + 5 = \boxed{9}$.

8. Since $6 = 3 \times 2$ and $9 = 3 \times 3$, for a number to be divisible by 9 and not divisible by 6, the number must be an odd multiple of 9. $200 \div 9$ is a little more than 22, so there are 22 multiples of 9 less than 200. Half of these are odd, so the count of numbers less than 200 that are divisible by 9 but not 6 is $22 \div 2 = \boxed{11}$.

9. There are two possibilities. The first possibility is that the number is between 21 and 30. Then the distance from 21 to 30, which is $30 - 21 = 9$, is split into two segments by Chip's number, with one segment twice as long as the other. Therefore the distance from Chip's number to 21 must be $9 \div 3 = 3$, which means Chip's number is $21 + 3 = 24$. The second possibility is that the number is less than 21. The distance of this number from 30 is always 9 more than the distance from 21, so for the distance from 30 to be twice the distance from 21, the distance from 21 must be 9, and Chip's number must be $21 - 9 = 12$. The sum of the two possible values for Chip's number is $12 + 24 = \boxed{36}$.

10. The sum of $\frac{1}{5}$ and $\frac{1}{4}$ is $\frac{4}{20} + \frac{5}{20} = \frac{9}{20}$, so the value of the third number is $\frac{1}{2} - \frac{9}{20}$, or $\frac{10}{20} - \frac{9}{20} = \frac{1}{20}$. The second greatest of $\frac{1}{4}$, $\frac{1}{5}$, and $\frac{1}{20}$ is $\frac{1}{5}$, and the least is $\frac{1}{20}$. The value of the second greatest minus the least is $\frac{1}{5} - \frac{1}{20} = \frac{4}{20} - \frac{1}{20} = \boxed{\frac{3}{20}}$.

11. Let Optimus Prime be represented by O, Bumblebee by B, Megatron by M, and Starscream by S. Consider where Bumblebee is placed. If Bumblebee is in the leftmost position, then Optimus must be next, so the only possibilities are $BOMS$ and $BOSM$, for 2 possibilities. Similarly, if Bumblebee is in the rightmost position, the only possibilities are $SMOB$ and $MSOB$, for 2 possibilities. If Bumblebee is in the second leftmost position, the only possibilities are $OBSM$ and $SBOM$, for 2 possibilities. Similarly, if Bumblebee is in the second rightmost position, the only possibilities are $MOBS$ and $MSBO$, for 2 possibilities. Altogether, the total number of possible arrangements is $2 + 2 + 2 + 2 = \boxed{8}$.

12. The dimensions of the large rectangle are $4 + 6 = 10$ and $8 + 3 = 11$, so the area of the large rectangle is $10 \cdot 11 = 110$. The unshaded area of the large rectangle is two small right triangles, each with legs of length 3 and 4, having a total area of $3 \cdot 4 = 12$, and two large right triangles, each with legs of length 6 and 8, having a total area of $6 \cdot 8 = 48$. The area of the shaded rectangle is $110 - 12 - 48 = \boxed{50}$.

13. A ratio of $1 : 1$ means the number of fifth grade was equal to the number of sixth grade students. Because 4 fifth grade and 1 sixth grade student joined the team to make the ratio $1 : 1$, prior to these students joining there must have been 3 more sixth grade students than fifth grade students. Two numbers that are in the ratio of $5 : 6$ with a difference of 3 are 15 and 18. After the students join, the number of fifth and sixth grade students is $15 + 4$ and $18 + 1$, for a total of $19 + 19 = \boxed{38}$.

14. In the swimming race, Andrew finished in first place, and Brandon could not have finished in second place, since he finished in second place in the running race and did not finish in the same place in more than one race. Therefore Clint finished second place in the swimming race and Brandon finished in third place in the swimming race. In the cycling race, Brandon could not finish in third place, since he finished in third place in the swimming race, and he could not finish in second place, since he finished in second place in the running race. Therefore Brandon finished in first place in the cycling race. Clint could not finish in second place in the cycling race since he finished in second place in the swimming race. Therefore Clint finished in third place in the cycling race, and Andrew finished in second place in the cycling race, so the order of finish was $\boxed{B, A, C}$.

15. The value of X is $8 - 5 = 3$. The value of the square with 23 is equal to the sum of the 2 and the 3 from the bottom row, plus twice the value of the unknown square from the bottom row, as this number is included in the sum for each of the squares immediately below the 23. Therefore the value of the unknown square on the bottom row is $(23 - 2 - 3) \div 2 = 9$. The value of the middle square in the next-to-bottom row is $9 + 3 = 12$, and the value of the rightmost square in the next-to-top row is $12 + 8 = 20$. Finally, the value of the top square is $23 + 20 = \boxed{43}$.

16. There were 3 games in the first match, so the sum of Emily's digs for the first match is $11 \cdot 3 = 33$. In the second match, Emily had an additional $9 + 14 + 16 = 39$ digs, so her total number of digs for the two matches was $33 + 39 = 72$. She played a total of 6 games, so her average number of digs per game is $\frac{72}{6} = \boxed{12}$.

17. The perpendicular segment is the longer leg of a right triangle with a hypotenuse of length 13 and a shorter leg of length 5. By the Pythagorean Theorem, the length of this perpendicular segment is $\sqrt{13^2 - 5^2} = 12$. The side of the large triangle with an unknown length is the hypotenuse of a right triangle with legs of length 12 and 9. By the Pythagorean Theorem, the length of this side is $\sqrt{12^2 + 9^2} = 15$, and the perimeter of the large triangle is $13 + 5 + 9 + 15 = \boxed{42}$.

18. Because $\sqrt{200}$ is a little less than 14, the only primes that can possibly divide a composite number less than 200 are 2, 3, 5, 7, 11, and 13. The multiples of 2 are all even numbers, so those cannot be prime. The multiples of 5 include all numbers with a units digit of 5, so those cannot be prime. The multiples of 3 are all numbers with digits that sum to a multiple of 3. This condition eliminates 153, 159, 171, 177, 183, and 189. Not being a multiple of 7 eliminates 161. Not being a multiple of 11 eliminates 187. Not being a multiple of 13 eliminates 169. This leaves 151, 157, 163, 167, 173, 179, 181, 191, 193, 197, and 199, for a total of $\boxed{11}$.

19. Devan runs twice as fast as he walks, so walking any distance takes twice as much time as running. Had Devan walked the last $\frac{1}{4}$ mile, it would have taken him $2 \cdot 2\frac{1}{2} = 5$ minutes. Since Devan can walk $\frac{1}{4}$ mile in 5 minutes, he can walk 1 mile in $5 \cdot 4 = 20$ minutes. Thus the length of his trip to school, in minutes, was $2\frac{1}{2} + 20 = \boxed{22\frac{1}{2}}$.

20. Since there is a border on all four edges of the the mosaic, there are $27 + 1 = 28$ borders of 0.25 inches added to the width, for a total horizontal width of $27 + 28 \cdot 0.25 = 34$. Similarly, there are $17 + 1 = 18$ borders of 0.25 inches added to the height, for a total height of $17 + 18 \times 0.25 = 21.5$. The total area covered by the mosaic, in square inches, is 34×21.5, which is $17 \times 43 = \boxed{731}$.

21. The expression $4ab + 2a + 2b + 1$ can be factored as $(2a + 1)(2b + 1)$, so $126 \diamond 128 = (2 \cdot 126 + 1)(2 \cdot 128 + 1)$, or $253 \cdot 257$. This is equivalent to $250^2 + 3 \cdot 250 + 7 \cdot 250 + 3 \cdot 7 = 250 \cdot 260 + 21$, or $\boxed{65021}$.

22. The area of the base of the pyramid is $16^2 = 256$. Each triangular face of the pyramid is an isosceles triangle with two sides of length 17 and one side of length 16. Dropping an altitude from the vertex where the two equal sides of length 17 meet to the side of length 16 partitions the isosceles triangle into two congruent right triangles, each with a hypotenuse of length 17 and a leg of length $\frac{16}{2} = 8$. By the Pythagorean Theorem, the length of the second leg, which is also the length of the altitude of the isosceles triangle, is $\sqrt{17^2 - 8^2} = 15$. Therefore each of the four triangular faces of the pyramid has area $\frac{1}{2} \cdot 16 \cdot 15 = 120$, and the total surface area of the pyramid is $120 \cdot 4 + 256 = \boxed{736}$.

23. Let X be the location of a K, N, or B, and _ be the location of any other letter. Any arrangement not having a K next to a N, a K next to a B, and a N next to a B must be of the form $X\_X\_X\_$, $X\_X\_\_X$, $X\_\_X\_X$, or $\_X\_X\_X$. Altogether, this is 4 possible forms. Within each form, there are $3! = 6$ ways to position the K, N, and B, and $3! = 6$ ways to position the remaining letters. Therefore the total number of possible arrangements is $4 \cdot 6 \cdot 6 = \boxed{144}$.

24. The number 512 is 8^3, or the cube of 11_7. The cube of 11_7 is $(110_7 + 11_7) \cdot 11_7$, or $121_7 \cdot 11_7$. This is $1210_7 + 121_7 = 1331_7$. Huey's number in base 9 was 1331_9. This could be converted directly, but it is also the cube of 11_9, or 10. Therefore Huey's number was $10^3 = \boxed{1000}$.

25. The number 10! is $10 \cdot 9 \cdot 8 \cdot 7 \cdot 6 \cdot 5 \cdot 4 \cdot 3 \cdot 2 \cdot 1$. As a prime factorization, this is $2^8 \cdot 3^4 \cdot 5^2 \cdot 7$. For a divisor to be a perfect square, the divisor must have a prime factorization with exponents that are all even. Therefore it must have a prime factor of 2 with an exponent of 0, 2, 4, 6, or 8, for 5 possibilities. It must have a prime factor of 3 with an exponent of 0, 2, or 4, for 3 possibilities, and it must have an prime factor of 5 with an exponent of 0 or 2, for 2 possibilities. The total number of divisors of 10! that are perfect squares is $5 \cdot 3 \cdot 2 = \boxed{30}$.

26. Each time Dan passes Dave, the father and son have, together, completed 1 lap around the track. In 65 seconds, Dan completes $\frac{65}{90} = \frac{13}{18}$ of a lap. Therefore Dave must complete $1 - \frac{13}{18} = \frac{5}{18}$ of a lap in 65 seconds. If Dave completes $\frac{5}{18}$ of a lap in 65 seconds, then his time to complete 1 lap is $65 \div \frac{5}{18} = 13 \cdot 18$, which is $\boxed{234}$.

27. The larger hexagon is comprised of six equilateral triangles with altitudes of length 6. The side lengths of each of these equilateral triangles is $\frac{6}{\sqrt{3}} \cdot 2 = 4\sqrt{3}$. The smaller hexagon is comprised of six equilateral triangles with sides of length 6. The area of an equilateral triangle with side length s is $\frac{s^2 \cdot \sqrt{3}}{4}$. The area of the larger hexagon is $6 \cdot \frac{(4\sqrt{3})^2 \cdot \sqrt{3}}{4}$, and the area of the smaller hexagon is $6 \cdot \frac{6^2 \cdot \sqrt{3}}{4}$. The area region within exactly one of the hexagons is the difference between these two values, or $\frac{6}{4} \cdot \sqrt{3} \cdot \left((4\sqrt{3})^2 - 6^2\right) = \frac{3}{2} \cdot \sqrt{3} \cdot (48 - 36)$, which is $\boxed{18\sqrt{3}}$.

28. Since the numbers in the list form an arithmetic sequence and the first number is 3, the remaining six numbers can be expressed as $3+k$, $3+2k$, $3+3k$, $3+4k$, $3+5k$, and $3+6k$. The sum of the first three numbers is $9 + 3k$, so the average is $3 + k$, and the sum of the last four numbers is $12 + 18k$, so the average is $3 + \frac{9}{2}k$. Because the latter average is three times the former average, $3 \cdot (3+k) = 3 + \frac{9}{2}k$, and $6 = \frac{3}{2}k$, so $k = 4$. Then the fourth number is $3 + 3 \cdot 4 = 15$ and the fifth number is $15 + 4 = 19$, and their sum is $15 + 19 = \boxed{34}$.

29. Multiplying the entire expression by 2 yields $2 \cdot \sqrt{1.5 + 0.5\sqrt{5}} - \sqrt{5} + 1$, or $\sqrt{6 + 2\sqrt{5}} - \sqrt{5} + 1$. Considering only $\sqrt{6 + 2\sqrt{5}}$, suppose this is equal to $\sqrt{a} + \sqrt{b}$ for some positive whole numbers a and b. Then, squaring, $6 + 2\sqrt{5} = a + b + 2\sqrt{ab}$. The right side is equivalent to the left side if either of a or b equals 5 and the other is 1, so $\sqrt{6 + 2\sqrt{5}} = \sqrt{1} + \sqrt{5}$, or $1 + \sqrt{5}$. Substuting back into the original expression yields $1 + \sqrt{5} - \sqrt{5} + 1 = 2$. Since the original expression was multiplied by 2, this is twice the original value, which is $\boxed{1}$.

30. A line is unique if the ratio of the vertical distance from the lower left dot to the horizontal distance from the lower left dot is unique. The ratio is unique if, when expressed as a fraction, it cannot be reduced. The vertical distance may be any value from 0 through 9, and the horizontal distance may also be any value from 0 through 9. Consider the lines with such a positive ratio less than 1. There is 1 such ratio with a denominator of 2, 2 such ratios with a denominator of 3, and an additional 2 such ratios with a denominator of 4. There are 4 with a denominator of 5, 2 with a denominator of 6, and 6 with a denominator of 7. Finally, there are 4 with a denominator of 8 and 6 with a denominator of 9. This is a total of $1 + 2 + 2 + 4 + 2 + 6 + 4 + 6 = 27$ lines. By symmetry, there are an equal number of lines with such a ratio greater than 1. Additionally, there is a horizontal line, a vertical line, and a line along the diagonal of the grid. Therefore the total number of unique lines is $27 \cdot 2 + 1 + 1 + 1 = \boxed{57}$.

Target Round Solutions

1. There are 9 cookies in a packet, 2 packets per column, and 2 columns per box. The total number of cookies in the box is $2 \times 2 \times 9 = 36$. If Maddy ate 3 cookies per day, then the number of days it took her eat all of the cookies in the box was $36 \div 3 = \boxed{12}$.

2. Any number that is a multiple of both 7 and 11 must be a multiple of $7 \times 11 = 77$. Any number that has a remainder of 2 when divided by 13 is $13 - 2 = 11$ less than a multiple of 13. Because 77 is 1 less than a multiple of 13, $77 \times 11 = 847$ is 11 less than a multiple of 13, so the number that Thomas chose was $\boxed{847}$.

3. At end of January, Captain Marbles weighed $4 + 1 = 5$ pounds. In February, Captain Marbles gained $1 + \frac{1}{2} = 1\frac{1}{2}$ pounds, so his weight at the end of February was $5 + 1\frac{1}{2} = 6\frac{1}{2}$ pounds. In March, Captain Marbles gained $1\frac{1}{2} + \frac{1}{2} = 2$ pounds, so his weight at the end of March was $6\frac{1}{2} + 2 = 8\frac{1}{2}$ pounds. In April, Captain Marbles gained $2 + \frac{1}{2} = 2\frac{1}{2}$ pounds, so his weight at the end of April, in pounds, was $8\frac{1}{2} + 2\frac{1}{2} = \boxed{11}$.

4. The hour hand and minute hand form a right angle when the minute hand is either $90°$ counterclockwise from the hour hand, or the minute hand is $90°$ clockwise from the hour hand. In the 2 o'clock hour, the minute hand will never be $90°$ counterclockwise from the hour hand, but it will be $90°$ clockwise from the hour hand, for 1 right angle formed. This will occur at a time shortly after $2 : 25$. In the 3 o'clock hour, the minute hand will be $90°$ behind the hour hand at exactly 3 o'clock, and be $90°$ ahead later in the hour, at a time shortly after $3 : 30$, for 2 right angles. In the 4 o'clock, 5 o'clock, and 6 o'clock hours, 2 right angles are formed for each hour. The total number of right angles formed is $1 + 2 \cdot 4 = \boxed{9}$.

5. For the two palindromes to differ by less than 1000, the four-digit palindrome must be between 1000 and 2000, so both the thousands digit and units digit of the four-digit palindrome are 1. If the four-digit palindrome has a units digit of 1, and the difference with the three-digit palindrome is 544, then the three-digit palindrome must have a units digit of $11 - 4 = 7$. This is also the hundreds digit of the three-digit palindrome. Thus the four-digit palindrome is of the form $1AA1$, where A is a digit, and the three-digit palindrome is of the form $7B7$, where B is a digit. Since $544 + 707$ is greater than 1221, and $544 + 797$ is less than 1441, the four-digit palindrome must be 1331, so the value of the three-digit palindrome, Mala's number, is $1331 - 544 = \boxed{787}$.

6. The sum of the exterior angles of any convex polygon is $360°$. If an interior angle at a vertex is not obtuse, then it is acute or right, and the exterior angle at that vertex must be greater than or equal to $90°$. If 4 exterior angles are greater than or equal to $90°$, then, after including the acute exterior angles at the four given vertices, the sum of the exterior angles would be greater than $360°$. Therefore the greatest number of exterior angles that can be greater than or equal to $90°$, and therefore interior angles less than or equal to $90°$, is 3, so there are at most 3 other vertices, and the greatest possible value for the number of sides is $4 + 3 = \boxed{7}$.

7. Since $32^2 = 1024$ and $99^2 = 9801$, any four-digit perfect square must be the square of a number greater than or equal to 32 and less than or equal to 99. Given the conditions, the units digit should be as small as possible and the thousands digit should be as large as possible. The only way to have a units digit of 1 is to square a number with a units digit of 1 or 9. Checking 39, 41, 49, 51, 59, 61, 69, 71, 79, 81, 89, 91, and 99, none meet the given conditions. The next smallest possible value of the units digit of a square is 4, which can only occur when squaring a number with a units digit of 2 or 8. However, if the units digit is a 4, then the thousands digit must be at least 4, eliminating squares of numbers less than $\sqrt{4000} \approx 63$. Checking 68, 72, 78, 82, and 88, the value of 88^2 is 7744. Therefore, the only four-digit perfect square with digits that meet the stated conditions must be $\boxed{7744}$.

8. The hundreds digit of the smaller number must be 1, 2, 3, or 4, since adding any two numbers greater than or equal to 500 requires a carry. Similarly, the tens digit of the smaller number must be 0, 1, 2, 3, or 4, or the tens and units digits of the smaller number together must be 99. Finally, the units digit of the smaller number must be 0, 1, 2, 3, 4, or 9. Counting the possibilities for the smaller number when no digit is a 9, there are 4 possibilities for the hundreds digit, 5 for the tens digit, and 5 for the units digit, for $4 \cdot 5 \cdot 5 = 100$ possibilities. Counting the possibilities for the smaller number when the tens and units digits are 99, there are 4 possibilities, namely 199, 299, 399, and 499. Counting the possibilities for the smaller number when only the units digit is a 9, there are 4 possibilities for the hundreds digit and 5 possibilities for the tens digit, for 20 possibilities. Therefore the total number of possible pairs is $100 + 4 + 20 = \boxed{124}$.

Team Round Solutions

1. The distance traveled from Houston to Dallas and then Dallas to Little Rock was $246 + 324 = 570$ miles. The distance from Little Rock to Houston, however, was $570 - 131 = 439$ miles. The total distance traveled, in miles, was $570 + 439 = \boxed{1009}$.

2. The digit 2 occurred in 10 numbers from 20 through 29, and also occurred in the numbers 2, 12, 32, and 42, for a total of 14. Because 32 was already counted, the digit 3 occurred in 9 uncounted numbers from 30 through 39, and also occurred in the uncounted numbers 3, 13, and 43, for a total of 12. Altogether, the total number of numbers that contain either the digit 2 or the digit 3 is $14 + 12 = \boxed{26}$.

3. Because $B + B$ sums to A in the units digit, the value of A must be even. But the sum of A and A in the tens digit must be less than 10, as there is no hundreds digit, so the greatest possible value of A is 4. This will also maximize C, since C is either $A + A$ or, if there is a carry from the units digit, $A + A + 1$. There are two possible values of B that produce a value of A that is 4. The first is $B = 2$. This yields $42 + 42 = 84$. The second is $B = 7$. This yields $47 + 47 = 94$. The second produces the greatest possible sum of A, B, and C, which is $4 + 7 + 9 = \boxed{20}$.

4. The entire triangle is partitioned into 14 smaller triangles. Using exactly 2 of the small triangles, there are 3 triangles that exist, one on the left side of the figure, one on the right side of the figure, and one in the middle of the figure. Using exactly 3, 4, 5, 6, 7, or 8 of the triangles, there are 2 of each, one on the left side of the figure and one on the right side of the figure. This accounts for $6 \cdot 2 = 12$ triangles. There is also 1 largest triangle formed by all of the small triangles. Altogether, the total number of triangles is $14 + 3 + 12 + 1 = \boxed{30}$.

5. Because $29 \times 7 = 203$, the greatest number of 29 cent coins that could be used is 6. If 6 coins worth 29 cents are used, they have a value of $6 \times 29 = 174$, and 1 coin worth 23 cents could be added to bring the total to 197 cents. If only 5 are used, then the value is $29 \times 5 = 145$, and only 2 of the coins worth 23 cents could be added to bring the total to $145 + 2 \times 23 = 191$ cents. If only 4 are used, then the value is $29 \times 4 = 116$, and only 3 of the coins worth 23 cents could be added to bring the total to $116 + 3 \times 23 = 185$. If only 3 are used, then the value is $29 \times 3 = 87$, and only 4 of the coins worth 23 cents could be added to bring the total to $87 + 4 \times 23 = 179$. If only 2 are used, then the value is $29 \times 2 = 58$, and only 6 of the coins worth 23 cents could be added to bring the total to $58 + 6 \times 23 = 196$. If only 1 is used, then the value is $29 \times 1 = 29$, and only 7 of the coins worth 23 cents could be added to bring the total to $29 + 7 \times 23 = 190$. Finally, if none are used, then the greatest total could be $23 \times 8 = 184$ cents. The greatest whole number of cents less than 200 cents that is possible using these coins is therefore $\boxed{197}$.

6. Let Elizabeth's current age be E. Then Elizabeth's mother's current age is $4E$. Four years ago, Elizabeth's age was $E - 4$, and Elizabeth's mother's age was $4E - 4$. But since Elizabeth's mother's age was 7 times Elizabeth's age four years ago, $7 \cdot (E - 4) = 4E - 4$, or $3E = 24$, and $E = 8$. Then Elizabeth's mother's current age is $4 \cdot 8 = 32$. Since Elizabeth is always $32 - 8 = 24$ years younger than her mother, Elizabeth's mother will be twice the age of Elizabeth when Elizabeth is 24. The number of years from now that this will occur is $24 - 8 = \boxed{16}$.

7. When rolling two standard dice, the number of ways to have a sum of 8 is 5, a sum of 9 is 4, a sum of 10 is 3, a sum of 11 is 2, and a sum of 12 is 1. Therefore the dice show one of $5 + 4 + 3 + 2 + 1 = 15$ outcomes. Of these, the outcomes $(4, 4)$, $(4, 5)$, $(5, 4)$, $(4, 6)$ and $(6, 4)$ include at least one 4. There are 5 such outcomes, for a probability of $\frac{5}{15} = \boxed{\dfrac{1}{3}}$.

8. If the lesser of the two numbers was 6, then the other number could be any multiple of 6 less than 50, for 8 possibilities. If the lesser of the two numbers was 12, then the other number could be any odd multiple of 6, for 3 possibilities. If the lesser of the two numbers was 18, then the other number could be any multiple of 6 other than 36, for 4 possibilities. If the lesser of the two numbers was 24, then the other number could be any odd multiple of 6, for 2 possibilities. If the lesser number was 30, then the other number could be any multiple of 6, for 3 possibilities. Finally, if the lesser number was 36, then the other number could be 42, for 1 possibility, and if the lesser number was 42, then the other number could be 48, for 1 possibility. Altogether, the number of possible pairs is $8 + 3 + 4 + 2 + 3 + 1 + 1 = 22$ pairs. However, Jalen could have either the greater or lesser number, except for the pair where both Jalen and Jason pick the number 6. Therefore the total number of different pairs is $22 \cdot 2 - 1 = \boxed{43}$.

9. Because $28^2 + 45^2 = 53^2$, the triangle is a right triangle. Additionally, the right triangle with a right angle at the lower left corner of the square and a hypotenuse of length 45 is similar to the right triangle with a right angle at the upper left corner of the square and a hypotenuse of length 28. Let the length of a side of the square be x. This is the longer leg of the right triangle with a hypotenuse of length 45. The longer leg of the right triangle with a hypotenuse of length 28 is $\frac{28}{45}x$. But this longer leg plus the shorter leg of the right triangle with the hypotenuse of length 45 are the side of the square, so the shorter leg of the right triangle with the hypotenuse of length 45 is $x - \frac{28}{45}x = \frac{17}{45}x$. By the Pythagorean Theorem, $\left(\frac{17}{45}x\right)^2 + x^2 = 45^2$. This is approximately $1.1427x^2 = 2025$. Then x^2, or the area of the square, is $\frac{2025}{1.1427}$, which to the nearest whole number is $\boxed{1772}$.

10. If the leftmost number of row n of Pascal's Triangle is called the $0th$ number in that row, then the kth number in the nth row is $\binom{n}{k}$. Let $\binom{n}{k}$ be the middle number of the three consecutive numbers in the ratio $2 : 3 : 4$. Then $\frac{3}{2} \cdot \binom{n}{k-1} = \binom{n}{k}$, and $\frac{4}{3} \cdot \binom{n}{k} = \binom{n}{k+1}$. The first equation becomes $\frac{3}{2} \cdot \frac{n!}{(k-1)! \cdot (n-(k-1))!} = \frac{n!}{k! \cdot (n-k)!}$, or $3 \cdot k! \cdot (n-k)! = 2 \cdot (k-1)! \cdot (n-(k-1))!$. This is $3 \cdot k = 2 \cdot (n-k+1)$, or $n = \frac{5}{2}k - 1$. The second equation becomes $\frac{n!}{k! \cdot (n-k)!} = \frac{3}{4} \cdot \frac{n!}{(k+1)! \cdot (n-(k+1))!}$, or $4 \cdot (k+1)! \cdot (n-(k+1))! = 3 \cdot k! \cdot (n-k)!$. This is $4 \cdot (k+1) = 3 \cdot (n-k)$. Substituting $n = \frac{5}{2}k - 1$ for n yields $4 \cdot (k+1) = 3 \cdot (\frac{5}{2}k - 1 - k)$, and $k = 14$, so n is $\frac{5}{2} \cdot 14 - 1 = \boxed{34}$.

Number Sense
12228

Place ID Sticker
Inside This Box

Name _____

Grade _____

School _____

1. $212 + 21 - 12 =$ _____.

2. The units digit of 942478 is _____.

3. $376 + 245 =$ _____.

4. $422 - 243 =$ _____.

5. The remainder of $166 \div 4$ is _____.

6. $9 + 12 \times 9 =$ _____.

7. $32 + 32 + 48 + 49 =$ _____.

8. The quotient of 119 divided by 7 is _____.

9. $30 \times 19 =$ _____.

10. (estimate) $2409 + 1314 + 2847 =$ _____.

11. $19^2 =$ _____.

12. $616 - 224 - 225 =$ _____.

13. The remainder of $174 \div 9$ is _____.

14. $82 \times 11 =$ _____.

15. $155 + 93 + 62 =$ _____.

16. $1.82 \div 0.013 =$ _____.

17. $35 \times 38 =$ _____.

18. *MMXXII* in Arabic numerals is _____.

19. $18 \times 19 \times 5 =$ _____.

20. (estimate) $249 \times 601 =$ _____.

21. $15 \times 42 \div 30 =$ _____.

22. The greater of $\frac{2}{17}$ and $\frac{3}{26}$ is _____ (fraction).

23. $585 \div 13 =$ _____.

24. The GCD of 65 and 39 is _____.

25. $28^2 =$ _____.

26. $42 + 35 + 28 + 21 + 14 + 7 =$ _____.

27. If 1 ounce is equal to $\frac{1}{16}$ of a pound, then 256 ounces is equal to _____ pounds.

28. $\frac{1}{6} + \frac{1}{10} + \frac{1}{15} =$ _____ (fraction).

29. $99 \times 61 =$ _____.

30. (estimate) $27 \times 303 \times 11 =$ _____.

31. 2520 minutes is _____ hours.

32. The perimeter of a rectangle with width 8 and area 24 is _____.

33. $115^2 =$ _____.

34. 15% of 40 is _____.

35. $41^2 =$ _____.

36. $82 \times 88 =$ _____.

37. The number of odd whole numbers between 100 and 222 is _____.

38. $\frac{24}{25} =$ _____ %.

39. The LCM of 65 and 39 is _____.

40. (estimate) $393852 \div 129 =$ _____.

41. $77 \times 37 =$ _____.

42. The seventeenth term in the arithmetic sequence $12, 25, 38, \ldots$ is _____.

43. $101 \times 213 =$ _____.

44. The remainder of $1454 \div 11$ is _____.

45. $18 \times 13 + 34 \times 9 =$ _____.

46. The perimeter of an isosceles triangle with sides of length 3 and 8 is _____.

47. $61^2 - 38^2 =$ _____.

48. $2^3 \times 5^4 =$ _____.

49. 13311_4 in base 10 is _____.

50. (estimate) $8333 \times 48 =$ _____.

51. The area of a right triangle with a hypotenuse of length 29 and a leg of length 21 is _____.

52. $105 \times 117 =$ _____.

53. $26\frac{2}{3}\%$ of 30 is _____.

54. $\sqrt[3]{140608} =$ _____.

55. The median of the list $14, 3, 8, 22, 19, 18$ is _____.

56. $375 \times 72 =$ _____.

57. The measure of an interior angle in a regular polygon with 20 sides is _____ $^\circ$.

58. $96 \times 76 =$ _____.

59. 10000111_2 in base 16 is _____ $_{16}$.

60. (estimate) $857142 \times 3 =$ _____.

61. $0.\overline{074} =$ _____ (fraction).

62. The number of different outcomes showing exactly 3 heads when flipping 5 fair coins is _____.

63. $414 \times 111 =$ _____.

64. 94 in base 3 is _____ $_3$.

65. If $u = 15$, then $u^2 + 32u + 256 =$ _____.

66. $5\frac{2}{3} \times 13\frac{2}{3} =$ _____ (mixed number).

67. $\frac{5}{12} =$ _____ % (mixed number).

68. The area of an equilateral triangle with side length $6\sqrt[4]{3}$ is _____.

69. $16 \times 24 \times 23 =$ _____.

70. (estimate) $\sqrt{11^5} =$ _____.

71. The number of positive whole number divisors of 102 is _____.

72. $1023 \times 1017 =$ _____.

73. $9^{3.5} =$ _____.

74. If $8^{x-2} = 125$, then $2^{2x+1} =$ _____.

75. The number of proper subsets of the set $\{J, U, S, T, W, I, N\}$ is _____.

76. $52 \times 31 \times 75 =$ _____.

77. The reciprocal of 0.0625 is _____.

78. The sum of the terms of the infinite geometric sequence $8, -\frac{8}{3}, \frac{8}{9}, \ldots$ is _____.

79. $\sqrt{2} \times \sqrt{54} \times \sqrt{3} =$ _____.

80. (estimate) The surface area of a right circular cylinder with radius 7 and height 10 is _____.

Sprint Round
12228

Place ID Sticker
Inside This Box

Name _____

Grade _____

School _____

1. (A) (B) (C) (D) (E)   11. (A) (B) (C) (D) (E)   21. (A) (B) (C) (D) (E)

2. (A) (B) (C) (D) (E)   12. (A) (B) (C) (D) (E)   22. (A) (B) (C) (D) (E)

3. (A) (B) (C) (D) (E)   13. (A) (B) (C) (D) (E)   23. (A) (B) (C) (D) (E)

4. (A) (B) (C) (D) (E)   14. (A) (B) (C) (D) (E)   24. (A) (B) (C) (D) (E)

5. (A) (B) (C) (D) (E)   15. (A) (B) (C) (D) (E)   25. (A) (B) (C) (D) (E)

6. (A) (B) (C) (D) (E)   16. (A) (B) (C) (D) (E)   26. (A) (B) (C) (D) (E)

7. (A) (B) (C) (D) (E)   17. (A) (B) (C) (D) (E)   27. (A) (B) (C) (D) (E)

8. (A) (B) (C) (D) (E)   18. (A) (B) (C) (D) (E)   28. (A) (B) (C) (D) (E)

9. (A) (B) (C) (D) (E)   19. (A) (B) (C) (D) (E)   29. (A) (B) (C) (D) (E)

10. (A) (B) (C) (D) (E)   20. (A) (B) (C) (D) (E)   30. (A) (B) (C) (D) (E)

1. What is the tens digit of the product of $2 \times 3 \times 5 \times 7 \times 9 \times 11$?

(A) 7   (B) 9   (C) 5   (D) 1   (E) 0

2. For his summer cookout, Nathan purchased nine packs of hot dogs. There were ten hot dogs in each pack. He also purchased eleven packs of hot dog buns. There were eight hot dog buns in each pack. How many more hot dogs than hot dog buns did Nathan purchase?

(A) 5   (B) 4   (C) 0   (D) 2   (E) 1

3. Which of the following expressions is odd?

(A) $5 \times 7 + 8$ (B) $9 \times 1 + 5$ (C) $4 \times 3 + 6$ (D) $8 \times 3 + 4$ (E) $9 \times 3 + 11$

4. Quarters are coins worth 25 cents and dimes are coins worth 10 cents. Penny has seven quarters and ten dimes. She wants to purchase some candy that costs 400 cents. How many additional quarters does Penny need to purchase the candy?

(A) 4   (B) 3   (C) 7   (D) 1   (E) 5

5. Two triangles have the same perimeter. One triangle has sides of length 10, 17, and 21. The other triangle has one side of length 18, and the other two sides have equal length. What is the length of one of the two other sides?

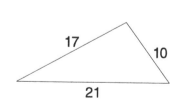 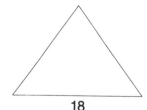

(A) 18   (B) 16   (C) 19   (D) 15   (E) 14

6. Matthew and Mark are learning how to solve a Rubik's Cube. Matthew can scramble and then solve a Rubik's Cube in five minutes, and Mark can scramble and then solve a Rubik's Cube in six minutes. Last week, Matthew and Mark each spent one and a half hours scrambling and then solving a Rubik's Cube. How many more times than Mark did Matthew solve the Rubik's Cube last week?

   (A) 1   (B) 2   (C) 5   (D) 4   (E) 3

7. How many positive whole numbers less than 100 are evenly divisible by 3 and evenly divisible by 5, but not evenly divisible by 9?

   (A) 2   (B) 4   (C) 6   (D) 5   (E) 3

8. Danielle wrote down all of the positive whole numbers less than 100 that were 3 more than multiples of 4. The first number Danielle wrote down was 3, the second was 7, and the third was 11. Danielle made sure that every two-digit number she wrote was greater than the last number she wrote. How many numbers did Danielle write before she wrote the number 67?

   (A) 18   (B) 16   (C) 15   (D) 17   (E) 19

9. The square below has an area of 48 and is divided into a number of triangles by two diagonals and two segments connecting the middle points of opposite sides. What is the total area of the shaded triangles?

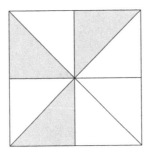

   (A) 16   (B) 15   (C) 20   (D) 21   (E) 18

10. Sebastian is preparing a sports drink for his soccer team. The recipe for the sports drink requires adding $\frac{1}{8}$ cup of the sports drink powder for every 1 quart of water. There are 4 quarts in 1 gallon, and Sebastian wants to make 5 gallons of sports drink for his soccer team. How many cups of sports drink powder does Sebastian need?

(A) $1\frac{1}{2}$ (B) 2   (C) $2\frac{1}{2}$ (D) 5   (E) $3\frac{1}{2}$

11. What is the remainder when $11 \times 22 \times 33 \times 44$ is divided by 9?

(A) 6   (B) 0   (C) 3   (D) 8   (E) 2

12. As illustrated below, a gear with 10 teeth is connected to a gear with 9 teeth. The gear with 9 teeth is connected to a gear with 8 teeth. When the gear with 10 teeth makes 180 full turns, how many full turns will the gear with 8 teeth make?

(A) 225   (B) 250   (C) 144   (D) 240   (E) 200

13. The year in which the Continental Army won the Battle of Saratoga, the first major American victory of the Revolutionary War, was a prime number that occurred in the decade of the 1770s. Which of the following was the number of that year?

(A) 1775   (B) 1771   (C) 1773   (D) 1779   (E) 1777

14. Sasha received a book on Monday that he needed to read for a language arts test on Friday. He read $\frac{1}{3}$ of the book on Monday, $\frac{1}{4}$ of the book on Tuesday, and $\frac{1}{5}$ of the book on Wednesday. He read the final 52 pages of the book on Thursday. How many pages long was the book?

(A) 210   (B) 240   (C) 224   (D) 252   (E) 180

15. A rectangle and right triangle have the same area. The rectangle has side lengths of 8 and 9. The length of one leg of the right triangle is four times the length of the other leg of the right triangle. What is the sum of the lengths of the legs of the right triangle?

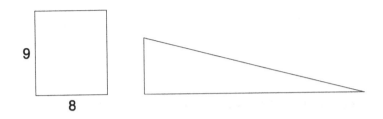

(A) 24   (B) 28   (C) 30   (D) 32   (E) 26

16. Sylvia was born on May 4th, 2010, which was a Tuesday. Sylvia turned one year old on May 4th, 2011, which was a Wednesday. On what day of the week did Sylvia turn twelve years old?

(A) Saturday   (B) Wednesday   (C) Monday   (D) Sunday   (E) Tuesday

17. If $a \heartsuit b = 4ab + 2b - 2a$, then what is the value of $23 \heartsuit 22$?

(A) 2022   (B) 2025   (C) 2021   (D) 2024   (E) 2020

18. Jason, Kyla, Lara, Nick, and Mason are classmates that will be sitting around a circular table. Jason does not want to sit next to Kyla, and Mason does not want to sit next to Lara. If a seating arrangement is only considered different if at least one person has someone different sitting on their right, then how many different ways can the five classmates be seated around the circular table?

(A) 12   (B) 9   (C) 6   (D) 10   (E) 8

19. A circular wheel with a radius of 3 centimeters rolls, without slipping, along a path that is a quarter-circle of radius 12 centimeters, a semicircle of radius 12 centimeters, and a second quarter-circle of radius 12 centimeters, as illustrated below. How many complete turns does the wheel make when rolling along this path?

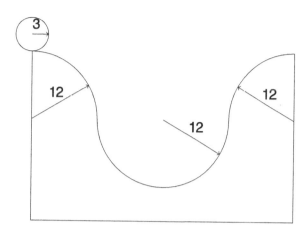

(A) 12   (B) 8   (C) 6   (D) 3   (E) 4

20. How many digits are required to write the value of $5^8 \cdot 9^7 \cdot 8^3$?

(A) 15   (B) 13   (C) 14   (D) 16   (E) 12

21. In any triangle, the sum of the lengths of any two sides of the triangle must be greater than the length of the third side. A triangle is a scalene triangle if no two sides of the triangle have the same length. How many different scalene triangles have positive whole number side lengths and perimeters less than 13? Two triangles are considered different only if the lengths of their sides are different.

(A) 5   (B) 3   (C) 2   (D) 6   (E) 4

22. When the product of 195 and 273 is written in binary, or base 2, how many more ones than zeros are used?

(A) 7   (B) 5   (C) 8   (D) 6   (E) 4

23. To celebrate her grandchildren coming to visit, a grandmother is going to give a Snickums candy bar, a Dr. Goodbar candy bar, a Four Musketeers candy bar, and a Kat Kit candy bar to her three grandchildren. But to be nice, the grandmother is going to make sure every child receives at least one of the candy bars. How many different ways can the grandmother give the candy bars to her grandchildren?

(A) 72   (B) 48   (C) 36   (D) 18   (E) 24

24. From a piece of paper in the shape of a right triangle with legs of length 16 centimeters and 12 centimeters, a smaller right triangle is cut out and removed. The sides of the smaller right triangle are parallel to the sides of the piece of paper. After the smaller triangle is cut out and removed, the area of the remaining piece of paper is 42. To the nearest whole number, what is the perimeter, in centimeters, of the smaller right triangle?

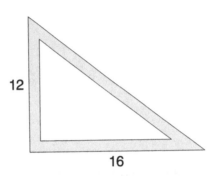

(A) 40   (B) 39   (C) 38   (D) 37   (E) 36

25. How many odd whole numbers evenly divide 2022^{22}?

(A) 484   (B) 1012   (C) 1058   (D) 506   (E) 529

26. Sean has a small motorboat that he uses to travel upstream and downstream in a river. The motorboat travels at a constant speed of 10 miles per hour in still water. One day when the river current was moving at a constant speed, Sean piloted his motorboat $2\frac{2}{5}$ miles downstream and then immediately turned around and piloted the motorboat back to his starting location. The total time for this trip was 30 minutes. What speed, in miles per hour, was the river current?

(A) 3   (B) 1   (C) 5   (D) 2   (E) 4

27. How many positive whole numbers are less than one million and have digits that increase in value from left to right? For example, 1489, 267, and 5 are three such numbers, but 1448 is not, since there is no increase from the 4 in the hundreds digit to the 4 in the tens digit.

(A) 451   (B) 511   (C) 484   (D) 465   (E) 475

28. In a circle of radius 10 units, a point is located 8 units from the center of the circle. How many chords include that point and have a length that is a whole number of units? One such chord is the diameter shown below.

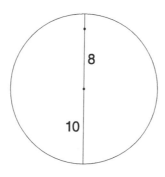

(A) 8   (B) 16   (C) 18   (D) ∞ (E) 2

29. Lenny and Benny were investigating the diagonals of various rectangles with perimeters of 12. Lenny told Benny, "If you tell me the length of the diagonal, I can multiply the square of that length by this first number, and then subtract that result from this second number, and the result will always be the area of the rectangle!" What is the product of Lenny's first number and Lenny's second number?

(A) 12   (B) 9   (C) 24   (D) 18   (E) 6

30. If x and y are positive whole numbers such that $y^2 - x^2 = 7y + 6x + 9$, then what is the value of xy?

(A) 256   (B) 96   (C) 216   (D) 192   (E) 144

Target Round
12228

Name _____

Grade _____

School _____

Problems 1 & 2

1. Mackenzie gave some stickers to her friends. She gave Susan seven stickers. She gave Regina two more stickers than she gave Susan. She split the remaining stickers evenly between Kelly, Loraina, and Josephine, so that each received the same number of stickers. Josephine received five fewer stickers than Regina received. How many stickers did Mackenzie give to her friends?

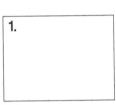

1.

2. The diagram below shows two squares, with circles at the corners of the squares. One circle is shared by both squares. Edgar places each of the numbers 1, 2, 3, 4, 5, 6, and 7 into the circles, so that each number is written in exactly one circle. He then sums the numbers in the four circles at the corners of one square, and also sums the numbers in the four circles at the corners of the other square. Edgar's two sums were the same. What is the greatest possible value of one of Edgar's sums?

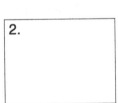

2.

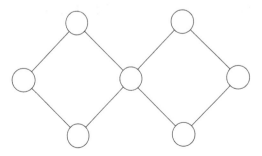

Place ID Sticker
Inside This Box

Name _____

Grade _____

School _____

Problems 3 & 4

3. Chris wrote down a three-digit whole number greater than 800 but less than 900. Chris swapped the hundreds and units digits of the number, creating a new three-digit number. He then added that new three-digit number to his original three-digit number, and the sum was 1150. What was Chris' original three-digit number?

3.

4. How many positive whole number divisors of 36036 are multiples of 12?

4.

Place ID Sticker
Inside This Box

Name _____

Grade _____

School _____

Problems 5 & 6

5. For how many minutes in the five hours between 11:00 and 4:00 do the hour and minute values displayed on a digital clock have digits that sum to 6? For example, one such minute is 3:12, since $3 + 1 + 2 = 6$.

5.

6. A 100×60 rectangle is divided into a number of 10×10 squares as shown. A shaded triangle is drawn with vertices that coincide with corners of the squares, also as shown. A region of four squares is highlighted. What is the area of the portion of the shaded triangle that lies within that region of four squares?

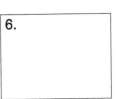

6.

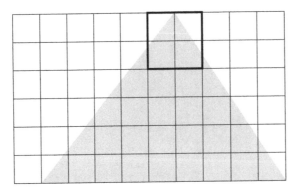

Place ID Sticker
Inside This Box

Name _____

Grade _____

School _____

Problems 7 & 8

7. The rectangle below is divided into eight squares as shown. The shaded square has an area of 1. What is the area of the entire rectangle?

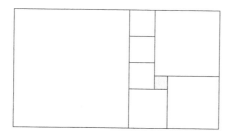

7.

8. On El-Al-Gebra Airlines, there is no cost for a bag that weighs no more than a certain weight limit, but there is a extra fee for each pound that a bag weighs above the weight limit. Amy and Bryan each brought a bag on their El-Al-Gebra flight, and the combined weight of their bags was 120 pounds. Each of their bags was over the weight limit. Amy had to pay an extra fee of $20, and Bryan had to pay an extra fee of $10. If Amy and Bryan together had one bag that weighed 120 pounds, the extra fee for being over the weight limit would have been $90. How many pounds is the weight limit for a bag that can be brought on El-Al-Gebra Airlines without an extra fee?

8.

Team Round
12228

School or Team	Name _____
	Name _____
	Name _____
	Name _____

Place ID Sticker
Inside This Box

Place ID Sticker
Inside This Box

Place ID Sticker
Inside This Box

Place ID Sticker
Inside This Box

1.

2.

3.

4.

5.

6.

7.

8.

9.

10.

1. Sam wrote down all of the numbers from 1 through 100. How many numbers that Sam wrote had the digit 4, the digit 5, or the digit 6?

2. Travis began watching the final three episodes of *The Book of Boba Fett* at 5:45 PM. The first episode he watched was 50 minutes long, and the second episode was 47 minutes long. If Travis took a break of 5 minutes between one episode and the next, and he finished watching all three episodes at 8:31 PM, then how many minutes long was the third episode?

3. Pierre wrote down three two-digit prime numbers. Pierre used each of the digits 1, 3, 4, 5, 7, and 9 exactly once to write these three numbers. What is the greatest possible sum of Pierre's three prime numbers?

4. Four squares of side length 6 are arranged as shown. The centers and two of the corners of each of the squares are all on the same line, and corners of two squares lie at the center of each of the two middle squares. What is the total area of the region that lies within at least one of the squares?

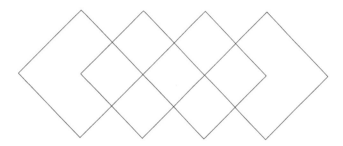

5. Will has a special deck of 59 cards. Each of the numbers from 1 through 59 appears on exactly one of the cards. Will sorted all of the cards into separate groups, and no group of cards had two cards that summed to a multiple of 10. What is the fewest number of groups of cards that Will could have?

6. In the boxes below, the value of each box is a positive whole number, and the value of each of the three rightmost boxes is the average, or mean, of the values of the two boxes immediately to the left. For example, the value of the box labeled C is the average of the values of the boxes labeled A and B. If the rightmost box has a value of 12, as shown, and the value of the box labeled D is not 12, then how many different positive whole number values are possible for the box labeled A?

| A | B | C | D | 12 |

7. The nine dots below are arranged in a 3 × 3 grid of three evenly-spaced rows and three evenly-spaced columns. How many triangles can be formed by using three dots as vertices?

```
  .    .    .

  .    .    .

  .    .    .
```

8. A shipping clerk had to weigh five boxes before shipment. Unfortunately, the shipping clerk only had a scale that could accurately weigh items with weights greater than 80 pounds. The shipping clerk decided to weigh the items in pairs. The shipping clerk weighed every possible pair of boxes, and the scale showed weights, in pounds, of 95, 98, 101, 104, 105, 107, 108, 110, 111, and 117. Using these results, the clerk was able to determine the weight of each of the five boxes. What is the remainder when the product of the five weights, in pounds, of the boxes is divided by 100?

9. Pentagon *ABCDE* is shown below. The interior angle at vertex *A* measures 120°, and the interior angles at vertices *B* and *E* each measure 90°. The measures of the interior angles at vertices *C* and *D* are equal, and the length of side *AE* is 18. Also, the lengths of sides *BC*, *CD*, and *DE* are equal to each other. To the nearest whole number, what is the area of *ABCDE*?

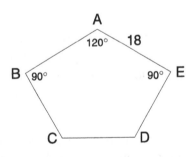

10. Octavius has three fair eight-sided dice, each with sides numbered 1 through 8. Octavius rolls the three dice and then sums the numbers shown. What is the probability that Octavius's sum is divisible by 3? Express your answer as a common fraction.

Sprint Round

1. B	11. A	21. B	
2. D	12. A	22. C	
3. A	13. E	23. C	
4. E	14. B	24. E	
5. D	15. C	25. E	
6. E	16. B	26. D	
7. B	17. A	27. D	
8. B	18. E	28. B	
9. E	19. E	29. B	
10. C	20. A	30. E	

Target Round

1. 28
2. 17
3. 872
4. 16
5. 24
6. 265
7. 144
8. 48

Team Round

1. 51
2. 59
3. 191
4. 117
5. 6
6. 5
7. 76
8. 76
9. 456
10. $\frac{85}{256}$

Number Sense

1. 221	21. 21	41. 2849	61. $\frac{2}{27}$
2. 8	22. $\frac{2}{17}$	42. 220	62. 10
3. 621	23. 45	43. 21513	63. 45954
4. 179	24. 13	44. 2	64. 10111
5. 2	25. 784	45. 540	65. 961
6. 117	26. 147	46. 19	66. $77\frac{4}{9}$
7. 161	27. 16	47. 2277	67. $41\frac{2}{3}$
8. 17	28. $\frac{1}{3}$	48. 5000	68. 27
9. 570	29. 6039	49. 125	69. 8832
10. [6242, 6898]	30. [85492, 94490]	50. [379985, 419983]	70. [382, 421]
11. 361	31. 42	51. 210	71. 8
12. 167	32. 22	52. 12285	72. 1040391
13. 3	33. 13225	53. 8	73. 2187
14. 902	34. 6	54. 52	74. 800
15. 310	35. 1681	55. 16	75. 127
16. 140	36. 7216	56. 27000	76. 120900
17. 1330	37. 61	57. 162	77. 16
18. 2022	38. 96	58. 7296	78. 6
19. 1710	39. 195	59. 87	79. 18
20. [142167, 157131]	40. [2901, 3205]	60. [2442855, 2699997]	80. [711, 785]

Sprint Round Solutions

1. The product of 2 and 5 is 10, so the tens digit of the entire product is the units digit of the product of the remaining terms. The units digit of 3×7 is 1, the units digit of 9×11 is 9. Therefore the tens digit of the entire product is $1 \times 9 = \boxed{9}$.

2. Nathan purchased $9 \times 10 = 90$ hot dogs, and $11 \times 8 = 88$ hot dog buns. The number of hot dogs exceeded the number of hot dog buns by $90 - 88 = \boxed{2}$.

3. Each of the expressions is a product followed by a sum. A sum is only odd if one term is even and one term is odd. For $9 \times 3 + 11$, both 9×3 and 11 are odd. For $4 \times 3 + 6$, both terms are even. For $9 \times 1 + 5$, both terms are odd. And for $8 \times 3 + 4$, both terms are even. But 5×7 is odd, and 8 is even, so the expression that is odd is $\boxed{5 \times 7 + 8}$.

4. The total value of Penny's quarters and dimes is $7 \times 25 + 10 \times 10 = 275$ cents. She needs an additional $400 - 275 = 125$ cents. The number of quarters required is $125 \div 25 = \boxed{5}$.

5. The perimeter of the first triangle is $10 + 17 + 21 = 48$. The perimeter of the second triangle is also 48, so the two other sides of the second triangle have a total length of $48 - 18 = 30$. Since these two sides have an equal length, the length of each is $30 \div 2 = \boxed{15}$.

6. A period of 1 and $\frac{1}{2}$ hours is $60 + 30 = 90$ minutes. In 90 minutes, Matthew can scramble and solve a Rubik's Cube $90 \div 5 = 18$ times, while Mark can scramble and solve a Rubik's Cube $90 \div 6 = 15$ times. Matthew's count exceeds Mark's count by $18 - 15 = \boxed{3}$.

7. If a number is divisible by both 3 and 5, then it is divisible by $3 \times 5 = 15$. The multiples of 15 less than 100 are 15, 30, 45, 60, 75, and 90, for a total of 6. However, both 45 and 90 are divisible by 9, so the total count of numbers divisible by both 3 and 5 but not 9 is $6 - 2 = \boxed{4}$.

8. The number 3 is 1 less than 4, or 4×1, the number 7 is 1 less than 8, or 4×2, and the number 11 was 1 less than 12, or 4×3. The number 67 is 1 less than 68, or 4×17. Therefore 67 was the seventeenth number Danielle wrote down, and the count of numbers she wrote prior to 67 is $17 - 1 = \boxed{16}$.

9. The diagonals and segments partitioning opposite sides divide the square into 8 triangles, all of equal area. The area of one of these triangles is $48 \div 8 = 6$, so the shaded area, which is 3 of these triangles, is $6 \times 3 = \boxed{18}$.

10. The total number of quarts in 5 gallons is $5 \times 4 = 20$. Therefore Sebastian needs $20 \times \frac{1}{8}$ cups of sports drink powder. In cups, this is $\frac{20}{8} = \boxed{2\frac{1}{2}}$.

11. The expression can be rewritten as $(9+2) \times (2 \times 9 + 4) \times (3 \times 9 + 6) \times (4 \times 9 + 8)$. Every term in the expansion of this product is divisible by 9 except $2 \times 4 \times 6 \times 8 = 384$, which, when divided by 9, has a remainder of $\boxed{6}$.

12. When the gear with 10 teeth makes 180 full turns, exactly $180 \cdot 10 = 1800$ teeth of the gear pass the point where the gear is connected to the gear with 9 teeth. The same number of teeth on the gear with 9 teeth must pass that same point, so the gear with 9 teeth will make $\frac{1800}{9} = 200$ turns. Similarly, when the gear with 9 teeth makes 200 turns, the number of turns made by the gear with 8 teeth is $\frac{200 \cdot 9}{8} = \boxed{225}$.

13. The number 1775 has a units digit of 5, and is therefore divisible by 5, so it cannot be prime. The numbers 1773 and 1779 both have digits that sum to multiples of 3, and are therefore divisible by 3, so neither can be prime. Finally, the number 1771 has alternating digit sums that differ by a multiple of 11. That is, the difference between the sum of the units digit and the hundreds digit, 8, and the sum of the tens digit and the thousands digit, also 8, is 0, which is a multiple of 11. Therefore 1771 is divisible by 11. The only remaining possibility, which must be the prime, is $\boxed{1777}$.

14. On Monday, Tuesday, and Wednesday, Sasha read $\frac{1}{3} + \frac{1}{4} + \frac{1}{5} = \frac{47}{60}$ of the book. The remaining portion of the book was $1 - \frac{47}{60} = \frac{13}{60}$ of the book. Since this was 52 pages, the length of the entire book, in pages, was $52 \div \frac{13}{60} = \boxed{240}$.

15. The area of the rectangle is $8 \cdot 9 = 72$. The right triangle has the same area, so the product of the lengths of the legs of the right triangle is $72 \cdot 2 = 144$. If one leg has a length 4 times the length of the other, the square of the length of the shorter leg must be $\frac{144}{4} = 36$, so the shorter leg has length 6. The longer leg has length 24, and the sum of the lengths of the legs is $6 + 24 = \boxed{30}$.

16. A non-leap year is 365 days, or 52 weeks and 1 day. Therefore in a non-leap year, the day of the week for Sylvia's birthday is one day later in the week than it was the previous year. But a leap year is 366 days, so since May 4th is after February 29th, the day of the week for Sylvia's birthday is two days later in the week than it was the previous year. Sylvia turned 12 years old in $2010 + 12 = 2022$. The leap years between 2010 and 2022 are 2012, 2016, and 2020. Therefore Sylvia's birthday will be $12 + 3 = 15$ days later in the week than it was in 2010. This is equivalent to $15 - 7 - 7 = 1$ day later in the week, which is $\boxed{\text{Wednesday}}$.

17. The expression $4ab + 2b - 2a - 1$ can be rewritten as $(2a + 1)(2b - 1) + 1$. Then $23 \heartsuit 22 = (2 \cdot 23 + 1)(2 \cdot 22 - 1) + 1$, or $47 \cdot 43 + 1 = \boxed{2022}$.

18. Seat Jason at the table. Then there are 2 possibilities for where Kyla sits, as she must not be in one of the two seats next to Jason. Once Kyla is seated, either Mason or Laura must be in the single seat that is between Kyla and Jason, so there are 2 possibilities for this seat. Finally, once that seat is filled, the remaining two classmates can be seated in the remaining two seats in 2 ways. Therefore the total number of different ways the classmates can be seated is $2 \cdot 2 \cdot 2 = \boxed{8}$.

19. Because two quarter-circles and one semicircle are altogether one entire circle, the total length of the path is equal to the circumference of a circle of radius 12, which is $2 \cdot 12 \cdot \pi = 24\pi$. The circumference of the wheel is $2 \cdot 3 \cdot \pi = 6\pi$, so the number of complete turns by the wheel is $\frac{24\pi}{6\pi} = \boxed{4}$.

20. Because $2^3 = 8$, the number 8^3 can be written as $\left(2^3\right)^3 = 2^9$. Each power of 2 paired with a power of 5 creates a power of 10, and there are 9 powers of 2 and 8 powers of 5, so the entire expression can be rewritten as $10^8 \cdot 2 \cdot 9^7$. The factor of 10^8 will append 8 instances of the digit 0 at the right end of the number. Because $3^2 = 9$, the number 9^7 can be written as $\left(3^2\right)^7$, or $\left(3^7\right)^2$. The value of 3^7 is 2187, and since $21^2 = 441$ while $22^2 = 484$, the value of $\left(3^7\right)^2$ is a little less than $4,840,000$. Therefore the value of $2 \cdot \left(3^7\right)^2$ is a little less than $9,700,000$, and requires 7 digits. When multiplied by 10^8, the total number of digits required is $7 + 8 = \boxed{15}$.

21. If the shortest side of the triangle has length 1, then the other two sides must have equal length, and the triangle is not scalene. If the shortest side of the triangle has length 2, then the other two sides can differ by at most 1, and the possible side lengths are 2, 3, and 4, as well as 2, 4, and 5, for 2 possible triangles. Any greater lengths for the other two sides results in a perimeter not less than 13. If the shortest side of the triangle has length 3, then the other two sides can differ by at most 2, and the possible side lengths are 3, 4, and 5, for 1 possible triangle. Any greater lengths for the other two sides results in a perimeter not less than 13. The total number of possible triangles is $2 + 1 = \boxed{3}$.

22. As the sum of powers of 2, the number 195 is $128 + 64 + 2 + 1$. In binary, this is 11000011_2. As the sum of powers of 2, the number 273 is $256 + 16 + 1$. In binary, this is 100010001. The product of these two binary values is $1100001100000000_2 + 110000110000_2 + 11000011_2 = 1100111111110011_2$. This binary number is 16 digits, with 12 ones and 4 zeros, so the number of ones exceeds the number of zeros by $12 - 4 = \boxed{8}$.

23. There are 4 different candy bars and 3 grandchildren, and since every grandchild will receive at least one candy bar, exactly 1 child will receive 2 candy bars. There are 3 ways to pick this grandchild, and $\binom{4}{2} = 6$ ways to select the candy bars this child receives. There are 2 ways to distribute the remaining two candy bars among the other two grandchildren, so the total number of ways the grandmother can give the candy bars to her grandchildren is $3 \cdot 6 \cdot 2 = \boxed{36}$.

24. Because the smaller right triangle has sides that are parallel to the larger triangle, the smaller triangle is similar to the larger triangle. The area of the larger triangle is $\frac{1}{2} \cdot 12 \cdot 16 = 96$, so the area of the smaller triangle is $96 - 42 = 54$. This is $\frac{54}{96} = \frac{9}{16}$ of the area of the larger triangle. Because the two triangles are similar, the side lengths of the smaller triangle must be $\sqrt{\frac{9}{16}} = \frac{3}{4}$ of the side lengths of the larger triangle. Therefore the legs of the smaller triangle are $\frac{3}{4} \cdot 12 = 9$ and $\frac{3}{4} \cdot 16 = 12$, and by the Pythagorean Theorem, the hypotenuse of the smaller triangle is $\sqrt{9^2 + 12^2} = 15$, for a perimeter of exactly $9 + 12 + 15 = \boxed{36}$.

25. The prime factorization of 2022 is $2 \cdot 3 \cdot 337$, so the prime factorization of 2022^{22} is $2^{22} \cdot 3^{22} \cdot 337^{22}$. For a divisor to be odd, it can include no powers of 2 in its prime factorization. However, any number that is a product of a power of 3 from 3^0 through 3^{22}, for 23 possible powers of 3, and a power of 337 from 337^0 through 337^{22}, for possible 23 powers of 337, will be an odd divisor of 2022^{22}. Therefore the number of odd divisors is $23 \cdot 23 = \boxed{529}$.

26. Expressed as a decimal, $2\frac{2}{5}$ is 2.4. Time is equal to distance divided by rate. If r is the speed of the river current in miles per hour, the rate Austin travels downstream is $10 + r$, and the time, in hours, for Austin to travel downstream is $\frac{2.4}{10+r}$. Similarly, the time, in hours, for Austin to travel upstream is $\frac{2.4}{10-r}$. Since the entire journey lasted 30 minutes, these times must sum to 0.5 hours, so $\frac{2.4}{10+r} + \frac{2.4}{10-r} = 0.5$, or $\frac{24}{10+r} + \frac{24}{10-r} = 5$. This equation could be solved directly, but consideration of divisors of 24 reveals that $10 - r$ is 8 and $10 + r$ is 12, so the speed of the river current, in miles per hour, is $\boxed{2}$.

27. Since the digits increase from the left to right, the digit 0 cannot appear in any of the numbers. Only the digits 1 through 9 may appear. When given a set of 6 or fewer distinct digits, there is exactly 1 way to order the digits in increasing value from left to right. Therefore there are $\binom{9}{6} = 84$ such numbers that use 6 digits, $\binom{9}{5} = 126$ such numbers that use 5 digits, $\binom{9}{4} = 126$ that use 4, $\binom{9}{3} = 84$ that use 3, $\binom{9}{2} = 36$ that use 2, and $\binom{9}{1} = 9$ that use 1. Altogether, the count of such numbers less than one million is $84 + 126 + 126 + 84 + 36 + 9 = \boxed{465}$.

28. The shortest possible length of the chord occurs in the chord that is perpendicular to the diameter that includes the point. The length of half of this chord is, by the Pythagorean Theorem, $\sqrt{10^2 - 8^2} = 6$, so the length of the chord is 12. As a chord including the point is rotated about the point, its length can be any value between the minimum of 12 and the maximum of the diameter, which is 20. Additionally, each length between 12 and 20 occurs in exactly 2 chords, one by rotating the chord clockwise and the other by rotating the chord counterclockwise. Therefore the total number of chords with a length that is a whole number of units is 1, for the chord of minimal length, plus 1, for the diameter, plus $2 \cdot (19 - 13 + 1) = 14$, which sums to $\boxed{16}$.

29. Let the length of the rectangle be x and the width be y. Then the area is xy, and the square of the diagonal is $x^2 + y^2$. Because the perimeter is 12, $x + y = 6$, and $x^2 + 2xy + y^2 = 36$. Therefore $2xy$, or twice the area, is equal to 36 minus the square of the diagonal. Letting the length of the diagonal be d, this is $2xy = 36 - d^2$, so the area, or xy, is $18 - \frac{1}{2}d^2$. Lenny's first number is $\frac{1}{2}$ and his second number is 18, and their product is $\frac{1}{2} \cdot 18 = \boxed{9}$.

30. The given expression can be rewritten as $y^2 - 7y = x^2 + 6x + 9$, or $y \cdot (y - 7) = (x + 3)^2$. If y and $y - 7$ are factor pairs of a perfect square, then one number is odd and the other is even. The even factor must be the square of an even number v times an odd number s, and the odd factor must be the square of an odd number d times the same odd number s. Therefore $(v^2 \cdot s) - (s \cdot d^2) = \pm 7$, or $s \cdot (v^2 - d^2) = \pm 7$. But 7 is prime and both s and $v^2 - d^2$ are whole numbers. Since v and d are positive, the difference of their squares cannot be 1, so s must be 1, and $v^2 - d^2 = \pm 7$. Furthermore, if $v^2 - d^2 = -7$, but v and d are positive, then $v - d = -1$ and $v + d = 7$. This results in $v = 3$, an impossibility since v is even. Thus $v^2 - d^2 = 7$, and $v = 4$ and $d = 3$. Then $y = 16$ and $y - 7 = 9$, so $(x + 3)^2 = 16 \cdot 9$. Since x is positive, $x + 3 = 12$, and $x = 9$. The value of xy is $9 \cdot 16 = \boxed{144}$.

Target Round Solutions

1. Susan received 7 stickers, so Regina received $7 + 2 = 9$ stickers. Josephine received 5 fewer sticker than Regina, so Josephine received $9 - 5 = 4$ stickers. Kelly and Loraina also received 4 stickers. The total number of stickers Mackenzie gave to her friends was $7 + 9 + 4 + 4 + 4 = \boxed{28}$.

2. The sum of the numbers 1, 2, 3, 4, 5, 6, and 7 is $1 + 2 + 3 + 4 + 5 + 6 + 7 = 28$. When the number in the circle shared by both squares is removed from this sum, the remaining total must be even, since the sum of the remaining three circles must be the same for both squares. For the greatest possible sum, the number in the circle shared by both squares should be as large as possible. Therefore the number in the circle shared by both squares must be 6, and the sum of the remaining three circles for each square must be $(28 - 6) \div 2 = 11$. The partitioning of the remaining numbers is 7, 3, and 1 for one square, and 5, 4, and 2 for the other square. The greatest value of the sum for one square is $6 + 11 = \boxed{17}$.

3. The hundreds digit of Chris' number was an 8. Since the sum was 1150, and the units digit of the sum is the sum of the hundreds and units digits of the original number, the units digit of Chris' number was $10 - 8 = 2$. The sum of $802 + 208$ is 1010, and $1150 - 1010 = 140$. The tens digit of the original number is counted twice, as it occurs in both the original number and the new number. Therefore the tens digit is $140 \div 20 = 7$, and Chris' original three-digit number was $\boxed{872}$.

4. The number 36036 is $36 \cdot 1001$, and has a prime factorization of $2^2 \cdot 3^2 \cdot 7 \cdot 11 \cdot 13$. For a number to be a multiple of 12, it must have at least one factor of 3 and at least two factors of 2 in its prime factorization. Thus the divisor of 36036 must have a prime factorization of 2 factors of 2, for 1 possibility, and 1 or 2 factors of 3, for 2 possibilities. Additionally, the divisor may have 0 or 1 factors of each of 7, 11, or 13, for 2 possibilities for each. Altogether, the number of possible divisors of 36036 that are also multiples of 12 is $1 \cdot 2 \cdot 2 \cdot 2 \cdot 2 = \boxed{16}$.

5. Since $1 + 1 = 2$ and $1 + 2 = 3$, the count for the 2 o'clock hour is the same as the count for the 11 o'clock hour, and the count for the 3 o'clock hour is the same as the count for the 12 o'clock hour. If the sum of the hour digits is 2, then the tens digit of the minute value can be any value from 0 through 4, for 5 possibilities. But if the sum of the hour digits is a 3, then the tens digit of the minute value can only be any value from 0 through 3, for 4 possibilities. Finally, if the sum of the hour digits is a 1, as it is in the 1 o'clock hour, then the tens digit of the minute value can be any value from 0 through 5, for 6 possibilities. Altogether, the number of minutes where the hour and minutes digits displayed sum to 6 is $5 + 4 + 6 + 5 + 4 = \boxed{24}$.

6. The area of the entire region of four squares is $4 \cdot 10 \cdot 10 = 400$. In the upper right of the region of four squares is an unshaded right triangle. This triangle has a width of 10 and is similar to the larger unshaded triangle that has a width of 40 and a height of 60. The height of the smaller triangle is $10 \cdot \frac{60}{40} = 15$, and the area of the smaller triangle is $\frac{1}{2} \cdot 10 \cdot 15 = 75$. In the upper left of the region of four squares is another unshaded right triangle. This triangle has a width of 10 and is similar to the larger unshaded triangle that has a width of 50 and height of 60. The height of the smaller triangle is $10 \cdot \frac{60}{50} = 12$, and the area of the smaller triangle is $\frac{1}{2} \cdot 10 \cdot 12 = 60$. The area of the portion of the shaded triangle that lies within the region of four squares is $400 - 75 - 60 = \boxed{265}$.

7. The 3 identical squares have a side length that is 1 less than the square in the bottom middle of the rectangle. The square in the lower right of the rectangle has a side length that is 1 more than the side length of the square in the bottom middle. The square in the upper right has a side length that is both 1 more than the side length of the square in the lower right, and 1 less than 3 times the side length of the identical squares. Let the side length of the square in the bottom middle be x. The side length of the square in the upper right is $x + 2$ and the side length of the three identical squares is $x - 1$, so $3 \cdot (x - 1) - 1 = x + 2$. Solving, the side length of the middle bottom square is 3, so the side length of the three identical squares is 2, the side length of the lower right square is 4, and the side length of the large square is $3 + 2 + 2 + 2 = 9$. The width of the rectangle is $9 + 3 + 4 = 16$, and the height of the rectangle is 9, for an area of $16 \cdot 9 = \boxed{144}$.

8. Let the weight of Amy's bag, in pounds, be A and the weight of Bryan's bag, in pounds, be B. Additionally, let the weight limit be p and the cost per pound over the weight limit be c. Then $c \cdot (A - p) = 20$, and $c \cdot (B - p) = 10$. Additionally, $A + B = 120$, and $c \cdot (A + B - p) = 90$, or $cA + cB - cp = 90$. Summing the first two equations, $cA + cB - 2cp = 30$. Subtracting this from the last equation yields $cp = 60$, so $cA + cB = 90 + 60$. Since $A + B = 120$, the value of c is $\frac{90+60}{120} = 1.25$. Therefore $p = \frac{60}{1.25}$, so the weight limit, in pounds, is $\boxed{48}$.

Team Round Solutions

1. The digit 4 appears 10 times in the units place, and an additional 10 times in the tens place. But 44 has the digit 4 twice, so the digit 4 occurs in $10 + 10 - 1 = 19$ numbers. Similarly, the digit 5 also occurs in 19 numbers, and the digit 6 also occurs in 19 numbers, for a total of $19 + 19 + 19 = 57$. However, 54, 45, 46, 64, 56, and 65 each occur in two counts, so the total of numbers that have the digit 4, the digit 5, or the digit 6 is $57 - 6 = \boxed{51}$.

2. The time between 5:45 and 8:45 is 3 hours, or $3 \cdot 60 = 180$ minutes. But 8:31 is $45 - 31 = 14$ minutes before 8:45, so the total time Travis spent watching the episodes was $180 - 14 = 166$ minutes. The first two episodes lasted a total of $47 + 50 = 97$ minutes, and the 2 breaks between the first and second episodes and the second and third episodes were $5 + 5 = 10$ minutes, for a total of $97 + 10 = 107$ minutes. Therefore the length of the third episode, in minutes, was $166 - 107 = \boxed{59}$.

3. No two-digit prime number can have a units digit of 5 or 4, so these two digits must be the tens digits of two of the three primes. To maximize the sum, the tens digit of the third number should be as large as possible. Therefore the third prime would have to be 97, as that is the only two-digit prime number with a tens digit of 9. The remaining two primes must be 41 and 53, so the greatest possible sum of the three primes is $97 + 41 + 53 = \boxed{191}$.

4. The diagram can be partitioned into a number of squares of side length $6 \div 2 = 3$. Of these these smaller squares, 7 are already visible in the diagram, and each of the two squares on either end of the diagram can be partitioned into 3 additional smaller squares. The total number of smaller squares is $7 + 3 + 3 = 13$. Each has an area of $3 \cdot 3 = 9$, so the total area of the region that lies within at least one of the squares is $9 \cdot 13 = \boxed{117}$.

5. Each of the cards numbered 5, 15, 25, 35, 45, and 55 must be in a separate group, as any two of those numbers will always sum to a multiple of 10. Place these cards into 6 groups. Each of the cards numbered 10, 20, 30, 40, and 50 must be placed into a different one of these 6 groups. The remaining cards can be sorted into those groups in any number of ways. One such way is to place the cards with a units digit of 1, 2, 3, or 4 in one group, and those with a units digit of 6, 7, 8, or 9 in another. Therefore the fewest number of groups required is $\boxed{6}$.

6. The value of C is $\frac{A+B}{2}$, and the value of D is $\frac{1}{2} \cdot \left(B + \frac{A+B}{2}\right) = \frac{A+3B}{4}$. The value of 12 is $\frac{1}{2} \cdot \left(\frac{A+B}{2} + \frac{A+3B}{4}\right) = \frac{3A+5B}{8}$. Then $3A + 5B = 96$. If A is positive, then $3A$ must be both less than 96 and 1 more than a multiple of 5. The possible values of $3A$ are 6, 21, 36, 51, 66, and 81. But when $3A$ is 36, A is 12, and all other boxes have a value of 12, so this possibility must be discarded. Therefore the total number of possible values of A is $\boxed{5}$.

7. There are $\binom{9}{3} = 84$ possible sets of 3 dots. However, 3 dots will not form a triangle if the dots lie on the same line. Each of the 3 columns, each of the 3 rows, and each of the 2 diagonals have 3 dots on the same line. Therefore the total number of triangles that can be formed is $84 - 8 = \boxed{76}$.

8. Since each box is weighed with each of the 4 other boxes, each box is weighed four times. The total weight of all the weighings is $95 + 98 + 101 + 104 + 105 + 107 + 108 + 110 + 111 + 117 = 1056$ pounds, so the total weight of all five boxes is $\frac{1056}{4} = 264$. The two heaviest boxes must together weigh 117 pounds, and the two lightest boxes must together weigh 95 pounds. The weight of the third heaviest box must be $264 - 117 - 95 = 52$ pounds. The weight of the third heaviest box and the heaviest box must be 111 pounds, so the weight of the heaviest box must be $111 - 52 = 59$ pounds. The weight of the third heaviest box and lightest box must be 98 pounds, so the weight of the lightest box must be $98 - 52 = 46$ pounds, and the weight of the second lightest box must be $95 - 46 = 49$ pounds. The five boxes have weights of 46, 49, 52, 58, and 59 pounds. The product of the five weights is $46 \cdot 49 \cdot 52 \cdot 58 \cdot 59 = 401085776$, and the remainder when this value is divided by 100 is $\boxed{76}$.

9. The sum of the measures of the interior angles in a convex pentagon is $180° \cdot (5 - 2) = 540°$, so the measure of the interior angles at vertices C and D are each $\frac{1}{2} \cdot (540° - 120° - 90° - 90°) = 120°$. The pentagon is symmetrical about a segment perpendicular to CD that passes through A, so side AB has length 18, and triangle ABE is isosceles. Let a segment from A that is perpendicular to BE meet BE at X. Triangle EAX is a $30 - 60 - 90$ triangle, as is triangle BAX, so the length of AX is $\frac{18}{2} = 9$, and the length of EX is $9\sqrt{3}$. The area of ABE is twice the area of EAX, or $2 \cdot \frac{1}{2} \cdot 9 \cdot 9\sqrt{3} = 81\sqrt{3}$. Quadrilateral $BCDE$ is an isosceles trapezoid, and segments CX and DX partition this trapezoid into three equilateral triangles, each with side length $9\sqrt{3}$. The total area of these three triangles is $3 \cdot \frac{(9\sqrt{3})^2 \cdot \sqrt{3}}{4} = \frac{729\sqrt{3}}{4}$. The total area of $ABCDE$ is $81\sqrt{3} + \frac{729\sqrt{3}}{4} = \frac{1053\sqrt{3}}{4}$, which when rounded to the nearest whole number is $\boxed{456}$.

10. There are $8 \cdot 8 \cdot 8 = 512$ possible outcomes when rolling the three dice. On each die, there are 3 sides that have a remainder of 1 when divided by 3, 3 sides that have a remainder of 2 when divided by 3, and 2 sides that have a remainder of 0 when divided by 3. The sum of the numbers shown will be divisible by three if all three dice show numbers that have the same remainder when divided by 3. The sum will also be divisible by 3 if each die shows a number that has a different remainder when divided by 3. There are $3 \cdot 3 \cdot 3 = 27$ outcomes where all three dice show a number with a remainder of 1, and an additional 27 outcomes where all three dice show a number with a remainder of 2. There are only $2 \cdot 2 \cdot 2 = 8$ outcomes where all three dice show a number with a remainder of 0. There are $3 \cdot 3 \cdot 2 = 18$ ways to select three numbers that have different remainders when divided by 3, and those three numbers can be permuted in $3! = 6$ ways among the three dice, for a total of $18 \cdot 6 = 108$ outcomes. Altogether, the total number of outcomes with sums that are divisible by 3 is $27 + 27 + 8 + 108 = 170$, for a probability of $\frac{170}{512} = \boxed{\frac{85}{256}}$.

Number Sense
12229

Place ID Sticker
Inside This Box

Name _____

Grade _____

School _____

1. $22 + 212 + 21 =$ _____.

2. $768 + 344 =$ _____.

3. The product of the tens and units digits of 45825 is _____.

4. $6 + 6 \times 13 =$ _____.

5. $621 - 295 =$ _____.

6. $67 + 41 + 53 + 51 =$ _____.

7. The remainder of $132 \div 5$ is _____.

8. $16 \times 40 =$ _____.

9. The quotient of $136 \div 8$ is _____.

10. (estimate) $1710 + 3705 + 3135 =$ _____.

11. $638 - 221 - 339 =$ _____.

12. $11 \times 91 =$ _____.

13. $18 \times 55 =$ _____.

14. The remainder of $731 \div 8$ is _____.

15. $18^2 =$ _____.

16. $82 + 123 + 205 =$ _____.

17. $1.4 \times 0.004 =$ _____ (decimal).

18. *CDLXXIX* in Arabic numerals is _____.

19. $5 \times 9 \times 16 =$ _____.

20. (estimate) $401 \times 349 =$ _____.

21. $62 \times 25 =$ _____.

22. The lesser of $\frac{3}{13}$ and $\frac{4}{17}$ is _____ (fraction).

23. $15 \times 77 \div 21 =$ _____.

24. $1312 \div 41 =$ _____.

25. If 1 yard is equal to 36 inches, then 1080 inches is equal to _____ yards.

26. $1 - \frac{1}{4} - \frac{2}{3} =$ _____ (fraction).

27. $31^2 =$ _____.

28. $41 + 43 + 45 + 47 + 49 + 51 =$ _____.

29. The GCD of 24 and 56 is _____.

30. (estimate) $9 \times 51 \times 55 =$ _____.

31. $45^2 - 3 =$ _____.

32. 75% of 56 is _____.

33. The area of a square with perimeter 52 is _____.

34. $\frac{22}{25} =$ _____ %.

35. $73 \times 77 =$ _____.

36. 96 hours is _____ days.

37. The number of even whole numbers between 113 and 227 is _____.

38. $74 \times 99 =$ _____.

39. The LCM of 24 and 56 is _____.

40. (estimate) $54 \times 6667 =$ _____.

41. $24 \times 7 + 26 \times 12 =$ _____.

42. $314 \times 101 =$ _____.

43. The remainder of $6719 \div 11$ is _____.

44. $81 \times 21 =$ _____.

45. $51^2 - 26^2 =$ _____.

46. 122_{12} in base 10 is _____.

47. The perimeter of an isosceles triangle with sides of length 4 and 9 is _____.

48. $2^3 \cdot 3^3 \cdot 5^3 =$ _____.

49. The eleventh term in the arithmetic sequence $11, 20, 29, \ldots$ is _____.

50. (estimate) $759190 \div 189 =$ _____.

51. $\sqrt{7056} =$ _____.

52. The perimeter of a right triangle with area 60 and a leg of length 15 is _____.

53. $128 \times 103 =$ _____.

54. The mean of the list $25, 19, 31, 13$ is _____.

55. $36\frac{4}{11}\%$ of 121 is _____.

56. 333_4 in base 8 is _____ $_8$.

57. $98 \times 64 =$ _____.

58. The measure of an interior angle in a regular polygon with 15 sides is _____ $^\circ$.

59. $811 \times 125 =$ _____.

60. (estimate) $51^3 =$ _____.

61. The number of different ways to arrange the letters *KAYAK* is _____.

62. $17\frac{2}{11} \times 5\frac{2}{11} =$ _____ (mixed number).

63. 125 in base 4 is _____ $_4$.

64. $.\overline{370} =$ _____ (fraction).

65. $\sqrt[8]{65536} =$ _____.

66. $17 \times 36 \times 21 =$ _____.

67. If $y = 22$, then $y^2 + 18y + 81 =$ _____.

68. $222 \times 22 =$ _____.

69. The area of a rhombus with perimeter 20 and a diagonal of length 6 is _____.

70. (estimate) $714285 \times 8 =$ _____.

71. $981^2 =$ _____.

72. If $9^{1-x} = \frac{9}{2}$, then $3^{2x+1} =$ _____.

73. $\frac{2}{5}$ of 18 is $\frac{3}{10}$ of _____.

74. The number of positive whole number divisors of 1296 is _____.

75. $2401^{0.75} =$ _____.

76. The surface area of a cube with a volume of 1728 is _____.

77. $89 \times 15 \times 54 =$ _____.

78. The sum of the terms of the infinite geometric sequence $4, \frac{16}{5}, \frac{64}{25}, \ldots$ is _____.

79. $\sqrt{2} \times \sqrt{54} \times \sqrt{12} =$ _____.

80. (estimate) $\sqrt{2.022 \times 20.22 \times 202.2 \times 2022} =$ _____.

Sprint Round
12229

Place ID Sticker
Inside This Box

Name _____

Grade _____

School _____

1. Ⓐ Ⓑ Ⓒ Ⓓ Ⓔ   11. Ⓐ Ⓑ Ⓒ Ⓓ Ⓔ   21. Ⓐ Ⓑ Ⓒ Ⓓ Ⓔ

2. Ⓐ Ⓑ Ⓒ Ⓓ Ⓔ   12. Ⓐ Ⓑ Ⓒ Ⓓ Ⓔ   22. Ⓐ Ⓑ Ⓒ Ⓓ Ⓔ

3. Ⓐ Ⓑ Ⓒ Ⓓ Ⓔ   13. Ⓐ Ⓑ Ⓒ Ⓓ Ⓔ   23. Ⓐ Ⓑ Ⓒ Ⓓ Ⓔ

4. Ⓐ Ⓑ Ⓒ Ⓓ Ⓔ   14. Ⓐ Ⓑ Ⓒ Ⓓ Ⓔ   24. Ⓐ Ⓑ Ⓒ Ⓓ Ⓔ

5. Ⓐ Ⓑ Ⓒ Ⓓ Ⓔ   15. Ⓐ Ⓑ Ⓒ Ⓓ Ⓔ   25. Ⓐ Ⓑ Ⓒ Ⓓ Ⓔ

6. Ⓐ Ⓑ Ⓒ Ⓓ Ⓔ   16. Ⓐ Ⓑ Ⓒ Ⓓ Ⓔ   26. Ⓐ Ⓑ Ⓒ Ⓓ Ⓔ

7. Ⓐ Ⓑ Ⓒ Ⓓ Ⓔ   17. Ⓐ Ⓑ Ⓒ Ⓓ Ⓔ   27. Ⓐ Ⓑ Ⓒ Ⓓ Ⓔ

8. Ⓐ Ⓑ Ⓒ Ⓓ Ⓔ   18. Ⓐ Ⓑ Ⓒ Ⓓ Ⓔ   28. Ⓐ Ⓑ Ⓒ Ⓓ Ⓔ

9. Ⓐ Ⓑ Ⓒ Ⓓ Ⓔ   19. Ⓐ Ⓑ Ⓒ Ⓓ Ⓔ   29. Ⓐ Ⓑ Ⓒ Ⓓ Ⓔ

10. Ⓐ Ⓑ Ⓒ Ⓓ Ⓔ   20. Ⓐ Ⓑ Ⓒ Ⓓ Ⓔ   30. Ⓐ Ⓑ Ⓒ Ⓓ Ⓔ

1. Which of the following is equal to 12×14?

   (A) 16×28 (B) 24×6 (C) 28×9 (D) 7×18 (E) 21×8

2. In the grid of numbers below, the sums of the three numbers in the top row, the bottom row, the left column, and the right column are all equal. What is the sum of the three numbers that belong in the three empty, unshaded squares?

5	1	4
3		2

   (A) 12   (B) 9   (C) 11   (D) 8   (E) 10

3. Two rectangles are shown below. The first rectangle has a width of 9 and a length of 6. The second rectangle is 2 units wider and 1 unit shorter than the first rectangle. What is the perimeter of the second rectangle?

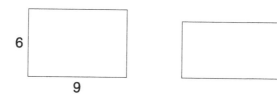

   (A) 30   (B) 36   (C) 32   (D) 34   (E) 28

4. Erica purchased a case of M&N's candy at PriceCo Wholesale for $32. The case contained 36 packs of M&N's. Erica sold all of the M&N's in her neighborhood for $2 per pack. How many more dollars did Erica receive selling the M&N's than she spent buying the M&N's?

   (A) $38   (B) $42   (C) $41   (D) $40   (E) $36

5. The sum of two positive whole numbers is 18, and the product of the same two numbers is 45. What is the value of the larger number minus the smaller number?

(A) 12   (B) 11   (C) 9   (D) 10   (E) 8

6. What is the greatest possible number of digits in the product of a five-digit positive whole number and a four-digit positive whole number?

(A) 9   (B) 8   (C) 11   (D) 12   (E) 10

7. The first day of May in the year 2022 was a Sunday, and the month of May has 31 days. Stephen jogged five miles every Saturday and Sunday in May and jogged two miles every other day of the month. How many total miles did Stephen jog in the month of May?

(A) 80   (B) 89   (C) 86   (D) 83   (E) 92

8. The figure below can be divided into two rectangles, and all side lengths are as shown. What is the area of the figure?

(A) 1200   (B) 950   (C) 850   (D) 900   (E) 1000

9. Mrs. Robinson has to grade quizzes from her history classes. She graded the first 27 quizzes in 54 minutes. If she spends the same number of minutes per quiz grading the remaining 32 quizzes, then how many total minutes will it take Mrs. Robinson to grade all of the quizzes?

(A) 108   (B) 118   (C) 128   (D) 148   (E) 138

10. What is the remainder when $31 \times 33 \times 35 \times 37$ is divided by 13?

(A) 11   (B) 9   (C) 5   (D) 3   (E) 7

11. Alfonso writes the letters of *MATHLEAGUE* in order, but he repeats the first letter three times, the second letter four times, the third letter five times, and so on, writing the next letter one more time than he wrote the previous letter. The first twelve letters Alfonso writes are *MMMAAAATTTTT*. What is the 50th letter Alfonso writes?

(A) *G*   (B) *A*   (C) *U*   (D) *L*   (E) *E*

12. Francine chose a positive whole number and then divided the number by 22. Francine's result was greater than $20\frac{4}{5}$ but less than $20\frac{5}{6}$. What was Francine's number?

(A) 457   (B) 456   (C) 454   (D) 458   (E) 455

13. Barry, Garry, Harry, Jerry, and Larry played a round of golf together. Both Jerry and Barry had a lower score than Garry. Larry's score was lower than Barry's, but higher than Harry's. Jerry scored lower than Larry, but higher than Harry. Which player had the second-lowest score?

(A) Larry   (B) Harry   (C) Jerry   (D) Barry   (E) Garry

14. As shown below, two right triangles share a leg of length 16, and the other leg of each triangle has length 12. What is the area of the region common to both triangles?

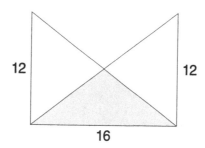

(A) 42   (B) 48   (C) 60   (D) 36   (E) 54

15. Two positive whole numbers are relatively prime if 1 is the only whole number that divides both numbers. For example, 8 and 15 are relatively prime, since the only whole number that evenly divides both numbers is 1. How many whole numbers greater than 28 and less than 56 are relatively prime to 56?

(A) 15   (B) 14   (C) 12   (D) 17   (E) 16

16. How many four-digit positive whole numbers less than 1234 have four different digits?

(A) 64   (B) 67   (C) 65   (D) 66   (E) 63

17. A distance of 1 mile is equal to 5280 feet. A car is traveling at a constant speed of 75 miles per hour on the freeway. How many feet does the car travel in four seconds?

(A) 480   (B) 520   (C) 440   (D) 500   (E) 420

18. A square has an area of 1764. A second square is drawn inside that square, with all four corners of the second square on sides of the original square, as shown. The shortest distance between a corner of the original square and a corner of the second square is 13. What is the area of the second square?

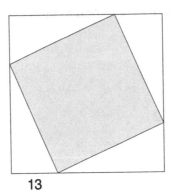

13

(A) 953   (B) 1010   (C) 1069   (D) 1000   (E) 1024

19. In Mr. Ramirez's AP Calculus class, there are four times as many 11th grade students as there are 9th and 10th grade students combined. There are twice as many 12th grade students as 9th grade students, and eight times as many 11th grade students as 12th grade students. There are 22 total students in the class, and all of the students are in the 9th, 10th, 11th, or 12th grade. How many more 10th grade students than 9th grade students are in Mr. Ramirez's AP Calculus class?

(A) 3   (B) 0   (C) 4   (D) 2   (E) 1

20. If $a \heartsuit b = a^4 + 4a^3b + 7a^2b^2 + 4ab^3 + b^4$, then what is the value of $6 \heartsuit 5$?

(A) 15151   (B) 14641   (C) 14671   (D) 15541   (E) 14941

21. To prepare for the mathleague.org Elementary National Championship, Javier did practice worksheets, with ten Sprint Round questions on each worksheet. For the ten practice worksheets, Javier averaged answering 5.8 questions correctly. Javier couldn't remember all of his scores, but he remembered that he had at least three practice worksheets with exactly 7 correct answers, at least two with exactly 6 correct answers, and at least one with exactly 8 correct answers. What is the sum of all possible values of Javier's median number of correct answers on the ten practice worksheets?

(A) 13   (B) 12.5   (C) 19.5   (D) 13.5   (E) 25

22. A small clock has an hour hand with a length of 42 millimeters and a minute hand with a length of 63 millimeters. To the nearest square millimeter, what is the total area of the region covered by the hour and minute hands as they move from a time of 4:36 to a time of 4:56?

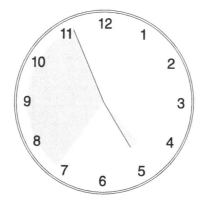

(A) 4310   (B) 4552   (C) 4090   (D) 4464   (E) 4156

23. Vivek converted a 3-digit number from base 10 to base 7. Naya converted the same number to base 9. Naya noticed that the digits of her result in base 9 were the same digits as Vivek's result in base 7, but in reverse order. What was the sum of the digits of the original number in base 10?

(A) 14   (B) 18   (C) 17   (D) 16   (E) 15

24. How many positive whole numbers less than 100 have exactly 8 positive whole number divisors?

(A) 9   (B) 8   (C) 7   (D) 10   (E) 11

25. Tommy and Ricky are painting bedrooms in a new high rise to earn money for college. Working together, Tommy and Ricky can paint a bedroom in $\frac{3}{5}$ of the time it would take Tommy working alone, and Ricky can paint a bedroom in 5 hours alone. When working alone, how many hours does it take Tommy to paint a bedroom?

(A) 4   (B) $\frac{11}{3}$ (C) $\frac{8}{3}$ (D) 3   (E) $\frac{10}{3}$

26. How many positive whole numbers are powers of 2, greater than 3^7, and less than 3^{28}? For example, one such number is 4096, since $2^{12} = 4096$, and 4096 is greater than 3^7 and less than 3^{28}.

(A) 33   (B) 37   (C) 34   (D) 35   (E) 36

27. A circle passes through two vertices of a square of side length 16 and is tangent to a side of the square. To the nearest whole number, what is the area of the circle?

16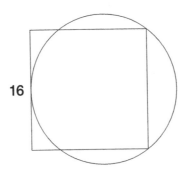

(A) 330   (B) 362   (C) 314   (D) 298   (E) 346

28. A cake has been cut into twelve identical pieces, and four friends are sharing the pieces amongst themselves. To be fair, the friends want to guarantee that everyone receives at least one piece. But the friends also do not want anyone to receive more pieces than the other three friends have in total. How many different ways can the friends share the pieces of cake?

(A) 155   (B) 125   (C) 165   (D) 145   (E) 135

29. The value of $\frac{(2025!+2024!)(2023!+2022!)}{(2025!-2024!)(2023!-2022!)}$ is equal to a common fraction. What is the value of the numerator of that fraction minus the denominator of that fraction?

(A) 4   (B) 1   (C) 3   (D) 2   (E) 5

30. Robert and Roberta each chose a positive whole number. Roberta remarked, "If you take the square root of my number and add it to your number, Robert, I got 733 as the result!" Robert added, "And if you take the square root of my number and add it to your number, Roberta, I got 3275 as the result!" What is the sum of Robert's and Roberta's numbers?

(A) 3940   (B) 3965   (C) 3920   (D) 4010   (E) 3925

Place ID Sticker
Inside This Box

Name _____

Grade _____

School _____

Problems 1 & 2

1. How many positive whole numbers greater than 100 but less than 300 have digits that sum to 17?

1. [   ]

2. For a science project, Wes recorded the weight, in pounds, of five dogs in his neighborhood and then calculated the average weight. He recorded this data in a table in his notebook, but the page accidentally got wet and Wes could not read two of the digits. The table is copied below, with a ~ in place of a digit that Wes could not read. What is the product of the two digits that Wes could not read?

2. [   ]

Dog	Weight
Stuffers	23
Cookie	31
Watson	50
Piper	34
Ozzie	1~
Average	~1

 Place ID Sticker
Inside This Box

Name _____

Grade _____

School _____

Problems 3 & 4

3. Raphael has a length of string that has a length of 60 centimeters, and he cuts the string into four pieces. The length of the second piece is twice the length of the first piece, the length of the third piece is half the length of the first piece, and the length of the fourth piece is three times the length of the third piece. How many centimeters longer is the longest piece than the shortest piece?

3.

4. Piere wants to paint four square regions on the wall of his room, as illustrated below. Piere has red paint, blue paint, yellow paint, and green paint. He wants to paint two of the squares one color and two of the squares another color, but he does not want two squares that are the painted the same color to share a side. How many different ways can Piere paint the four square regions?

4.

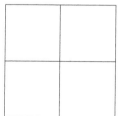

 Place ID Sticker
Inside This Box

Name _____

Grade _____

School _____

Problems 5 & 6

5. In the multiplication problem below, each letter represents a different digit. What is the greatest possible sum of the values of the digits represented by *A*, *B*, and *C*?

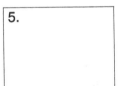

```
    B C
x     C
-------
A B C
```

6. Two equilateral triangles each share a side with the side of a square of side length 60, as shown below. To the nearest whole number, what is the area of the region common to both equilateral triangles?

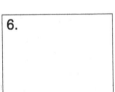

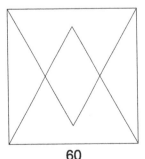

60

Place ID Sticker
Inside This Box

Name _____

Grade _____

School _____

Problems 7 & 8

7. The sum of ten consecutive positive whole numbers is the cube of a positive whole number. What is the least possible value for the greatest of the ten numbers?

7.

8. Gary and Lois each chose two positive whole numbers less than 49. The least common multiple of the two numbers was 12 times the greatest common divisor of the two numbers. How many different pairs of numbers could Gary and Lois have chosen? For example, one possible pair is Gary choosing 1 and Lois choosing 12, and another possible pair is Gary choosing 12 and Lois choosing 1.

8.

School or Team

Name _____

Name _____

Name _____

Name _____

Place ID Sticker
Inside This Box

Place ID Sticker
Inside This Box

Place ID Sticker
Inside This Box

Place ID Sticker
Inside This Box

1.	2.	3.	4.	5.
6.	7.	8.	9.	10.

1. How many positive whole numbers between 20 and 50 are divisible by 3 or have at least one digit that is 3?

2. Trey has three rectangular tiles. One tile measures 7 centimeters by 12 centimeters. Another measures 4 centimeters by 9 centimeters. The third measures 8 centimeters by 9 centimeters. Trey arranges the tiles into a larger rectangle, with no spaces between the tiles and no tiles that overlap. How many centimeters are in the perimeter of that rectangle?

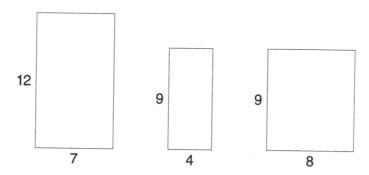

3. At Shelly's school graduation, seats for the graduates are arranged in a number of rows, with the same number of seats in each row. Shelly is sitting in the fifth row of chairs when counting rows from the front, which is also the twelfth row of chairs when counting rows from the back. When Shelly looks to her left, there are three other graduates sitting in her row, and when she looks to the right, there are five other graduates sitting in her row. Every seat has a graduate sitting in it. How many graduates are there?

4. In the array of numbers shown below, the first number on each row is a 3, and the last number on each row is an 8. Any other number is the sum of the two numbers just above it to the left and right. What is the sum of the numbers in row 9 of this array?

Row 1			3	8		
Row 2		3	11	8		
Row 3	3	14	19	8		

5. The Plainville Math Team sold school spirit t-shirts as a fundraiser. The team sold a total of 150 shirts in three weeks. The first week of the fundraiser, the team sold some of the shirts for $15 each, and the second week of the fundraiser, the team sold some of the shirts for $12 each. In the third week, the team sold the remaining 49 shirts for $8 each. The total amount of money collected from the t-shirt sales was $1706. How many more shirts did the team sell in the second week than in the first week?

6. Joseph, Kyla, and Lynn were candidates in the election for Class President. Each vote in the election was for exactly one of the three candidates, and there were 29 total votes for the three candidates. One candidate received more votes than the other two, and the number of votes for each candidate was a prime number. How many different ways could the votes have been received by the candidates? For example, one possible way is if Joseph received 17 votes, Kyla received 7 votes, and Lynn received 5 votes.

7. Diego and Ramon were each riding their bicycles toward each other along a long, straight road. Both were riding their bicycles at a constant speed, but Ramon was traveling three miles per hour faster than Diego. At 12:49 PM, Diego and Ramon were separated by a distance of 51 miles, and at 2:13 PM, the two cyclists were separated by a distance of 16 miles. What was Ramon's speed on his bicycle, in miles per hour?

8. How many perfect cubes evenly divide 22!?

9. In a square, the segments are drawn connecting corners of the square to the middle points of sides. This partitions the square into nine regions. Five of these regions are shaded, as shown below. What is the ratio of the combined area of the shaded regions to the area of the large square? Express your answer as a common fraction.

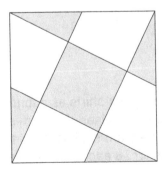

10. Sixteen dots are in a square grid so that each dot has a horizontal and vertical distance of 1 unit from neighboring dots, and the area of the entire grid is $3 \times 3 = 9$. One dot is chosen in each of the four columns. The chosen dots in neighboring columns are connected by a line segment, and the region of the grid below the segment is shaded. For how many different selections of four dots, one in each column, will exactly half of the grid be shaded? One such selection of four dots is shown below.

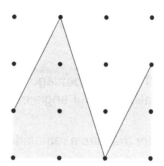

1. Two numbers sum to 2022. The value of the greater number minus the lesser number is 22. What is the lesser number?

2. The measures of the interior angles of a convex pentagon are in the ratio 22 : 23 : 24 : 25 : 26. What is the measure, in degrees, of the smallest interior angle of the pentagon?

3. What is the least positive whole number that has a remainder of 8 when divided by 9 and a remainder of 21 when divided by 22?

4. How many diagonals does a regular polygon with 22 sides have?

5. Alice and Bob each choose a positive whole number greater than or equal to 1 and less than or equal to 22. What is the probability that the product of the numbers Alice and Bob chose was even? Express your answer as a common fraction.

6. After working late the night before, Mala enjoyed a nap beginning at 1:49 PM and ending at 4:01 PM. How many hours was Mala asleep? Express your answer as a decimal to the nearest tenth.

7. What is the sum of the prime divisors of 2022?

8. Carnival tickets are worth either 2 points or 7 points. Andy has a collection of carnival tickets worth 124 points. What is the fewest number of carnival tickets that Andy could have?

9. A rhombus has a diagonal of length 22 and a perimeter of 244. What is the area of the rhombus?

10. At B & R Ice Cream, Steve is selecting three different flavors of ice cream from the 22 available flavors. How many different selections of three flavors can Steve select?

11. What is the units digit of 2022^{2022}?

12. Allison is making pancakes for a community pancake breakfast. Her recipe calls for $3\frac{1}{2}$ teaspoons baking powder. Allison wants to make 22 times her usual recipe. There are 3 teaspoons in one tablespoon, and 16 tablespoons in 1 cup. How many cups of baking powder will Allison need? Express your answer as a common fraction.

13. What is the least positive whole number that has exactly 22 positive whole number divisors?

14. Starting with a full gas tank in his SUV, Mason drove a distance of 396 miles. He then stopped and refilled the gas tank in his SUV, and calculated that his fuel efficiency on the drive was 22 miles per gallon. How many gallons of gas did Mason purchase?

15. A right triangle has legs of length 20 and 22. What is the smallest whole number greater than the length of the hypotenuse?

16. A large bag contains one hundred blue marbles, one hundred red marbles, and one hundred green marbles. How many marbles must Pidge remove from the bag in order to guarantee that he has at least 22 marbles that are the same color?

17. The squares of two positive whole numbers sum to 202. What is the positive difference between the two numbers?

18. At WallyMart, shoes were on sale for 20% off their original price. David used a coupon for an additional 10% off the sale price. The price David paid for shoes was what percent of the original price?

19. What is the 22nd term in the arithmetic sequence $1, 20, 39, \ldots$?

20. Four standard dice are rolled. What is the probability the sum of the numbers shown is greater than 22? Express your answer as a common fraction.

21. Jason rode his bike 22 miles east, 27 miles north, 34 miles west, and then 22 miles south. How many miles was Jason from his starting point?

22. Three positive whole numbers are in the ratio $1 : 3 : 7$. If the difference between the largest number and the smallest number is 2022, then what is the value of the middle number?

23. Ethan cut a large circular pizza into a number of pieces with four straight cuts. What is the greatest possible number of pieces of pizza created by Ethan's cuts?

24. Josh can mow his family's large lawn using his riding lawnmower in 26 minutes. Josh's brother James can mow his family's large lawn using his push lawnmower in 143 minutes. How many minutes will it take the two brothers to mow the lawn when working together?

25. What is the sum of the hundreds, tens, and units digits of 2022^2?

26. Three rectangles have whole number side lengths and equal area. One side of the first rectangle has length 22, one side of the second rectangle has length 12, and one side of the third rectangle has length 15. What is the least possible value for the area of one of the rectangles?

27. How many different ways can the letters *GIGEMAGGIES* be arranged?

28. January 1st of the year 2022 was a Saturday. Thanksgiving in the United States is celebrated on the fourth Thursday of November. What day of November in 2022 is Thanksgiving in the United States?

29. Three prime numbers have a sum of 122. What is the least possible value for the greatest of the three numbers?

30. A triangle with whole number side lengths has two sides of length 6 and 11. What is the sum of the greatest possible value for the length of the third side and the least possible value for the length of the third side?

31. Twelve consecutive whole numbers sum to 2022. What is the greatest of the twelve numbers?

32. A collection of 22 identical 1×1 square tiles is arranged, without overlapping and with no empty space between tiles, into a polygon. What is the least possible perimeter of that polygon?

33. A total of 22 princes and princesses are seated randomly in 22 seats around a circular table. What is the probability that Jasmin sits next to Aladdin? Express your answer as a common fraction.

34. What is the value of $21^3 + 3 \cdot 21^2 + 3 \cdot 21 + 1$?

35. Francisco averaged a score of 20 on his first six quizzes. What score does Francisco need to average on his next nine quizzes if he wants to average a score of 22 for all fifteen quizzes? Express your answer as a decimal to the nearest tenth.

36. What is the greatest positive whole number that is both a power of 4 and a divisor of 22!?

37. The circumference of half of a circle is 22. To the nearest whole number, what is the area of the entire circle?

38. The Comboville Middle School math team has 22 sixth graders and 10 fifth graders. How many different teams of 2 sixth graders and 1 fifth grader can be selected from members of the math team?

39. Of the first 2022 positive whole numbers, how many are not divisible by either 2 or 3?

40. Jace and Steph are both jogging at a constant speed. Jace is running at 2.2 meters per second, and Steph is running at 2.8 meters per second. However, Jace is currently 2022 meters ahead of Steph. To the nearest minute, in how many minutes will Steph catch up to Jace?

41. One angle in an isosceles triangle measures $36°$. What is the sum, in degrees, of all possible values for the measure of any other angle in the triangle?

42. When the base 10 number 2022 is written in binary, how many more ones than zeroes are used?

43. A regular hexagon has a side length of 22. What is the area of the hexagon? Express your answer in simplest radical form.

44. If every child must receive at least one candy bar, then how many different ways can 22 identical candy bars be distributed among 20 different children?

45. A cube has an edge of length 22. To the nearest whole number, what is the length of an interior diagonal of the cube?

46. What is the seventh term in the geometric sequence $\frac{337}{7776}, \frac{337}{1296}, \frac{337}{216}, \cdots$?

47. The number 2022 is 3 less than a perfect square. The number 2022 is how much greater than the greatest perfect square less than 2022?

48. Two circles with the same center have radii of 20 and 22. To the nearest whole number, what is the area of the region that lies within exactly one of the circles?

49. What is the value of $999 \times 2.\overline{022}$?

50. The smallest prime number is 2. The second smallest prime number is 3. What is the 22nd smallest prime number?

51. The Bandit made a 2022 mile drive from San Francisco, California to Beaumont, Texas. The Bandit averaged a speed of 72 miles per hour for the first 22 hours of his drive. What minimum speed, in miles per hour, does The Bandit need to average for the remainder of the drive to complete the drive in no more than 28 hours?

52. How many digits are required to write the whole number equal to 20^{22}?

53. A right triangle has side lengths that are positive whole numbers. The shortest side of the triangle has length 22. What is the area of the triangle?

54. A crowd of 106,815 watched Texas A&M beat Alabama in 2021. The number 106,815 has exactly 8 positive whole number divisors. What is the greatest prime divisor of 106815?

55. When training for a 10K run, Maria ran 4 miles on her first training run, 4.1 on the second, 4.2 on the third, and so on, running 0.1 mile farther on each run than the previous run. To the nearest whole number, how many total miles did Maria run on her first 22 training runs?

56. How many positive whole numbers have square roots greater than 20 and less than 22?

57. The ratio of fourth graders to fifth graders at Yearville Elementary is 22 : 21. There are 20 more fourth graders than fifth graders. How many total fourth and fifth graders are there at Yearville Elementary?

58. Thomas was riding his bicycle at a speed of 22 feet per second. There are 5280 feet in 1 mile. To the nearest whole number, what was Thomas' speed in miles per hour?

59. Two interior angles of a convex quadrilateral measure 20°, and one of the remaining two interior angles has a measure 22° greater than the measure of the other. What is the measure, in degrees, of the largest interior angle of the quadrilateral?

60. There are a number of teams in a local recreational softball league. In the regular season, each team plays every other team in the league twice. Two additional games are played between league teams in a postseason tournament. A total of 22 games are played. How many teams are in the league?

61. How many four-digit positive whole numbers less than 2022 have digits that sum to three?

62. All sides of a rectangle have lengths that are even whole numbers. If the area of the rectangle is 2200, then what is the least possible perimeter of the rectangle?

63. Shannon had 22 stamps. She first gave four steps to Tessa, and then gave $16\frac{2}{3}$% of what remained to Ella. She split the remaining evenly between Joanna, Cassie, and Kate. How many more stamps than Ella did Cassie receive?

64. Two sides of an isosceles triangle have length 22 and the third side has length 20. What is the area of the triangle? Express your answer in simplest radical form.

65. How many perfect squares are greater than 22 and less than 2022?

66. The population of a certain bacteria increases by 22% every 24 hours. To the nearest whole number, what is the percent increase in the population of the bacteria in 48 hours?

67. There are 26 letters in the English alphabet, and 22 of them are not used to spell the word *MATH*. If two, not-necessarily-different letters are randomly selected from the alphabet, then what is the probability that at least one occurs in the word *MATH*? Express your answer as a common fraction.

68. What is the value of $\frac{22!-21!}{20!}$?

69. How many times between 2:22 AM and 4:22 AM of the same day do the hour and minute hands of an analog clock form a right angle?

70. How many positive whole numbers greater than 1 and less than 22×2022 evenly divide 22×2022?

71. Mrs. Permuta has 22 students in her fourth grade class. If no student may hold more than one position, how many different ways can a class president, vice president, and secretary be selected?

72. If numbers may not appear more than once in any particular set and the order of numbers in the set does not matter, then how many different sets of prime numbers sum to 22?

73. A list of 337 consecutive whole numbers sums to 2022. What is the smallest number in the list?

74. An isosceles right triangle has a leg of length 22. The altitude to the hypotenuse of this right triangle partitions the triangle into two smaller triangles. What is the area of one of these smaller triangles?

75. Kevin summed the first 2022 perfect squares. What was the units digit of Kevin's sum?

76. There are three prime numbers greater than 2000 and less than 2022. What is the greatest of these three prime numbers?

77. In a special deck of 20 cards, each card is labeled with a unique whole number from 1 through 20. Chance is dealt a pair of cards from the deck. What is the probability that the numbers on Chance's cards sum to at least 22? Express your answer as a common fraction.

78. The shortest side of a rectangle has a length that is an even whole number, and the area of the rectangle is 4052. What is the positive difference between the greatest possible perimeter of the rectangle and the least possible perimeter of the rectangle?

79. A positive fraction that is at most 1 has a denominator of 30, and that fraction is equal to another fraction with a denominator less than 30. How many different values are possible for the numerator of the original fraction?

80. James has plenty of tokens worth 22 points and plenty of tokens worth 20 points. What is the greatest even number of points that James cannot make with his tokens?

Sprint Round

1. E	11. A	21. C
2. C	12. D	22. A
3. C	13. C	23. A
4. D	14. B	24. D
5. A	15. C	25. E
6. A	16. A	26. A
7. B	17. C	27. C
8. B	18. B	28. B
9. B	19. D	29. D
10. E	20. D	30. E

Target Round

1. 7
2. 21
3. 18
4. 12
5. 15
6. 557
7. 17
8. 32

Team Round

1. 18
2. 56
3. 144
4. 2816
5. 33
6. 24
7. 14
8. 112
9. $\frac{2}{5}$
10. 28

Number Sense

1. 255	21. 1550	41. 480	61. 30
2. 1112	22. $\frac{3}{13}$	42. 31714	62. $89\frac{4}{121}$
3. 10	23. 55	43. 9	63. 1331
4. 84	24. 32	44. 1701	64. $\frac{10}{27}$
5. 326	25. 30	45. 1925	65. 4
6. 212	26. $\frac{1}{12}$	46. 170	66. 12852
7. 2	27. 961	47. 22	67. 961
8. 640	28. 276	48. 27000	68. 4884
9. 17	29. 8	49. 101	69. 24
10. [8123, 8977]	30. [23983, 26507]	50. [3817, 4217]	70. [5428566, 5999994]
11. 78	31. 2022	51. 84	71. 962361
12. 1001	32. 42	52. 40	72. 6
13. 990	33. 169	53. 13184	73. 24
14. 3	34. 88	54. 22	74. 25
15. 324	35. 5621	55. 44	75. 343
16. 410	36. 4	56. 77	76. 864
17. 0.0056	37. 57	57. 6272	77. 72090
18. 479	38. 7326	58. 156	78. 20
19. 720	39. 168	59. 101375	79. 36
20. [132952, 146946]	40. [342018, 378018]	60. [126019, 139283]	80. [3885, 4292]

Countdown

1. 1000	21. 13	41. 216	61. 8
2. 99($°$)	22. 1011	42. 5	62. 188
3. 197	23. 11	43. $726\sqrt{3}$	63. 2
4. 209	24. 22	44. 210	64. $80\sqrt{6}$
5. $\frac{3}{4}$	25. 16	45. 38	65. 40
6. 2.2	26. 660	46. 2022	66. 49(%)
7. 342	27. 415800	47. 86	67. $\frac{48}{169}$
8. 22	28. 24	48. 264	68. 441
9. 1320	29. 61	49. 2020	69. 4
10. 1540	30. 22	50. 79	70. 22
11. 4	31. 174	51. 73	71. 9240
12. $\frac{77}{48}$	32. 20	52. 29	72. 4
13. 3072	33. $\frac{2}{21}$	53. 1320	73. -162
14. 18	34. 10648	54. 7121	74. 121
15. 30	35. 23.3	55. 111	75. 5
16. 64	36. 262144	56. 83	76. 2017
17. 2	37. 154	57. 860	77. $\frac{9}{19}$
18. 72	38. 2310	58. 15	78. 2022
19. 400	39. 674	59. 171($°$)	79. 22
20. $\frac{5}{1296}$	40. 56	60. 5	80. 178

Solutions
12229

Sprint Round Solutions

1. The product 12×14 is $2 \times 2 \times 3 \times 2 \times 7$. These factors can be rearranged as $7 \times 3 \times 2 \times 2 \times 2$, or $\boxed{21 \times 8}$.

2. The sum of the numbers in the top row is $5 + 1 + 4 = 10$. The missing number in the bottom row is $10 - 3 - 2 = 5$. The missing number in the left column is $10 - 5 - 3 = 2$. The missing number in the right column is $10 - 4 - 2 = 4$. The sum of the three missing numbers is $5 + 2 + 4 = \boxed{11}$.

3. The width of the second rectangle is $9 + 2 = 11$, and the length is $6 - 1 = 5$, so the perimeter is $11 + 11 + 5 + 5 = \boxed{32}$.

4. Erica received $36 \times 2 = 72$ dollars selling the M&N's, and she spent 32 dollars buying the M&N's. The difference between these two amounts is $\$72 - \$32 = \boxed{\$40}$.

5. Because 45 is a multiple of 5, one of the numbers must be 5 or 15. Since $5 \times (18 - 5) = 65$ and $15 \times (18 - 15) = 45$, the other number must be 3, and $15 - 3 = \boxed{12}$.

6. The greatest five-digit positive whole number is 99999, and the greatest four-digit positive whole number is 9999. Since $100000 \times 9999 = 999900000$, and $999900000 - 9999$ has 9 digits, the greatest possible number of digits is $\boxed{9}$.

7. Sundays occurred on days 1, 8, 15, 22, and 29 of May, and Saturdays occurred on days 7, 14, 21, and 28, so there were a total of 9 Saturdays and Sundays in May. On these days, Stephen jogged $9 \times 5 = 45$ miles. There were $31 - 9 = 22$ days that were not a Saturday or Sunday, and on these days Stephen jogged $22 \times 2 = 44$ miles. The total number of miles that Stephen jogged in May was $44 + 45 = \boxed{89}$.

8. Consider the figure as a rectangle with width 40 and height 30, with a rectangle with width 25 and height 10 that has been removed. The area of the original rectangle is $40 \times 30 = 1200$, and the area of the removed rectangle is $25 \times 10 = 250$, so the area of the figure is $1200 - 250 = \boxed{950}$.

9. Grading 1 quiz requires $54 \div 27 = 2$ minutes, and there are a total of $27 + 32 = 59$ quizzes, so the total time required, in minutes, is $59 \times 2 = \boxed{118}$.

10. This is $(26 + 5) \times (26 + 7) \times (26 + 9) \times (26 + 11)$. Every term in the expansion of this product is a multiple of 13 except for $5 \times 7 \times 9 \times 11$. This is 63×55, or $(52 + 11) \times (52 + 3)$, so the remainder when this product is divided by 13 is the remainder when 11×3 is divided by 13, which is $\boxed{7}$.

11. Letters 13 through $13 + 6 - 1 = 18$ are H. Letters 19 through $19 + 7 - 1 = 25$ are L. Letters 26 through $26 + 8 - 1 = 33$ are E. Letters 34 through $34 + 9 - 1 = 42$ are A. Finally, letters 43 through $43 + 10 - 1 = 52$ are G, so the 50th letter Alfonso writes is $\boxed{G}$.

12. The value of 20×22 is 440. The value of $\frac{4}{5} \cdot 22$ is $\frac{88}{5} = 17\frac{3}{5}$, and the value of $\frac{5}{6} \cdot 22$ is $\frac{110}{6} = 18\frac{1}{3}$. Therefore Francine's number must have been greater than $440 + 17\frac{3}{5}$ but less than $440 + 18\frac{1}{3}$, so Francine's number was $440 + 18 = \boxed{458}$.

13. Since both Jerry and Barry had a lower score than Garry, Garry did not have the second-lowest score. Larry's score was lower than Barry's and higher than Harry's, so at least Harry and Larry had lower scores than Barry, and Barry did not have the second-lowest score. Of the remaining three possibilities, Jerry's score was lower than Larry and higher than Harry, so the second-lowest score belonged to $\boxed{\text{Jerry}}$.

14. Consider a segment connecting the two top ends of the legs of length 12. The figure is now a rectangle, and the hypotenuses of the two triangles are diagonals of the rectangle. The shaded triangle has a base of length 16 and an altitude that is half the height of the rectangle, or 6. Therefore, the area of the region common to both triangles is $\frac{1}{2} \cdot 6 \cdot 16 = \boxed{48}$.

15. The prime factorization of 56 is $2^3 \cdot 7^1$, so a number will share a common divisor other than 1 with 56 only if the number is divisible by at least one of 2 or 7. There are $55 - 29 + 1 = 27$ whole numbers greater than 28 and, since both 29 and 55 are odd, 14 of those numbers are odd, and therefore do not have a divisor of 2. The odd multiples of 7 between 28 and 56 are 35 and 49, and both will not be relatively prime to 56. Therefore, the number of whole numbers greater than 28 and less than 56 that are also relatively prime to 56 is $14 - 2 = \boxed{12}$.

16. If the thousands and hundreds digits are 1 and 0, there are $10 - 2 = 8$ possibilities for the tens digit and then, once the tens digit is selected, $10 - 3 = 7$ possibilities for the units digit. This yields $7 \cdot 8 = 56$ possibilities. The thousands and hundreds digit cannot both be 1. However, if the thousands and hundreds digit are 1 and 2, the tens digit can be either 0 or 3. If the tens digit is 0, there are $10 - 3 = 7$ possibilities for the units digit, and if the tens digit is a 3, there is only 1 possibility for the units digit, as the units digit can only be 0. Altogether, the total count of four-digit numbers less than 1234 with four different digits is $56 + 7 + 1 = \boxed{64}$.

17. There are 60 minutes in 1 hour, and 60 seconds in 1 minute, so 1 hour is equal to $60 \cdot 60 = 3600$ seconds. A car traveling 75 miles per hour will travel $75 \cdot 5280$ feet in one hour, or $\frac{75 \cdot 5280}{3600}$ feet in one second. In 4 seconds, the car will travel $\frac{75 \cdot 5280}{3600} \cdot 4 = \frac{75 \cdot 5280}{900}$ feet. Since 900 is equal to $75 \cdot 12$, this is $\frac{5280}{12}$, and the total number of feet traveled in 4 seconds is $\boxed{440}$.

18. The side length of the original square is $\sqrt{1764} = 42$, so the longer distance between a corner of the second square and a corner of the original square is $42 - 13 = 29$. These two lengths form the leg lengths of a right triangle, and the hypotenuse of that right triangle is a side of the second square. The area of the second square is the square of the length of this hypotenuse which, by the Pythagorean Theorem, is $13^2 + 29^2 = \boxed{1010}$.

19. Because there are 2 times as many 12th grade students as 9th grade students, the number of 12th grade students must be even. Additionally, there are 8 times as many 11th grade students as 12th grade students. Therefore, there are 16 times as many 11th grade students as 9th grade students, and the only multiple of 16 less than 22, the total number of students, is 16. So there are 16 11th grade students, $\frac{16}{8} = 2$ 12th grade students, and $\frac{2}{2} = 1$ 9th grade student. The number of 10th grade students is $22 - 16 - 2 - 1 = 3$, so the number of 10th grade students exceeds the number of ninth grade students by $3 - 1 = \boxed{2}$.

20. The expansion of $(a + b)^4$ is $a^4 + 4a^3b + 6a^2b^2 + 4ab^3 + b^4$. Therefore, $a \heartsuit b$ can be rewritten as $(a + b)^4 + a^2b^2$, or $(a + b)^4 + (ab)^2$. Then $6 \heartsuit 5$ is $(6 + 5)^4 + (6 \cdot 5)^2$, or $14641 + 900 = \boxed{15541}$.

21. The sum of the number of correct answers for all 10 practice tests is $5.8 \cdot 10 = 58$, and the sum of the 6 known scores is $6 + 6 + 7 + 7 + 7 + 8 = 41$. Therefore, the remaining $10 - 6 = 4$ scores must sum to $58 - 41 = 17$. The median value of a list of 10 numbers is the mean of the fifth and sixth numbers in the list. There are 6 known values with the least and second least value both being 6. As it is possible to have the 4 unknown values each be no greater than 6 and sum to 17, the fifth and sixth values in the list can both be 6, for a median of 6. Similarly, one of the 4 unknown values could be 7, and the other 3 could sum to $17 - 7 = 10$ and be less than 6, producing a fifth value of 6 and a sixth value of 7, for a median of 6.5. Finally, it is possible for 2 of the unknown values to be 7, and the other two could sum to $17 - 7 - 7 = 3$, producing a fifth value of 7 and a sixth value of 7, for a median of 7. The sum of all possible values of the median is $6 + 6.5 + 7 = \boxed{19.5}$.

22. The time elapsed from 4:36 to 4:56 is 20 minutes, or $\frac{1}{3}$ of an hour. In this time, the minute hand will cover an area equal to $\frac{1}{3}$ of a circle of radius 63, and the hour hand will cover an area equal to $\frac{1}{3} \cdot \frac{1}{12} = \frac{1}{36}$ of circle of radius 42. The area covered by the minute hand is $\frac{1}{3} \cdot 63^2 \cdot \pi = 21 \cdot 63 \cdot \pi$, which is 1323π. The area covered by the hour hand is $\frac{1}{36} \cdot 42^2 \cdot \pi = 7 \cdot 7\pi$, which is 49π. The total area is $1323\pi + 49\pi = 1372\pi$. Using $\frac{22}{7}$ as an approximation for π yields $1372 \cdot \frac{22}{7} = 196 \cdot 22$, which is 4312. While this is a very slight overestimate, the only answer choice near this value is $\boxed{4310}$.

23. Let the number be ABC_7, where A, B, and C are digits. Then the number is also CBA_9, and $49A + 7B + C = 81C + 9B + A$. Simplifying, $48A = 80C + 2B$, or $24A = 40C + B$. Both $24A$ and $40C$ are multiples of 8, so B must also be a multiple of 8. However, B is also a valid digit in base 7, so B can only be 0. If B is 0, then $24A = 40C$, or $3A = 5C$. Since both A and C must be valid digits in base 7, A must be 5 and C must be 3. The base 9 number is 305_9, and the base 7 number is 503_7. The number in base 10 is $3 \cdot 9^2 + 5 = 248$, and $2 + 4 + 8 = \boxed{14}$.

24. For a number to have 8 positive whole number divisors, the number must have a prime factorization of p^7, where p is prime, a prime factorization of $p \cdot q \cdot r$, where p, q, and r are prime, or a prime factorization of $p^3 \cdot q$, where p and q are prime. In the first case, $2^7 = 128$, so there are no whole numbers less than 100 that have a prime factorization of p^7. In the second case, the possibilities are $2 \cdot 3 \cdot 5$, $2 \cdot 3 \cdot 7$, $2 \cdot 3 \cdot 11$, $2 \cdot 3 \cdot 13$, and $2 \cdot 5 \cdot 7$, for a total of 5. In the third case, the possibilities are $2^3 \cdot 3$, $2^3 \cdot 5$, $2^3 \cdot 7$, $2^3 \cdot 11$, and $3^3 \cdot 2$, for a total of 5. Altogether, the number of positive whole numbers less than 100 with exactly 8 positive whole number divisors is $5 + 5 = \boxed{10}$.

25. Let the number of hours Tommy requires to paint a bedroom alone be T. Then in 1 hour, Tommy can paint $\frac{1}{T}$ bedrooms, and Ricky can paint $\frac{1}{5}$ bedrooms. Together, in one hour they can paint $\frac{1}{\frac{3}{5}T}$ bedrooms.

Thus $\frac{1}{5} + \frac{1}{T} = \frac{1}{\frac{3}{5}T}$, so $\frac{3}{5} + \frac{3}{T} = \frac{5}{T}$. Finally, $3T + 15 = 25$, so T is $\boxed{\dfrac{10}{3}}$.

26. The value of 3^7 is 2187, and the value of 2^{11} is 2048. So the least power of 2 that is greater than 3^7 is 2^{12}. Because $(3^7)^4 = 3^{28}$, the value of 3^{28} is equal to $(2^{11})^4 \cdot (\frac{2187}{2048})^4$. The value of $\frac{2187}{2048}$ is only slightly more than 1, and this value to the power of 4 is less than 2. Therefore, the greatest power of 2 less than 3^{28} is 2^{44}. The count of numbers that are powers of 2, greater than 3^7, and less than 3^{28} is $44 - 12 + 1 = \boxed{33}$.

27. Let the radius of the circle be r. Consider the segment perpendicular to the side of the square at the point of tangency with the circle that meets the rightmost side of the square. That segment is parallel to two sides of the square and passes through the center of the circle. The distance from the center of the circle to the point of tangency is r, and the distance from the center of the circle to the other end of the segment is $16 - r$. Additionally, the distance from the center of the circle to one of the two vertices of the square that the circle passes through is r. A right triangle can be constructed with vertices at the center of the circle, one of the two vertices of the square that the circle passes through, and the rightmost end of the perpendicular segment. This triangle has legs of length $16 - r$ and $\frac{16}{2} = 8$, and a hypotenuse of length r. By the Pythagorean Theorem, $(16 - r)^2 + 8^2 = r^2$, so $256 - 32r + r^2 + 64 = r^2$. Therefore $320 = 32r$ and $r = 10$. The area of the circle is $10^2 \cdot \pi$, which to the nearest whole number is $\boxed{314}$.

28. If everyone receives at least one piece of cake, there are $12 - 4 \cdot 1 = 8$ pieces left to distribute. By sticks-and-stones, this can be done in $\binom{8+4-1}{4-1} = 165$ ways. But some of these distributions have someone receiving 7 or more pieces of cake, which is not allowed. Once one person receives 7 pieces and everyone else receives 1 piece, there are $12 - 7 - 3 \cdot 1 = 2$ pieces left to distribute. By sticks-and-stones, this can be done in $\binom{2+4-1}{4-1} = 10$ ways. Additionally, there are $\binom{4}{1} = 4$ ways to select the person receiving 7 or more pieces. Therefore, $10 \cdot 4 = 40$ of the distributions have someone receiving more pieces than the other three friends have in total, so the number of different ways to share the pieces of cake is $165 - 40 = \boxed{125}$.

29. Begin by dividing both the numerator and denominator by $(2022!)^2$, leaving $\dfrac{(2025 \cdot 2024 \cdot 2023 + 2024 \cdot 2023)(2023 + 1)}{2025 \cdot 2024 \cdot 2023 - 2024 \cdot 2023)(2023 - 1)}$. The numerator is equal to $2024 \cdot (2025 \cdot 2023 + 2023) \cdot 2024$, or $(2024)^2 \cdot 2026 \cdot 2023$. The denominator is equal to $2024 \cdot (2025 \cdot 2023 - 2023) \cdot 2022$, or $2024^2 \cdot 2023 \cdot 2022$. Both the numerator and denominator can be divided by 2024^2 and 2023, leaving $\frac{2026}{2022} = \frac{1013}{1011}$, and $1013 - 1011 = \boxed{2}$.

30. Let Robert's number be a^2 and Roberta's number be b^2. Then $a^2 + b = 733$, and $a + b^2 = 3275$. Subtracting the first equation from the second yields $b^2 - b + a - a^2 = 2452$. This can be rearranged as $b^2 - a^2 - (b - a) = 2452$, or $(b + a)(b - a) - (b - a) = 2452$. Then $(b - a)(b + a - 1) = 2452$. Since both b and a are whole numbers, both $b - a$ and $b + a - 1$ must be divisors of 2452. The prime factorization of 2452 is $2 \cdot 31 \cdot 41$, with factor pairs of $(1, 2452)$, $(2, 1271)$, $(31, 82)$, and $(41, 62)$. The first two possibilities yield values of a and b that are far too large. If $a - b = 31$ and $a + b - 1 = 82$, then $a = 57$ and $b = 26$. If $a - b = 41$ and $a + b - 1 = 62$, then $a = 52$ and $b = 11$. Since $52^2 + 11$ is not near 3275, only $a = 57$ and $b = 26$ is a possibility. Confirming, $57^2 + 26 = 3275$, and $26^2 + 57 = 733$, and $57^2 + 26^2 = \boxed{3925}$.

Target Round Solutions

1. If the hundreds digit is a 1, then the tens and units digits must sum to $17 - 1 = 16$, and the possibilities are 179, 188, and 197. If the hundreds digit is a 2, then the tens and units digits must sum to $17 - 2 = 15$, and the possibilities are 269, 278, 287, and 296. The total number of possibilities is $3 + 4 = \boxed{7}$.

2. Since the units digit of the average of the 5 weights is a 1, the units digit of the sum of the 5 weights must be $5 \times 1 = 5$. The sum of the known units digits is $3 + 1 + 0 + 4 = 8$, so the units digit that could not be read must be a 7, since $8 + 7 = 15$. Now that we know that the units digit that could not be read is a 7, the sum of all 5 weights is $23 + 31 + 50 + 34 + 17 = 155$, and the average weight is $155 \div 5 = 31$, so the tens digit of the average is a 3. The product of the two digits that Wes could not read is $7 \times 3 = \boxed{21}$.

3. The length of the first piece is 2 times the length of the third piece, the length of the second piece is $2 \times 2 = 4$ times the length of the third piece, and the length of the fourth piece is 3 times the length of the third piece. Altogether, remembering that the length of the third piece must be included as well, the total length of the four pieces is $1 + 2 + 4 + 3 = 10$ times the length of the third piece. Therefore the length of the third piece, the shortest piece, is $60 \div 10 = 6$ centimeters, and the length of the longest piece is $4 \times 6 = 24$ centimeters. The longest piece exceeds the shortest piece by a length, in centimeters, of $24 - 6 = \boxed{18}$.

4. There are 6 possible selections for the 2 colors that can be used: red and blue, red and yellow, red and green, blue and yellow, blue and green, and yellow and green. Once Piere selects the two colors, there are 2 possible colors for the square in the upper left, since he can choose either color. But once that color is selected, the remaining three squares must be painted in a checkerboard pattern. Therefore the total number of ways Piere can paint the squares is $6 \times 2 = \boxed{12}$.

5. The product of C and C has a units digit of C. Therefore C must be 1, 5, or 6. But C cannot be 1, since a two-digit number times 1 is a two-digit number. If C is 6, then, considering the tens digit of the product, $6B + 3$ must have a units digit of B. There is no value of B for which this is true. Therefore C must be 5, and, again considering the tens digit of the product, $5B + 2$ must have a units digit of B. This is true when B is 2 or 7, but to maximize the sum of A, B, and C, B should be 7. Therefore BC is 75, C is 5, ABC is $75 \times 5 = 375$, and the sum of A, B, and C is $3 + 7 + 5 = \boxed{15}$.

6. The altitude of each equilateral triangle is $\frac{60}{2} \cdot \sqrt{3} = 30\sqrt{3}$. A horizontal line through the center of the square partitions the region common to both triangles into two congruent equilateral triangles, each with altitude $30\sqrt{3} - 30$. The area of an equilateral triangle given the altitude is the square of the altitude multiplied by $\frac{\sqrt{3}}{3}$, so the area of one of these two equilateral triangles is $(30\sqrt{3} - 30)^2 \cdot \frac{\sqrt{3}}{3} = 1200\sqrt{3} - 1800$. The total area of both equilateral triangles is $2400\sqrt{3} - 3600$, which to the nearest whole number is $\boxed{557}$.

7. The sum of 10 consecutive whole numbers is the average of the fifth and sixth numbers multiplied by 10. Since the numbers are whole numbers, the average of the fifth and sixth numbers is number with a decimal portion of 0.5, and 10 times that number must have a units digit of 5. The least cube with a units digit of 5 is $5^3 = 125$, so the average of the fifth and sixth numbers must be $\frac{125}{10} = 12.5$. If the sixth number is 13, then the tenth, or greatest number, must be $13 + 4 = \boxed{17}$.

8. The product of the greatest common divisor and least common multiple of two positive whole numbers is equal to the product of the two numbers. Let the greatest common divisor of the two numbers be G. Then the least common multiple must be $12G$, and the product of the two numbers must be $12G^2$. There are two possibilities. The first is that one number is G and the other is $12G$. The second is that one number is $3G$ and the other is $4G$. It is not possible for one number to be $2G$ and the other to be $6G$, because then the greatest common divisor would be $2G$, not G. In the first case, $12G$ must be less than 49, so G, can be 1, 2, 3 or 4. This number can be chosen by either Lois or Gary, for $4 \cdot 2 = 8$ possibilities. In the second case, $4G$ must be less than 49, so G must be less than or equal to 12. Again, since $4G$ can be chosen by either Lois or Gary, there are $12 \times 2 = 24$ possibilities. Altogether, the total number of possible pairs is $8 + 24 = \boxed{32}$.

Team Round Solutions

1. The numbers that have a digit that is a 3 are 23, 43, and all ten numbers from 30 through 39, for a total of 12. The numbers that are divisible by 3 and not already counted are 21, 24, 27, 42, 45, and 48, for a total of 6. Altogether, the total is $12 + 6 = \boxed{18}$.

2. Place the two rectangular tiles with height 9 centimeters next to one another, so that together the two form a 9 by $4 + 8 = 12$ rectangular tile. Then rotate that rectangle so that the height is 12 centimeters, and place it next to the 12 by 7 rectangle, so together the two form a 12 by $7 + 9 = 16$ rectangular tile. The perimeter of that tile, in centimeters, is $12 + 16 + 12 + 16 = \boxed{56}$.

3. When counting rows from the back and the front, Shelly's row is included in both counts, so there are $5 + 12 - 1 = 16$ rows. But when counting seats to the left and the right, Shelly's seat is not included, so there are $3 + 5 + 1 = 9$ seats in each row. Therefore, the number of graduates is $16 \times 9 = \boxed{144}$.

4. In each row, each of the numbers in a row contributes to the value of 2 numbers in the row below. For example, in row 2, the 3 contributes to the 3 and the 14 in row 3, the 11 contributes to the 14 and 19 in row 3, and the 8 contributes to the 19 and 8 in row 3. Therefore, the sum of the numbers in each row is twice the sum of the numbers in the previous row. The sum of the numbers in the first row is $3 + 8 = 11$, in the second row is $3 + 11 + 8 = 22$, and in the third row is $3 + 14 + 19 + 8 = 44$. The fourth row has a sum of $44 \times 2 = 88$, the fifth 176, the sixth 352, the seventh 704, the eighth 1408, and the sum of the numbers in row 9 is $\boxed{2816}$.

5. The team collected $49 \times 8 = 392$ dollars the third week. Therefore, the team collected $1706 - 392 = 1314$ dollars the first two weeks by selling $150 - 49 = 101$ t-shirts. If all of the t-shirts were sold the second week, the team would have collected $12 \times 101 = 1212$ dollars, but the team collected $1314 - 1212 = 102$ dollars more than that amount. For each t-shirt sold the first week, the team collected $15 - 12 = 3$ more dollars than if the t-shirt was sold the second week, so the team sold $102 \div 3 = 34$ t-shirts the first week, and $101 - 34 = 67$ t-shirts the second week. The increase in t-shirts sold in the second week from the first week was $67 - 34 = \boxed{33}$.

6. If the fewest number of votes received by a candidate was 2, the votes for the other two candidates must sum to $29 - 2 = 27$. But no two primes sum to 27. If the fewest number of votes received by a candidate was 3, the votes for the other two candidates must total $29 - 3 = 26$. The primes that sum to 26 are 3 and 23, 7 and 19, and 13 and 13. However, vote totals of 3, 13, and 13 are not possible, since one candidate received more votes than the other two. Vote totals of 3, 3, and 23 can occur among the three candidates in 3 different ways, and vote totals of 3, 7, and 19 can occur among the three candidates in 6 different ways. If the fewest number of votes received by a candidate was 5, the votes for the other two candidates must total $29 - 5 = 24$. The primes that sum to 24 are 5 and 19, 7 and 17, and 11 and 13. The first can occur in 3 ways, the second in 6, and the third in 6. If the fewest number of votes received by a candidate was 7, the votes for the other two candidates must total $29 - 7 = 22$, and the only two primes greater than 7 which sum to 22 are 11 and 11, which is not possible since, again, one candidate received more votes than the other two. Altogether, the total number of possible vote totals is $3 + 6 + 3 + 6 + 6 = \boxed{24}$.

7. The time elapsed from 12:49 PM until 2:13PM is $(60 - 49) + 60 + 13 = 84$ minutes, or $\frac{84}{60} = 1.4$ hours. In this time, Diego and Ramon traveled a combined distance of $51 - 16 = 35$ miles, so their combined speed was $\frac{35}{1.4} = 25$ miles per hour. Let Ramon's speed, in miles per hour, be R. Then Diego's speed is $R - 3$, and $R + R - 3 = 25$, so Ramon's speed, in miles per hour, is $\boxed{14}$.

8. The product $22!$ is $22 \cdot 21 \cdot 20 \cdot 19 \cdot 18 \cdot 17 \cdot 16 \cdot 15 \cdot 14 \cdot 13 \cdot 12$ times $11 \cdot 10 \cdot 9 \cdot 8 \cdot 7 \cdot 6 \cdot 5 \cdot 4 \cdot 3 \cdot 2 \cdot 1$. As a product of primes, this is $2 \cdot 11 \cdot 3 \cdot 7 \cdot 2^2 \cdot 5 \cdot 19 \cdot 2 \cdot 3^2 \cdot 17 \cdot 2^4 \cdot 3 \cdot 5 \cdot 2 \cdot 7 \cdot 13 \cdot 2^2 \cdot 3$ times $11 \cdot 2 \cdot 5 \cdot 3^2 \cdot 2^3 \cdot 7 \cdot 2 \cdot 3 \cdot 5 \cdot 2^2 \cdot 3 \cdot 2$, or $2^{19} \cdot 3^9 \cdot 5^4 \cdot 7^3 \cdot 11^2 \cdot 13 \cdot 17 \cdot 19$. For a divisor of $22!$ to be a perfect cube, each of the exponents of its prime factorization must be a multiple of 3 and less than or equal to the exponent of the same prime in the prime factorization of $22!$. Therefore the prime factorization must be 2 to a power of 0, 3, 6, 9, 12, 15, or 18, for 7 possible values, 3 to a power of 0, 3, 6, or 9, for 4 possible values, 5 to a power of 0 or 3, for 2 possible values, and 7 to a power of 0 or 3, for 2 possible values. Therefore the number of perfect cubes that evenly divide $22!$ is $7 \cdot 4 \cdot 2 \cdot 2 = \boxed{112}$.

9. Let the side length of the square be 20, so the area of the square is $20^2 = 400$. By the Pythagorean Theorem, the length of one of the segments drawn from a corner of the square to the middle point of a side is $\sqrt{20^2 + 10^2} = 10\sqrt{5}$. Consider one of the shaded right triangles. This triangle has a hypotenuse of length 10, and is similar to the right triangle with sides of length 10, 20, and $10\sqrt{5}$. The legs of the shaded triangle are therefore $\frac{10}{10\sqrt{5}} \cdot 10 = \frac{10}{\sqrt{5}}$ and $\frac{20}{10\sqrt{5}} \cdot 10 = \frac{20}{\sqrt{5}}$, so the area of one of the shaded triangles is $\frac{1}{2} \cdot \frac{10}{\sqrt{5}} \cdot \frac{20}{\sqrt{5}} = 20$. The side length of the shaded square has the same length as the longer leg of the shaded right triangle, so the area of the large square is $\left(\frac{20}{\sqrt{5}}\right)^2 = 80$, and the combined area of the shaded regions is $20 \cdot 4 + 80 = 160$. The ratio of the shaded regions to the area of the square is $\frac{160}{400} = \boxed{\frac{2}{5}}$.

10. Let the bottom dot in any column have a value of 0, the dot above it have a value of 1, the next highest dot have a value of 2, and the top dot have a value of 3. Then the area of the trapezoidal or triangular region between two columns is the average of the values of the dots in those columns. Let the value of the dot selected in the first column be a, the second be b, the third be c, and the fourth be d. For half the grid to be shaded, $\frac{a+b}{2} + \frac{b+c}{2} + \frac{c+d}{2} = \frac{9}{2}$, or $a + 2b + 2c + d = 9$. Since $2b + 2c$ is always even, and $a + d$ is even if both a and d are even or both are odd, exactly one of a and d must be odd. Suppose a is 1 and d is 0. Then $2b + 2c = 8$, and b can be any of 1, 2, or 3, for 3 possibilities. Suppose a is 1 and d is 2. Then $2b + 2c = 6$, and b can be any of 0, 1, 2, or 3, for 4 possibilities. Suppose a is 3 and d is 0. Then $2b + 2c = 6$, and b can be any of 0, 1, 2, or 3, for 4 possibilities. Suppose a is 3 and d is 2. Then $2b + 2c = 4$, and b can be any of 0, 1, or 2, for 3 possibilities. Altogether, if a is odd, then there are $4 + 3 + 3 + 4 = 14$ possibilities. By symmetry, if d is odd, there are also 14 possibilities, so the total number of possible selections is $2 \cdot 14 = \boxed{28}$.